A TWENTIETH-
CENTURY LIFE

···

FRANCES DONALDSON

....

A Twentieth-Century Life

WEIDENFELD & NICOLSON
London

First published in Great Britain in 1992 by
George Weidenfeld & Nicolson Limited
The Orion Publishing Group, Orion House,
5 Upper St Martin's Lane, London WC2H 9EA

All photographs are from the author's collection

A catalogue reference for this book is available
from the British Library.

ISBN 0 297 81098 7

Printed in Great Britain by Butler & Tanner Ltd,
Frome and London

CONTENTS

ACKNOWLEDGEMENTS

I would like to thank Peters Fraser & Dunlop for permission to quote from letters by Evelyn Waugh and Laura Waugh; Curtis Brown Ltd for permission to quote from letters by Daphne Du Maurier, copyright of the Estate of Daphne du Maurier; the John Betjeman Estate, c/o Desmond Elliott, for permission to quote from a letter by John Betjeman; Sir Isaiah Berlin for permission to quote from his letters; Auberon Waugh for permission to quote from an article by himself; and the heirs of Frederick Ashton and Sir Alan Lascelles to quote from their letters.

I also have to thank Candida Brazil, Gila Falkus, Allegra Huston and Elizabeth Blumer.

INTRODUCTION

· ·

Evelyn Waugh thought the motive for reading autobiographical books was to get an understanding of the immediate past.* I was born in the first decade of the twentieth century and I have survived into the last; thus my life coincides with a period of change which, in England at least, was in some ways greater than in a thousand years of history. I speak not of the technical advances, but of the social pattern – of the decline in an aristocratic order which had lasted since the beginning of recorded history, the changed attitudes to war, to poverty, to religion, to the rights of man, to colour, race and creed; above all to the alteration in the opportunities for women. We talk today of Thatcherism, but even Thatcherism cannot undo the social revolution which took place as a result of two world wars and the Labour government of 1945–51.

My intention is not to write a social history but an account of my own life in the consciousness that it reflects the history of the times. I shall not attempt a full-scale autobiography, which, when not about public events but concerned with the ordinary life of the writer, is nearer to the art of the novelist than of the biographer. To the latter the material is given and should be of interest in itself, but autobiography comes from within and can be devilishly difficult.

In fact, I jumped the gun. My first two books, published in 1941 and 1945, were about farming in the Second World War and were necessarily an account of my own experiences; *Freddy Lonsdale* was a biography of my father, and *Child of the Twenties* an account of my childhood and youth, both published in the fifties. I cannot escape some repetition here, partly because these books have been so long out of print, but chiefly because my father, a playwright, was both a dominant influence in my own life and an important representative of the twenties. But I have dealt fairly briskly with my early years and avoided altogether the history of my first marriage, when my life was given up to horses and dogs. I have written of that before and have nothing new to say.

I do not, as some authors do, find pleasure in reading my own work and when I read my early books recently it was for the first

* Evelyn Waugh, *A Little Learning*, Chapman & Hall (1964) p. 33.

time in thirty years. The first two were bestsellers and the others have often been praised, but I was disappointed in them all. The second of the farming books is a great improvement on the first, but both are rather sententious. I think this must have been only partly due to my youth and inexperience as a writer, because so many people bought and enjoyed them. Possibly the high-flown tone was acceptable then, because, however clumsy, it was inspired by emotions which other people shared. Only now, when the mood has changed, is it obvious that the skill of the writer is no match for the heroic sentiments.

I hope I can do better now. Towards the end of his life I asked Frederick Ashton whether he thought his best work was done when he was young or at the time we spoke. He replied that when he was young he was more spontaneous but that he went deeper now. I was reminded of telling Evelyn Waugh that I thought my father, when he was young, had been content merely to amuse, but had now begun to wonder whether one should not have some higher aim; a mood, I said, which did not suit him.

'Perhaps', Evelyn had replied lugubriously, 'perhaps he doesn't feel amusing any more.'

There will be a certain amount of name-dropping in this book, because, owing to the circumstances of my childhood and youth and also because I lived on a farm for nearly thirty years, I seem for much of my life to have known a few 'names' and almost nobody else. This matter is much added to by my incorrigible desire to please. I was taught by my father that the one unforgivable sin is to be a bore but the author of memoirs is always in the difficulty that, while the critics will castigate name-dropping, the public prefer to read about people they recognize. I have never kept a diary, a thing which, although there are notable exceptions, seems to me death to the writer of memoirs, who, having kept this reminder of small doings, too often feels bound to use it.

Certainly my own work was more spontaneous when I was young. I wrote *Approach to Farming* in six weeks, working after supper at the end of a long day's farming; and equally I go deeper now. Yet the compulsion today is not simply to try to do better something I have done before. On the contrary, except to the extent that it is necessary to the narrative form, or because I can now make use both of material not available to me earlier and of hindsight, I do not intend to go over ground I have covered before. Having written so much earlier, I may pick and choose.

In an interview given recently, V.S. Pritchett said, 'No one can be called a type; everyone is at least three people.'* I would add that most people live at least three lives, by which I mean that at different times their circumstances are so dissimilar that one of the three people is uppermost. For my own part I reckon I have had four distinct lives (this would be five if I counted the four years of my first marriage); they coincide with the mood of the periods they cover and necessarily reflect them.

The first followed very closely what one might term the popular or picturesque view of the period between the two wars in England. This was one of the most philistine periods in the history of a generally philistine country; and, although Bloomsbury and Cyril Connolly, and later Auden and Isherwood have historically assumed so much importance, the overall view even now is better represented by Noël Coward and Mr Cochrane's Young Ladies.

In this, the image evoked by the words 'the twenties' is entirely different from that of 'the thirties'. The twenties are regarded with nostalgia for a raffish kind of glamour, although much of this is based on fantasy, while the thirties are remembered as a time of political incompetence, of intense poverty and fear, of the appeasement of Germany and the gradual slide into war; the era which produced Blunt, Burgess and Maclean. The distinction between the two decades is not as it happens entirely well-founded but it accords with the pattern of my youth.

I have written of both periods before, but the events of those years look very different in retrospect. However, I no longer remember my youth either very accurately or, more important, with any real feeling, and, for this reason, when the necessity arises, I quote without apology from myself. The books I wrote about my experiences in the Second World War have proved useful as source material, but for these years I have the far more explicit account of my life given in my letters to my husband, Jack. He was abroad for the whole of the war and my daily letters to him form something like a diary, the only one I ever kept. They were not written for publication, but they recall things I had half-forgotten and others I cannot remember even in face of the evidence, and they give an authentic picture of life at the time. The fact that I bought a farm at the beginning of the war had the secondary effect that it settled the course of our lives for more than thirty years.

The period when we farmed in Gloucestershire and then in Buckinghamshire, as well as the time in London after we retired

---

* *Guardian*, 8 February 1990.

from farming, are still uncharted, but I have been fortunate in my opportunities to view the immediate past. When we went to London we were already over sixty, yet in every worldly sense the last of my lives must be counted the most successful and the most interesting of the five.

PART I

*Childhood
and
Youth*

1

....

Freddy Lonsdale

I was seven when the First World War began and eleven when it ended. We had no near male relations or friends that I remember, and, in comparison to the horrors which I have since read about, the war impinged on us very little. Aeroplanes on their way to bomb London flew regularly (or so it seems now) across the Kent coast near Birchington where we lived, and a rich neighbour built a deep shelter of some size in his garden. We were woken when the sirens went and taken to this shelter some twenty feet beneath the earth and given cups of cocoa. Sir Johnstone Forbes Robertson walked about the village and was said to be frightened of the air raids, although I have no reason to believe this was true. Later my elder sister and I were sent to school in Teddington in order to avoid the raids, and when my mother visited us we used to go to Hampton Court and afterwards to a teashop opposite. I remember very little else about this school, although I have one clear memory of standing on the playing fields and being told the armistice had been declared. I understood not much more than that this was good, just as four years earlier when my nurse told me the war had begun I had also had a feeling that this was good!

My father was the most permanent influence of my childhood, although at the time my mother was the most important. One of the most successful playwrights of his time, Freddy Lonsdale was very witty and amusing and to most people irresistible. I still meet people who say, 'I met your father once,' and, since towards the end of his life Freddy became an obsessive traveller, endlessly crossing the Atlantic, they usually add, 'We travelled on the same boat on our way to America. We used to dine together and he was so charming, so amusing.'

He was born in 1881 in a small cottage in Jersey – then an island of farmers and fishermen, largely descended from the Normans. His father, whose surname was Leonard, not Lonsdale, was an assistant in a tobacconist's shop belonging to his father-in-law. Later he opened a shop of his own and the family then moved to live over it. The Leonards had three sons, Jim who died of drink before he was thirty, George who lived a respectable and uneventful life, and Freddy, the youngest.

Freddy was a heartbreakingly wilful child and from the beginning his parents were unable to influence him. He constantly played truant from school, and, although on one day he would be caught and beaten, he was nearly always absent again on the next. In this way he denied himself even the moderate education he might have had. ('You appear to be on terms of intimacy with words that I have never heard of,' he wrote to me when he read my first book.) His parents thought him a bad boy and feared that he would come to a bad end.

Yet when he was twenty-seven he had two plays and a musical comedy on in London. He wrote twenty-four plays and musicals, and in his time was one of the most successful playwrights who ever lived, while several of his plays have survived. Rex Harrison was seen in London in *Aren't We All?* in 1985 (the last time he appeared here before he died), and Penelope Keith took *On Approval* on an extended tour of England in 1992. Both these plays were written more than sixty years ago.

Freddy told me that when he was a child he always intended to be a playwright, but it is difficult to understand how the thought can have entered his head. He can never have seen a play, yet even those critics who did not admire his work admitted he was a very able craftsman, with an instinctive knowledge of the technique of writing for the theatre. He did not learn this by watching other people's plays, nor by a struggle to learn his job: he simply jumped fully armed into the theatre of London.

He was a notable eccentric. When he was fourteen he left home and in later life he told various fantastical tales about what he did then. Whatever the truth was, in 1903, when he was twenty-one, he reappeared in Jersey with plenty of money in his pockets and took a room at the Grand Hotel. He was obviously a bit above himself, and standing in the doorway of his father's shop, he ogled my mother as she passed down the street.

This had the opposite of the intended effect. Leslie Hoggan was a colonel's daughter and she was offended by the attentions of a tobacconist's son. Colonel Hoggan had no money apart from his army pay, and, by negotiating exchanges with officers who wished to serve in England when their regiments were ordered abroad, he had managed to spend the whole of his army career in India. In his retirement he lived in Jersey and conducted a cramming school for young men wishing to join the army. He and his family occupied a respectable position about halfway up the intricate class scale, high enough to make them very conscious of their advantages and merits, but not so high as to give them that boundless confidence in their own superiority and the correctness of any behaviour they chose to adopt which so distinguished the highest ranks of society. They belonged almost exactly to what George Orwell described as the 'lower-upper-middle class', the close distinction being entirely one of money. Members of this class knew theoretically how to wear clothes and order a dinner, although in practice they 'could never afford to go to a decent tailor or a decent restaurant'; and theoretically they knew how to shoot and ride, 'although in practice [they] had no horses to ride and not an inch of ground to shoot over'. It was this, he says, which explained the attraction of India. 'They [the lower-upper-middle class] went there because in India, with cheap horses, free shooting, and hordes of black servants, it was so easy to play at being a gentleman.'*

This exactly describes the class to which my grandfather and his family belonged, but their lives had enabled them to regard themselves not as the 'lower-upper-middle class' but as the upper-middle class. My mother was never the least snobbish in the sense of wanting to know people, but she had a family pride which inspired an interest in the divisions of society and an exaggerated belief in the height of her own position. On the strength of her father, the colonel, she taught me to believe we belonged to a class called the gentry, one higher than the upper-middle class. There was no real truth in this, but the term 'middle class' had a different connotation then. It was used largely from above and was slightly derogatory. In the 1920s when Maureen Stanley, a daughter of Lord Londonderry married to a son of Lord Derby, told her weekend guests, brought together for reasons other than their social status, that she was giving 'a middle-class luncheon party', to my intense surprise the visitors turned out to be the local landowners, people

* George Orwell, *The Road to Wigan Pier*, Gollancz (1937), pp. 155–6.

9

who in other circumstances would have felt themselves infinitely superior to most of the houseguests.

Today, the term 'middle class' has a different connotation and is applied to all except the aristocracy and those still called the working class; it no longer has a patronising flavour and can be something one rises into. Hugh Gaitskell groaned when Dora told him she had asked the wife of Arthur Cousins, the trade union leader, whether she would like to come to a 'middle-class luncheon party' and said that she had undone the work of four years. He knew that Mrs Cousins would understand that she was being asked to meet people considered higher in the social scale than herself. But this was many years after my mother passed my father in the street.

Freddy had some reason at that time to be pleased with himself because he had come to Jersey for the production of a play called *Who's Hamilton?*, which he had written under the name of Lonsdale, and which had already toured many towns in England and drawn the attention of the well-known critic Clement Scott.* A few weeks after the events I have described, my grandmother, Mrs Hoggan, received a letter from a lady who ran the amateur dramatic society asking her to bring her daughter to tea to meet Mr Leonard. He had written a one-act play whose first performance he would allow her society to give, and he wanted Miss Hoggan to play the lead. Leslie was due to visit her fiancé who lived in Scotland and she could not act in the play, but she and her mother attended the tea party nevertheless. There, as sometimes happens in these relationships, my grandmother fell mildly in love with the young playwright; so, although Colonel Hoggan had to be kept in the dark about the extent of his visits to the house, Freddy began to see a good deal of my mother. Some months later, when she was again visiting her fiancé in Scotland, he followed her there and, prising her out of the house, ran away with her to Weymouth where (in 1904) they were married.

Freddy was twenty-three and my mother a year younger. They had so little money they had to borrow the fee for the licence from the parson who married them, and to send for Mrs Hoggan to take Leslie home. Freddy could not go with them because of a Jersey law which allowed a man to be imprisoned for debt.

They lived without any regular income for four years until Freddy had his first plays produced in London, and I was always unable to discover from my mother what they lived on. 'I don't know,' she

---

* Later my father took the name Lonsdale by deed poll. I was born Leonard but my name was changed with his.

replied in answer to questions, 'I simply can't remember. When things were too bad I went home to Jersey.' And she added, as though explaining everything: 'You must realize we always knew Freddy would be a success.' They were living in lodgings in Harrow when I was born, eleven months after my elder sister, Mavis. Two years later my younger sister was born and christened Mab.

Only confidence in his own ability could have enabled Freddy to survive this period. Harassed by debt, uncertain from one day to the next how he would feed his family, in one small room in lodgings, amidst the cries of newborn babies, he wrote four plays. Later, in comfortable surroundings, with the whole house hushed for fear of disturbing him, without worry and with every management in London competing for his work, he often found it impossible to write a word until the spur of poverty pricked him on. But by the time I was born, success was in sight and soon we moved out of lodgings to a house at Westgate-on-Sea in Kent.

I remember almost nothing about living in Westgate and not much more about the first of the houses we moved to in Birchington, three miles away, but I have been told a good deal about this period. The society in Westgate was much the same as it would have been in any other seaside town. My parents kept a cook, a housemaid and a nanny and began to live a thoroughly middle-class life, and one, not so unusual in those days, of leisure. They played golf and tennis (by the time I can first remember, Freddy was quite good at both), they played bridge, bathed in the sea in summer and entertained their neighbours.

All would have been well if Freddy had done any work. He was thought to be lazy and he certainly wrote only when forced to through lack of money. For some years he was kept by a rich Australian neighbour called Conran. This gentleman joined a club Freddy belonged to in Westgate and on his first visit there ordered himself a whisky and soda. The waiter explained that, owing to the licensing laws, he could not order and pay for a drink until he had been a member of the club for twenty-four hours. At this a fair-haired young man crossed the room.

'My name is Lonsdale,' he said. 'Please order anything you want and put it on my bill.'

This early exhibition of the style of the Jersey tobacconist's son paid tremendous dividends. Mr Conran soon learned that his benefactor was hardly in a position to pay for his own drinks much less those of a complete stranger. He asked Freddy to make a list of his debts and he paid all these and made him an allowance of five pounds a week until he no longer needed it. The terms of the loan were that it should be paid back as and when Freddy was able to do so.

Not long after this Freddy began to write musical comedies for George Edwardes at Daly's Theatre. In 1916 he wrote a musical play called *The Maid of the Mountains*, one of the greatest successes in theatrical history. It ran for 1,352 performances in its first London production and is said to have made a profit of some £100,000. With *The Maid of the Mountains* Freddy said goodbye to the vagrancy of his youth. He paid Mr Conran all he owed him and he never again owed large sums as long as he lived.

He continued to live a simple and domesticated life in Birchington and he was a surprisingly responsible family man. After the war we lived at 6 Beach Avenue, a semi-detached house opposite the tennis courts on the road leading to the sea. This would nowadays be thought a reasonably large house. Somewhere there was a kitchen and on the ground floor a drawing room and dining room. On the next floor my parents shared a double room and my elder sister and I another ; my younger sister must have slept somewhere, there was a day nursery, and I imagine the three servants lived in. One of these was a girl called Mabel who looked after us but was not grand enough to be called Nanny.

Freddy was almost impossible to live with because he was so moody, and my mother and he quarrelled terribly. He was soon unfaithful to her and in middle age he ceased to live with her, but he always looked after her and regarded her as his own. As a father he had all the textbook faults because he was so incalculable – what pleased one day was rebuked the next, and a joke which showed humour and spirit on one occasion might be treated on another as that gravest of all mistakes – showing off. Entirely unconventional himself, he was nervous of any unconventionality in us. He watched us hopefully for signs of character or talent, but fell upon any deviation from the norm.

Yet we all adored Freddy and he always loved us – or at least he loved me. I used to walk with him round Quex Park, doing my best to entertain him, and I can remember talking to him in the mornings while he shaved. 'Don't keep finishing your sentences,' he said to me once. 'I am not a bloody fool.'* In the light of all modern knowledge he would be counted an inexpert father, and probably this was so. My elder sister died of drink and/or drugs and my younger, although very happy in her second marriage to Rodney

---

* I quoted this remark in *Child of the Twenties* and it has since reached *The Oxford Dictionary of Quotations* attributed 'Lonsdale quoted Donaldson'.

Ackland, the playwright, was so neurotic that for the last ten years of her life she seldom left the house. My mother was of major importance in our childhood because she gave us all the love we needed and stood between us and Freddy and I have no recollection of being other than happy.

Throughout the whole of our childhood and youth we knew almost no one of our own age. Until I was fourteen and sent to boarding school for the second time, Daphne du Maurier was the only friend I ever had. Immediately after the First World War, because it was not yet possible to travel abroad, Birchington enjoyed a short period as a popular seaside resort. Freddy was the cause of this success, since it was because he lived there that Gerald du Maurier, whom he adored and who to a large extent returned his affection, brought his family to stay at the Bungalow Hotel in Birchington. They came several summers running and also one year for Christmas. Other members of the theatrical profession followed them and Birchington became fashionable.

Gerald was the son of George du Maurier, the author of *Trilby*, and he was the last of the great actor-managers. In 1910 he joined Frank Curzon in management at Wyndham's Theatre, and after a break during the First World War, remained there for most of his acting career. In looks and personality he was of quite exceptional distinction and, within the limits he imposed upon himself, a marvellous actor. He originated the naturalistic manner and in doing so killed off the melodramatic style of the nineteenth century, which had become an obstacle to the presentation of modern drama and even to a faithful portrayal of the classics. This was a vital contribution to the development of acting. He lived too early for there to be any major film record of him in his prime, but in 1969 an extract from *Lord Camber's Ladies*, shot in 1932, in which he played a small part, was shown on the BBC's *Omnibus* programme to a studio audience consisting of Sir John Gielgud, Dame Edith Evans, Donald Sinden and Vanessa Redgrave. Commenting, Edith Evans said : 'He was a very, very fine actor indeed. He could do every part better than they did. But he chose to be the sort of originator of the rather throw-away style.... A lot of people copied him ; all they did was throw away, but they didn't throw anything away, do you see. I'd great admiration for him.'

He was a natural leader of men, and his skill as a producer has been testified to again and again by the leading actors of the day. He taught the art of light comedy to actors such as Ronald Squire and actresses like Gladys Cooper, Tallulah Bankhead and Celia Johnson. He was, however, a product of the period in which he lived, one of the most uncultured in the history of the country. During the whole of his career he was responsible for no production of any intrinsic interest whatever; he never introduced a play which has remained in the repertory of English theatre; he neither acted in nor produced any of the classics.

At the time the du Mauriers came to Birchington Gerald was at the height of his career. Like my own parents, they had three daughters, roughly the same ages as ourselves, and we paired off naturally. Daphne was, like me, the middle one. She was an extraordinarily good-looking child, a mixture of her father and her mother, who had been a beauty in her youth. In photographs in some of the obituary notices she is shown with a hairdresser's head and a good deal of make-up. As a child she had corn-coloured hair cut in a long bob and wore a fringe. She looked like a medieval page.

Granddaughter of George du Maurier and daughter of Gerald, even at this age Daphne lived almost entirely in her imagination. We were all made to play Roundheads and Cavaliers in the shrubbery behind the tennis courts and we stood on trial in the dock before Freddy and Gerald for any faults. When they came at Christmas Daphne wrote a play and the great actor and the playwright were forced to watch us act it. Father and daughter were two of the most distinguished personalities I ever knew.

When in 1991 Daphne died, I felt disproportionately sad. Now that it was too late, I felt that in middle life I had failed sufficiently to respond to affectionate letters and, since she was almost entirely a recluse, an unusual offer of hospitality. I continued to see her until she married because I used to go with Freddy to luncheon on Sundays at Canon Hall in Hampstead, where the du Mauriers lived, but after she married Sir Frederick Browning and went to live in Cornwall I never saw her again. She came back into my life because of a passage in my book *Evelyn Waugh: Portrait of a Country Neighbour*. Evelyn was at this time obsessed by the income tax he had to pay and in my book I quoted the following letter he wrote to me to prove that it was impossible for a writer to earn more than a limited annual income, even allowing for certain concessions:

Piers Court Stinchcombe
8 May 54

Dear Frankie,
Lady Browning's income: 100,000 copies @ 12/6 produce a 20% royalty of £12,500 i.e. difference between sale of 100,000 and 150,000 = gross £6,250.

14

Suppose her previous thrift to qualify her for full Welfare rates of taxation:

Gross £6,250 = net (approx.) £156.

> Yours ever
> Evelyn

I had chosen Daphne du Maurier – Lady Browning – in conversation as one of the few writers who hit the jackpot with every book. The meaning of Evelyn's letter may not be entirely clear, nor the facts completely accurate. But the point is that, while on all his earnings the writer paid tax and supertax, he could neither by hard work nor unusual success raise these earnings in good years to save against bad. Evelyn had six children to educate.

When my book appeared in 1967 I received a long letter from Daphne from Menabilly, Par, Cornwall. In this she said: 'I was so amused at the reference, and how right Evelyn Waugh was about my Income Tax. I've got about £156 in the bank at the moment, and scream when the butcher's bill comes in, despite the fact that I live alone like a Trappist monk and eat cold ham for supper off a tray.' Then she went on:

> I've been thinking all afternoon about Birchington days, and you in a blue linen frock, with bare legs. We were great buddies after all, and thought alike on many subjects, were rather pleased with our joint status of being the middle daughters of three sisters. ...
> I always remember 13 January is your birthday and think 'Ah, Frankie's birthday' when I tear off the calendar, and 6th February was surely Mavis's.
>
> Possibly we are still alike – books on our fathers – both violently Left-Wing (Angela and Jeanne are screaming Tories). ...* Am also agnostic but rather faute de mieux, with a rooted feeling there is Something, Somewhere, and all those cells we are made up of must mean something. ... I never get used to people being dead. It's such a terrible waste. But I feel Gerald somehow hovers around me, and my darling Tommy too.† Rather as though they were in Australia and one can't telephone, and wouldn't know what to say if they were. ...
>
> I've never been back to Birchington, but I feel sure I could find

---

* Her sisters.
† Her name for Sir Frederick Browning.

my way about it blindfold. . . . * I don't suppose you ever come to Cornwall, or I to Gloucestershire for that matter, possibly we will meet in twenty years time in St Cuthbert's Home for the Senile – this is always my dread, that my daughters will be firm and say, 'The time has come, you can't live alone, it's for your own *good*.' and that will be that.

I think I must have replied to this that I, too, feared St Cuthbert's because she referred to it without explanation in other letters, and certainly it was a neurotic fear not uncommon in women brought up unable to keep themselves. In her next letter Daphne asked me to stay: 'If you could ever face the drive down to Cornwall and staying with me, we could meet and talk before St Cuthbert's. I can offer you a very comfortable spare-room (with electric blanket on bed) your own adjoining bathroom and lav, breakfast in bed, lunch cooked by the daily (who cooks well) and a forage for ourselves on trays in the evening.'

It was because I never went to Cornwall in response to this generous invitation that I felt disconsolate when Daphne died. I do not know why I did not go, but it was not only because of the distance. I think I felt uncertain that I could any longer please. As she said, we were alike in some things, but we were very different in others. She was so imaginative and I in many ways so stolid. I wrote to her once more, however. At the time of the television serial *Edward and Mrs Simpson* based on my book *Edward VIII*, there was also a new version of *Rebecca*. I found a cutting in some paper which said that the bestselling paperbacks for the week were these two books, and sent it to Daphne. 'How lovely to hear from you,' she wrote back, 'and I was so pleased with the cutting. Think of ourselves at Birchington, could we have seen into the future. "Good Lord! We are going to be real writers!" But I don't think I want to look into the future now. I see myself as a dotty old woman in some Nursing Home. . . .'

She died, in fact, at home, and I felt sad and unresponsive.

---

* In fact she could not have. I went to Birchington the other day and found the Bungalow Hotel no longer a bungalow, the tennis courts become an estate of small houses, and 6 Beach Avenue, where we lived, and its neighbours pulled down and replaced by what looks like blocks of flats.

16

2

··

Leonora Wodehouse

The only other friend I remember making in my childhood was Leonora Wodehouse, the stepdaughter of P.G. Wodehouse and daughter of his wife, Ethel. She was to have a far greater influence on my life.

The Wodehouses must have come for the summer in 1921, when I was fourteen. That was the time when all over England, and particularly in Birchington, the dancing began. A band played every night of the week at the Beresford and the Bungalow hotels, and one summer Jack Hylton played at the Bungalow. We had by now moved to a larger house on the seafront which had a drawing room of considerable size, and on Sundays my father hired a band and the dancing was continued there. My elder sister and I always attended these dances and had considerable success with the young men, so much so that my parents presently took fright. 'Freddy,' Gladys Cooper said to my father, 'those girls ought to be in bed.' Soon after that we were sent once more to boarding school.

My parents chose the school that Leonora Wodehouse went to because that was how, in their circle, the thing was done. I learn from some of the books written by my contemporaries, such as Elizabeth Longford, that it was possible for girls of the upper-middle and upper classes to be reasonably educated, but this was only when their parents had some intellectual ambition. I know also from others that, but for the exigencies of the class system, one might have acquired some education at a high school. The Old Palace, Bromley, to which Mavis and I were sent, was the fifth

17

school I attended, and I learned almost nothing at any of them. At the time there were a great many schools taking only about thirty girls, where the teaching was done by unqualified spinsters who had had almost no education themselves. All these schools were very snobbish – they had to be because that was how they attracted parents. At the school in Westgate I had attended as a day girl immediately after the war, there were at least two earls' daughters and two future marchionesses, and the teaching was the worst I ever experienced.

At all schools we wrote essays and, while I was still at Westgate, one of the teachers angered my father by saying that I had a natural prose style. Considerably talented himself, he regarded the ability to write as a gift from God, from which it followed that for any but the chosen to attempt it was an abominable conceit, to be stamped out of his children at any cost. 'Don't take any notice of these women,' he said to me. 'They know nothing about these things.' At the Bromley school my essays were always marked 'Very Good Indeed' or 'Excellent' but the competition was not high and I believed my father. Certainly I was taught very little and today know nothing of English grammar, although I learned the rudiments of correct prose from Rupert Hart-Davis, who edited two of my books when I was over fifty. I try, for instance, not to use five words when three would do and to avoid what Evelyn Waugh called 'the slipped participle'. (Fowler calls it the unattached participle.) The fault is very common and one can take a bet on finding an example in any week in the columns of *The Times* (this week, in a review of a book by Lord Lambton called *The Mountbattens*: 'Before reading this book, Lord Mountbatten stands, bemedalled and magnificent ...'). The rest is luck. Recently when I read a pamphlet written by George (Dadie) Rylands which discussed the use made by poets of the mixture of Saxon and Latin words in the English language, it was all, as it were, Greek to me. We were not introduced to English literature. I read a great deal when I was young, but only things that came my way – *The Prisoner of Zenda* and *Rupert of Hentzau*, *The Count of Monte Cristo* and *The Three Musketeers*, but not Dickens, Thackeray or even Jane Austen.

The Bromley school was owned by a Belgian woman, although run by an English one, and we learned a certain amount of Anglicized French, but nothing much else. When I went with Mary Dunn and Coney Jarvis (of whom more later) to Moulton Farm Institute during the Second World War, none of us could take the subject called 'Survey' because to us fractions and decimals were mysteries of the order of electrons. (I found out the secret of decimals and imparted this knowledge to Mary and Coney, who were as much surprised as I to find there was no difficulty.) A good deal of money was spent on having us learn the piano, but after four years Leonora Wodehouse could play *The Merry Peasant* and I the hymns in chapel – much too slowly.

The lack of professionalism extended to all subjects and to sports. I think we were taught some sewing but allowed to experiment only on unimaginative tasks such as hemming handkerchiefs; we could neither cook nor clean. I was taught to play golf but, although there were tennis courts at Bromley Palace where we played regularly, I never had a lesson; and, although I lived all my youth beside the sea, I never learned to swim except by a mongrel stroke of my own invention.

Apart from the ability to read and write, to add and subtract and to speak enough French to get through France with the help of a good deal of gesturing, I learned only one thing which would be of use in later life and that was through an initiative of my own. I begged to be excused from the Confirmation classes taken by the local vicar on the rather adventurous grounds that I was not a believer. The first time I did this it was considered original and I was allowed to get away with it. My request to be taught shorthand in the weekly hour in which I was thus free was agreed to, and for a whole year a little woman came once a week to give me lessons. When in the second year I tried this on again, the authorities had had enough and I was forced to take the Confirmation classes and to be confirmed. There must have been something more than a desire to be original in my reluctance, however, because, although following Confirmation I went once to Holy Communion, I have never been since.

Speaking purely as a writer, I think there may have been gains as well as losses in being so uneducated. In reply to a question in a fan letter asking him whether he thought that he would have become a writer if he had been to university, P.G. Wodehouse answered: 'Probably not.' This is not likely to have been true in his case, but it may be that for all but unconquerable talents it is better to write without rules. When Philip Williams, a don at Oxford, came to see me because he was writing a book about Hugh Gaitskell, he told me that he did all the research for a book first and started to write it only after this was complete; and he added, 'I'm sure this is the best method and I teach all my pupils to do the same.' I shivered at the thought, because although initially I get a good outline of the subject, I do the research in depth chapter by chapter as I write. This is absolutely necessary to me because I think writing is the difficult part and I would not have the confidence to spend two years in research without writing a line. I have since found that mine is a method used by other people at least as eminent as Philip Williams (who incidentally took fourteen years to write his book); but I am very law-abiding, and, if at a university I had been instructed to follow his method, I should probably never have written a book.

But this was the only good. The lack of education given to girls of the middle and upper classes left them entirely vulnerable and good only for being kept forever by their parents, or for marrying a man who would keep them instead. In my own case, the inability to fend for oneself was considerably added to by the fact that, partly because of the isolation of my parents' early life but also because of my father's eccentricities, except at school I never at any time knew people of my own age.

However, at Bromley Palace I did know Leonora Wodehouse. She was one of the most charming people I have ever met. Without apparent effort, she not only pleased everyone who met her and inspired idolatry in subordinates but was accepted by her equals as the leader of opinion. Because she was so well balanced her personality is extremely difficult to describe.

She was nine when she first met P.G. Wodehouse (Plummie to us), which disposes of any idea that he was in fact her father. But he adored her and brought her up and she took much colour from him. In his biography of Wodehouse, David Jasen says she was at school in England during the First World War,* but I have the impression she was in America. In any case, at school at this time her name was corrupted through Nora to S'nora and from there to Snorky or Snorkles. These corruptions of a rather beautiful name may not immediately please everyone but they were seized upon by Plummie, who never called her anything else. When she was young she stood too much on humour, which made her slightly unsympathetic to one's sadder moods, otherwise she had no perceptible faults. She was kind, generous and amusing, without malice or aggression. During the whole of her life she remained one of my greatest friends, but the peculiar significance of our youthful relationship was that, while we passed so much time in each other's company at Bromley, two boys, Peter Cazalet and Jack Donaldson, messed together at Eton.

* David Jasen, *P.G.Wodehouse: Portrait of a Master*, Continuum (1982).

3

···

Nobody Talks Politics

Between 1909 and 1923 Freddy wrote the libretti of six very successful musical plays. Then in 1923 he rewrote one of his early comedies and called it *Aren't We All?* This play has been revived several times up to the present day, but at its first performance in London it was only moderately successful, although much praised by the critics. A.B. Walkley voiced the general view when he said it was 'witty from end to end'.

The play was bought for New York by the great impresario Charles B. Dillingham, who had had a bad season. He billed it as follows:

CHARLES B. DILLINGHAM
announces
positively his last failure for this season
AREN'T WE ALL?

Aren't We All? was not a failure but a tremendous success. In New York most theatres close down in the summer because of the heat and only the greatest successes are run right through. *Aren't We All?*, which opened in May 1923, ran without a break until the end of January 1924.

After this our lives changed. We left Birchington in 1923 and lived in London, first in a sequence of rented houses and then in a house in Lowndes Square which my mother bought. My parents were now just over forty and had for the first time a considerable income. Their lives had been hard and uncertain for so long, and

21

now they simply threw themselves into spending the money Freddy earned so easily. They bought two Bentley cars – a saloon for my mother and an open car for Freddy – and acquired two chauffeurs and a butler.

I was nearly seventeen when all this happened and I left school immediately. I had never been particularly unhappy there, although both my sisters failed the course, Mavis by weeping incessantly until she was taken away, and Mab by the simple expedient of leaving Bromley Palace one morning and taking the train to London, where, to my loudly expressed disgust, she was allowed to stay. I left without regret. I knew that the whole matter of my education had been shoddily performed by spinsters without the qualifications to find any other work. It did not yet occur to me that I might end up in the same boat myself.

In London we knew even fewer people of our own age than we had before, because in Birchington families with children had sometimes come for the holidays. Our parents knew no one in London except theatre people, and could give us no version, however modified, of 'coming out'. Not only this, on the few occasions when I or one of my sisters brought some ordinary young man to the house Freddy sniffed around him, frightening him to death, and afterwards made no secret of his disapproval. 'You may not be very intelligent or attractive,' he said to my younger sister once, 'but you're worth better things than that.'

My case was rather different from my sisters', because although we made no new friends in London, Freddy quickly made many and he took me with him everywhere he went. I have never understood why this was, and now that sexual practices I had never heard of are openly discussed, I am sometimes asked whether there was a sexual element in his feeling for me. This was absolutely not so; during all this period Freddy was in love with Jean Norton and later with Maureen Stanley. But he was always very fond and, I suppose, in a foolish parental way, proud of me. In any case, he took me with him night after night and to meet all his friends.

Thus I played tennis with Ronald Squire, the actor, and golf with Lord Beaverbrook. Ronnie was an old friend and an unexpectedly good tennis player but lazy. From the time I was about twelve, we had played together at Canon Hall against Freddy and Gerald du Maurier, whom we normally beat. Now I went down to Golders Green where he temporarily lived and played singles with him, in which he fed me like a pro. Then one day Freddy took me to Hurlingham, to an eighteenth-century house with a garden and tennis court, where we picked up Lord Beaverbrook and went to play golf. Afterwards we had lunch in the house at Hurlingham and Max asked me questions. One of his great charms for other people was that he was so curious about their lives and genuinely interested in what they had to say. If for any reason you refused to tell him something, he put reporters on to find it out. After this, when Freddy was busy, I used sometimes to play alone with him. I was much better than he was and he played me for a pound a hole, which was simply a method of giving me money. My mother was, probably quite rightly, highly suspicious of all this, but she dealt with it in an undistinguished way, making me return the money. As a result of this kind of thing, Max quite quickly gave up bothering with me, but in the meantime he gave me the only real education I ever had. He told me that if I wished to form a literary taste, I must for one year read nothing but the great works of literature, after which I would never want to read anything else. The books he gave me were Samuel Butler's *Erewhon*, *The Life of Jesus* by Renan, and *The History of England* by J.A. Froude. Michael Arlen, also a friend at that time, added Proust, Dostoevsky and Anatole France to my reading list.

One other thing Max Beaverbrook said to me comes sometimes into my mind in these days when a number of people earn more every year than most of us can accumulate in a lifetime. He said that he and Jimmy Dunn – also a very rich man – had been interested to know how much you could spend in a year if you only did what you wanted to do : that is, no yacht unless you actually liked sailing, no horses unless you wanted to go racing. He said they both found it was surprisingly little.

The greatest influence on my youth were the Nortons, whom Freddy met on the boat returning from New York in 1923. Richard was the heir to Lord Grantley, Jean the daughter of Sir David Kinloch. Young, confident and attractive, they were typical of the society which in the aftermath of the war sought only amusement. They were immediately amused by Freddy and they took him up and introduced him to the wide circle of their friends. Unlike Ronnie Squire and Max Beaverbrook, they were nearer my age than his.

In the light of much opinion of today, Freddy and I must both be considered snobs. Neither he nor I ever went out of our way to meet people simply for their rank, but we liked, as Evelyn Waugh did, the qualities supported by what has recently been described as 'the inner self-confidence vouchsafed to those whose great expectations began from the moment of birth'.

At this time the aristocracy believed implicitly in their own superiority – something the rest of the world largely conceded. Not only were such concepts as 'blue blood' or 'good breeding' believed to have some real meaning, but money and position had ensured that children of the aristocracy were groomed to be at ease in public and private life; to meet royal personages with equanimity and to entertain the great of all nations; to manage estates and large households; to control crowds, make speeches, lead regiments. 'To meet them', H.G. Wells wrote, was 'like going to a flower show and seeing what space and care can do with the favoured strains of some familiar species.'

The upper classes all went to the same schools and shared characteristics of speech and mannerisms by which they recognized each other instantly. Largely a question of style and accent, these included the subtle shibboleths of what Nancy Mitford was to write about as 'U-speech'. In this matter, as in many others, they made their own rules. Thus the Mitford family thought it amusing to call their parents 'Farve' and 'Muv', yet they would have found it difficult to disguise their distaste if some innocent person had addressed one of them as 'luv'. The rules were also changed if the middle classes adopted some trick of upper-class speech, and words fashionable in one generation became 'non-U' in the next. These tricks gave extraordinary confidence, which made the upper classes very attractive when they chose to please.

Today the insensitivity, sometimes vulgarity, which often accompanies a sense of superiority is out of fashion, but on the night when I first dined with the Nortons I fell in love. Walking up the stairs after dinner, Jean said to Sheila Loughborough: 'This is the dress I bought in Paris. Do you like it?' and Sheila replied, 'Well, I would if it wasn't for that tarty bit of ribbon round the neck.' No one I had ever met before would have given that answer. Asked the question, my mother or her friends would have replied, 'Yes, I think it's lovely,' and given their real opinion to someone else. I think I already understood that, whereas my mother had two evening dresses, only one of them new, these women had dozens. Nevertheless, this speech had a dramatic effect on me, suggesting unimagined freedoms.

Clothes were a great bore in those days and a tremendous expense. One had to have different clothes for different occasions, and so many of them. My father gave my elder sister and me a dress allowance of £250 a year each, a sum which equals, I think, about £5,000 today, but we never had enough clothes. I was amused the other day to read, in a letter I wrote to my husband Jack at the beginning of the war in 1939, the description of a visit to the Ritz for a drink before luncheon. 'All the usual people were there but they wore country coats and skirts instead of London ones.' One of the unsung triumphs of the twentieth century is that the middle classes have lost their fears. They dress as they please and do as they please, and largely set the fashions rather than follow them.

Jean Norton was very beautiful and extremely spirited. She had dark blue, very short-sighted eyes, and, when she needed to see, wore horn-rimmed spectacles. She spent a lot of time in her bedroom – a glamorous room with soft pink quilts and white rugs. She wore pink satin pyjamas with a rounded Peter Pan collar, and she entertained fashionable London sitting up in bed. Cocktails would be brought there in the evenings and people would lie about at her feet, talking. She was the nearest thing to an Evelyn Waugh heroine ever to exist, except of course Diana Cooper who, as Mrs Stitch, actually was one. Evelyn did not invent this habit of entertaining in bed; it was a fashion of the times.

Women were in a transitional stage where they did much as they pleased but still kept up an Edwardian secrecy. The life of whole sections of London society was so frivolous and indeed so strange – Lady Stanley once boasted that she had not dined alone at home with her husband for two years – that a great deal of interchanging of partners was inevitable. Many of the young married couples were also short of the money needed to live the life they had been brought up to, and they, particularly the women, were not too scrupulous about how they acquired more. But in those days they all denied sexual intercourse, even when this was unobjectionable to a husband occupied elsewhere, usually saying, 'You see, darling, I don't much like that sort of thing.'

The parties I went to normally included either Sheila Loughborough with Buffles Milbanke, whom she afterwards married, or Edwina Mountbatten with Hugh Sefton. Sometimes we were joined by Freda Dudley Ward, accompanied by the Prince of Wales. Freda's husband, William Dudley Ward, a naval officer, had been stationed in Ramsgate during the war and we visited them at least once. Even as a child of seven or eight, I recognized Freda as a person of quite unusual individuality and charm, one element of which was her extreme good manners and kindness, more noticeable at the time because of the arrogance of fashionable manners. Now she remembered me, at least as my father's daughter, and later in life when she was asked why she confided certain matters to me, she replied in her small, squeaky voice: Well, I've known her since she was a child.'

If at this time the women of the upper classes did as they pleased, this was true only of married women. My own relationship with Richard Norton, which indirectly influenced my future considerably, cannot be explained unless it is understood that in those days it was necessary for girls to remain virgins if they wished to get married. I think now there may have been more who broke the rule than I realized then, but on the whole it was observed. It followed from this that for any man to seduce a virgin, even if not detrimental to his own career, it would impose the acceptance of a responsibility which most men preferred to avoid. It was therefore possible for me to have for some years a sentimental relationship with Richard which had the minimum of sexual content. This created a certain amount of scandal, since I was often one of a party in which all but Richard and I were paired off as lovers.

When my parents realized this, they stopped me from seeing him for a few weeks. But I mooned about the house and they could not keep it up. They believed that if they interfered too much with their daughters' lives we would never tell them anything and they would lose their influence over us, and they therefore abdicated without a trial. Their difficulties were much added to at the time by my sister, Mavis, who had a relationship, similar to mine with Richard, first with Herbert Buckmaster – Buck of Buck's Club – and then with Rupert Higgins, the son of a great Victorian figure, Harry Higgins, both the same age as her father. I think my parents lived in terrible fear of our future, a fear which caused them to become obsessed with the desire to see us married.

The parties I went to usually took place at the Embassy Club. I have described this in great detail in *Child of the Twenties* and it is enough to say here that it was the centre of an era of frivolity so fatuous that it is now impossible to understand, a time when people of all ages gave themselves up night after night to shuffling round the floor of a nightclub in partnership and in time to a band. At the Embassy Club, although the food was excellent, it was often allowed to grow cold on the table, since the moment the band struck up people rose to dance. Less wine was drunk, no vodka, but more whisky and gin. The manager of the club was called Luigi; he was a tremendous snob, whose knowledge of the social rating of his guests was equalled only by the arrogance with which he dealt with the lesser breeds. All the upper classes, actresses and famous men sat round the walls, but late at night, when people came in after the theatre, the tables encroached on the dance floor, and the discomfort of many of the lesser guests was extreme. Nothing but the desire to see and be seen could account for the willingness of so many people to take part in the crush, and nobody today would put up with the hauteur with which Luigi dealt with these difficulties. He was probably Italian, although he spoke perfect English, and he had a rather fine face. An unexpected light was thrown on him the other day by Camilla Cazalet, who told me that her father, George Gage, talking to a stranger out hunting, said:

'You know, you look exactly like Luigi.'

'I am Luigi,' the stranger replied.

The spirit of this society and this age is best depicted by Noël Coward in *The Vortex* and such songs as 'Dance, Dance, Dance Little Lady', and by Somerset Maugham in *Our Betters*, a play in which one of the characters was a 'gigolo' – a word much in use at the time to describe a man paid by a rich woman, if not to sleep with her then at least to dance with her, but not to be found in *The Shorter Oxford Dictionary* of 1933. Probably because they depict so accurately the spirit of a depraved yet essentially small and short-lived society, neither of these plays is much performed today. The number of people actually taking part in the nightlife of London was so small that they largely knew one another, if only by sight. The days are past, but only just, when old men could be heard complaining to each other: 'I dined at the Savoy last night. I didn't see a single soul I knew.'

In 1924 I went with Freddy to New York. Travelling with us on the boat were Jean Norton and Edwina Mountbatten. Freddy was going to produce a play, but Jean and Edwina were on their way to see the international polo matches between Great Britain and America. The Prince of Wales was there with the same object, and his general behaviour at that time was the first serious indication that he might lack some of the qualities necessary in the heir to the throne. 'Of course, New York was his undoing,' one of his equerries would say to me many years later. The Prince went out every night, on more than one occasion leaving the party arranged for him and disappearing until the early hours of the morning. All these proceedings were reported widely in the American press. Then, when rain delayed the polo matches, the Prince twice put off his arranged visit to Canada.

When Freddy and I visited Jean and Edwina in their hotel, they told us about these goings-on, and they, like the Prince's staff, were very disapproving. I have said enough to indicate that theirs was a fairly raffish society, but, no less than his own entourage, they felt their ways were quite unsuitable for the future King of England.

I seem quite quickly to have got bored with it myself, because soon after this I became an actress. At first I landed quite a good job in a new play with Ivor Novello and Constance Collier, but when my father heard of this he telephoned Ivor and told him that if I got the job neither he nor Constance Collier would ever get a play of his again. 'If you want to go on the stage,' he said to me, 'you can do what anyone else would have to do and go on tour.' I did go on tour for sixteen weeks in the smallest part in *The Last of Mrs Cheyney*, but I was very bad and I gave it up at the end.

At about this time Freddy left home. He said it was impossible to work at our house and he took a flat ostensibly for that purpose, but he spent more and more time there and finally moved in. Just before we left Birchington he had acquired a secretary, Miss Chesher, who was to become a factor in all our lives. She was very efficient and answered letters and kept accounts, but she proved surprisingly adaptable. In no time she was spending half her working day discussing with Freddy where he should go and what he should do, packing his clothes or unpacking them, and soon she joined parties of my sisters and myself when we crept up to Freddy's window to see what he was really doing when he was supposed to be working. All her life she was absolutely loyal to his interests, and when some financial crisis fell upon us it was often solved by Miss Chesher who had seized the fees from some past production and hoarded them against just such an occasion. Freddy also had a chauffeur-valet called Day who accompanied him wherever he went, and, in combination with Miss Chesher, filled all the gaps in a life where only the humdrum virtues, the most homely affections, might have been missed.

4

....

Maureen and Oliver Stanley

Freddy could not hold Jean Norton for long. She was after greater things, and it was widely said that she also fell much in love with Lord Beaverbrook. By a coincidence, it was at luncheon with Beaverbrook at Hurlingham that Freddy met Maureen Stanley, Jean's successor in his affections and the great love of his life.

'Will you come and dine one night?' she asked him as she got into her car to leave for London. 'I want to find out if all the terrible things Max says about you are true.'

Lady Maureen Stanley was the daughter of the Marquess of Londonderry, and was married to Oliver Stanley, the son of the Earl of Derby. Lord Derby and Lord Londonderry were at first highly suspicious of Freddy when he appeared too often in Maureen's company, but he proved as irresistible in this society as in any other. In no time he was staying with Lord Londonderry at Mount Stewart, and was playing golf with Lord Derby at Moujins. Inexplicably, given his family background, Freddy spoke like an English gentleman. I do not think he could have succeeded in this society if he had had any trace of the English Jerseyman's accent which, as opposed to the Norman Jerseyman's accent, is very unattractive.

The Stanleys had a house in Westmorland called Witherslack Hall, large enough to hold a great many people at weekend parties, and a London house in Dean Trench Street. They entertained extensively, and I went immediately to both their houses with Freddy. Maureen Stanley was very high-spirited and apparently free from any feelings of anxiety or guilt. She positively laughed at spilt milk, and she was no respecter of persons, a characteristic which endeared her to many of them. In London she conducted a largely political salon, keeping open house at six o'clock every evening, and at Witherslack she had anything up to eighteen guests for the weekend. Oliver told me once that he spent £1,000 a year on gin.

At that time Maureen was very dominant, but in retrospect one can see that Oliver was the more interesting of the two. When I first knew him he was a stockbroker and a backbencher in the House of Commons, but he became Under-Secretary to the Home Office in 1931 and after that, except when the Conservative Party was in opposition, was only once and for a short time without ministerial rank until he died. He held successively the posts of Minister of Transport 1933–4 (where he was responsible for the pedestrian crossings which were called Belisha beacons, after his successor, who actually introduced them), Minister of Labour 1934–5, President of the Board of Trade 1937–40, Secretary of State for war 1940, and Secretary for the colonies 1942–5.

When Oliver died in 1950, Winston Churchill, addressing the House of Commons, said that the tributes published in the news-papers showed how widely his exceptional and outstanding gifts were understood and admired, and went on to say that he regretted he had been unable to persuade Stanley to fill the Dominion Office on the formation of the National Government. And he went on: 'In the year before the war Oliver Stanley wrote to Mr Chamberlain, advising that the Government should be widened and strengthened in its composition, and placing his own office at the disposal of the Prime Minister in order to help that process.' Churchill said that he did not know of that until several years after, 'but it was a remark-able example of his bearing and his relation to public life, and a proof of the high level on which his actions proceeded'. He described Oliver as: 'A delightful companion, whose conversation never lost its dignity even in casual talk, and always preserved the spark of the unexpected, his memory will be long cherished by those who knew him ... They had lost a capable, experienced, attractive figure, who enriched their public life by a high character, disinterested service, and a commanding view of wide horizons.' It is customary to pay tributes to death in the House of Commons, yet sometimes these represent the truth. I have been struck, as would be anyone else who knew him, by this description of Oliver, who, born to every advantage, understood better than anyone else I have ever met the standards these imposed.

I was seventeen or eighteen when I first went to Witherslack, and I spent much time there until in 1939, at the outbreak of war, the house was lent to a school. One of the first people I met there was Tortor (Victoria) Gilmour, who was about five years older than me and who was to become a lifelong friend. After I left my first husband I spent two years living in her house. On the night I first met her, I stood aside at the door of the dining room to let her pass as we went into dinner. 'Don't stand aside for me, you chit,' she said, pushing me in.

Basically this was a serious society, very different from the frequenters of the Embassy Club, and still imbued with the belief in its hereditary right and duty to rule, both in its personal demesnes and in Parliament. Lord Derby was a king in Manchester and Oliver entered the House of Commons as a very young man. At Witherslack they were all unthinking Tories, by which I mean that on every subject they were stone-deaf to the arguments of any other political creed, and, even when at times they disapproved of some part of the policy of the Conservative Party, they never questioned where their loyalties lay. They numbered a few intellectual Liberals among their friends, but, as far as I know, no member of the Labour Party ever entered the house (although it was in these years that Lady Londonderry captivated Ramsay MacDonald). At the time of Munich the Stanleys belonged to a group which felt very strongly against appeasing the Germans, although publicly Oliver denied a rumour that he was unable to accept the agreement reached, saying that he was prepared to take a chance in the cause of peace. Normally kind and generous, they were more restricted in their power than their nineteenth-century ancestors, but their insensitivity to the lives of the working classes was hardly less. In the slump of 1929 and again in 1931, with two million unemployed, the Stanleys, like other country-house owners acting entirely from what they understood to be their duty, cut down the numbers of their house servants.

I had no difficulty in accepting these attitudes, because I too had never heard them questioned. I was brought up to have little thought about the working classes except when they were on strike and were regarded as enemies. Sometime in the years before 1926, my mother had shutters put on our London house, for fear of what she described as 'trouble'. Nor was this attitude unusual. In the 1931 election I went canvassing for Oliver in a seat, which, although it had a strong Conservative majority, included parts of an industrial town. We were told that some of the streets had been excluded from the canvass, because the inhabitants were believed to be so red as to be dangerous. When Tortor heard this, she

31

immediately volunteered to go, and, turning to me, said, 'And you will come with me.'

We spent all day in the slum streets, and during the whole of the day we met only apathy. The poverty was extreme, but no one believed that anything could be done about it. We received two stock replies to our questions: the first, 'None of it matters to us. It's all the same for us whoever gets in'; the second, 'Oh! we will vote Conservative. They are the people with the money, they must know best how to manage it.'

This second answer expressed exactly what the Tories felt themselves. They proceeded on the assumption that anything which adversely affected their profits was likely to be equally bad for the rest of the nation.

With all their advantages, these political families were, like the royal family itself, apt to be entirely philistine: without taste or culture or any feeling for the arts or music. (Tortor was the one exception I can remember to this rule. She loved music and went constantly to the opera: she also, as soon as she had any money, bought good modern pictures.) When Buck De La Warr stayed at Witherslack, he was shocked by the fact that there was not a single picture or object of any interest there; and my husband Jack, when I took him to dine with Lord Derby at the Villa Sansovino above Cannes, was equally shocked at the triviality of the conversation.

Both Maureen's and Oliver's families were of course very close to the royal family. Indeed, Maureen had been picked as a possible bride for the Duke of York, although she had refused this in order to marry a second son.

One thing I learned at that time – and it was to have some significance later in my life – was knowledge of the flaws in the character of the Prince of Wales. The Stanleys had very little time for him, although I have sometimes wondered how they would have felt if he had had more time for them. He stayed once at Witherslack, when he had royal business in the neighbourhood, and a room was specially done up for him. I was not there when he stayed, but I was told afterwards that he had been given Maureen's sitting room and spent much of his time there, ostensibly working. Once, when someone went in with a message, he was found dancing round the room by himself to the music of the gramophone.

Although the fact that my father took me about with him made my life more interesting than that of my sisters, we were all basically bored with living in London, since we knew so few people our own age. When I was still under twenty, we persuaded my mother to take a house in the country. My elder sister, Mavis, and I insisted on being given horses and, although we were quite inexpert, we soon took up hunting. Yet we still seldom met any young people and, because, like everyone else and all the heroines of Victorian novels, we had to get married, my mother began about now to take fright. In *Child of the Twenties* I described what happened as follows: 'It was in the following year, and largely as a result of the life we were leading, that my mother forced me, by the maximum of pressure, but also with extraordinary duplicity in the strangest set of circumstances, to marry a man twenty years older than myself, whom I did not want to marry.'

I do not now propose to go into this any further than I did then, except to say this: on the rare occasions on which I have told other people the details of what happened, they have been unable to understand how one could be forced as far as this. I can only say that parents then retained great authority – often lost nowadays when children are only two – and, in the case of my mother, affection and trust. I also counted on my father, who was at the time in America, to stop it when he came home, and here I quote again from *Child of the Twenties*: 'However, I misjudged him. When he arrived, he circled round the situation, suspicious, and with the manner of a dog who has just seen a ghost. He talked at length to my mother, but he did not talk to me. Then he left again for America.'

For most of my life I have believed that my mother's conduct was based on the shame of having three daughters not only unmarried, but with no prospect of marrying. Thinking about it lately, I realize that Freddy's income, although large, was uncertain, while nothing was saved, and she had no idea how we would live if anything happened to him or when he and my mother died.

After four years my marriage was annulled, but during that time I hunted all the winter, had a large number of dogs, and was not particularly unhappy. I knew that I had to leave in the end but I gave it long enough for my departure to be, as I thought, graceful. I have never regretted this marriage, because if my life had taken a different turn I might not have met Jack.

In the years immediately after I left my first husband, making use of the shorthand I had learned at school and also of my social position, I worked as a rather inefficient secretary to W. E. (Billy) Rootes. Again I wrote about this period in *Child of the Twenties*, and now I remember almost nothing about it. The ten-year gap in this narrative, apart from this short account, corresponds to the gap in my memory. The whole of this period of my life is now blank.

33

5

···

The Theory and Practice of Socialism

Leonora Wodehouse married Peter Cazalet in 1933 and with him acquired a country house called The Grange at Shipbourne in Kent. Peter had inherited Fairlawne, an eighteenth-century house and a thousand acres or so which went with it, but owing to death duties this house was let and the Cazalets lived for five or six years at The Grange. As I have explained earlier, Peter 'messed' with Jack Donaldson at Eton during the years that I was at school with Leonora, so it was inevitable that I met him in their house, and in 1935 we were married.

Jack came from a family of clergymen – his father was a master at Eton and later Master of Magdalene College, Cambridge, though he had taken Holy Orders, while his uncle was Bishop of Salisbury – and he had inherited the doomed but sustaining ambition to do good in the world. At this time he was working at the Pioneer Health Centre at Peckham, a family club and an experiment in medicine and sociology, run by Dr Williamson and Dr Pearse, with the primary object of doing research into health. The Centre had many attractions such as a large swimming pool, theatre and gymnasium, and the qualifications for joining were that the whole family should do so and that they should come together for a medical examination once a year. Jack ran the social floor in this club.

He had inherited £20,000 from his parents but he had already given half of this to ensure that the Pioneer Health Centre would open. When he asked me to marry him he told me that he did not propose to work primarily for money and that I would have to accept that condition. I did so and I think for the whole of our lives I have kept my part of the bargain, although this may have been made easier by the fact that by the time we had two children Jack himself had weakened a little on this point. At any rate, when he left the Pioneer Health Centre on the grounds that the social floors were running smoothly and no longer needed him, he went to a company called Transport Services, run by Philip Dunn, whose wife, Mary, later figures largely in this narrative.

We lived first in a small cottage in the village of Ivy Hatch, near Sevenoaks; but in 1936 we moved a few miles away to the Wood House at Shipbourne, which was built for us by Walter Gropius on land bought from Peter Cazalet. This house was the only country house Gropius built on his way through England to America, and is one of only three Gropius buildings in England, the others being a house in Church Street, Chelsea, since much altered, and the Village College at Cambridge. The Wood House was not much admired by the English, who dislike modern architecture too much to know the difference between good and bad, but it has been listed Grade Two and is often visited by foreigners.

It is worth recording that Gropius was a most modest man, admirable to deal with, and, unlike most architects of the present day, anxious to find out exactly what one wanted and to design the house accordingly. There was also a splendid builder called Durling, who finished the building in about six months. We lived there until war broke out in 1939. The Wood House was about ten minutes' walk from The Grange where P.G. Wodehouse often came, and I like to think we were part of what he called 'the gang'. Because we knew him so well then, his step-grandson, Edward Cazalet, asked me long after to write his biography.

Although it caused no breach between us, Jack and I held views which the rest of the gang could not share. I was once asked by Isaiah Berlin what first made me join the Labour Party, and I replied, 'Reading *The Coming Struggle for Power* by John Strachey.' Isaiah said then (as Tony Crosland has said in *The Future of Socialism*) that this was one of the most influential books of the century, responsible for the political conversion of hundreds of people.

However, I think it was probably Jack who was responsible for my conversion, although not directly. He had worked for six months in Liverpool staying at the University Settlement. Here he met radical social workers and helped in a survey of the slum areas. By the time I met him he was already a member of the Labour Party,

35

and, although like other people of opposite political views we merely quarrelled when we discussed these matters, it was he who supplied my reading matter. The time was also ripe. In another book of the thirties called *Nobody Talks Politics*, Geoffrey Gorer described a party, at a university which might well have been Cambridge, at which a young man is bitten by a lemur and falls asleep for ten years. At this party the conversation is rather pretentious, and concerned with aesthetics and intellectual matters, or else simply with gossip. Nobody talks politics. In 1934, when the young man awakes, nobody talks of anything else. Geoffrey Gorer was not so well informed as we are about the conversations at Cambridge in these years, but by the time his hero awakes most of the characters in his book had become either Communists or Fascists. The picture is exaggerated, but it represents a change which had actually occurred.

The stock market crash of 1929 caused a world slump and by the end of 1930 there were two and a half million unemployed in the United Kingdom. In 1931 a run on the pound brought about the end of the second Labour government. The National Government, a coalition of Conservatives with some Labour and some Liberal members, was formed to save the gold standard and to impose cuts of 10 per cent on unemployment benefit – something a Labour government could not have done. That the National Government immediately went off the gold standard it had promised to preserve caused little concern, but the cut in the dole changed the climate of the times.

I now believe that, although I must have read *The Coming Struggle for Power*, published in 1932, the book which converted me was *The Theory and Practice of Socialism*, also by Strachey but published in 1936. In any case, after my conversation with Isaiah I began to read these books again, and I now find the second one the easier to read and the more persuasive. John Strachey begins with an analysis of the faults of the economic and social system under which the British and American people lived, 'commonly called capitalism'; an analysis which remains curiously convincing even now. I shall return to this, but one cannot explain the extraordinary influence Strachey's analysis exerted on so many people in the mid-thirties unless one knows more of the conditions of that time than would nowadays be part of the natural understanding of anyone under the age of seventy.

First, there was the extreme poverty. Speaking of Britain and the United States as the two richest capitalist countries of the world,

Strachey makes the surprising statement that Great Britain was probably the richer and more prosperous of the two. Nevertheless, two-thirds of the British population, he tells us, had incomes averaging £25 per head per year. (Strachey gives sources for all his statements, although I will not quote them. A very rough guide to the value today of any figure given for the mid-thirties is to multiply by twenty-two.) This is about £550 in today's terms.

Even more influential than John Strachey in the formation of the political opinions of the thirties was his publisher, Victor Gollancz, who published each month a list of books for members of the Left Book Club. Living as Jack and I did, we saw very little real hardship. Peckham had been chosen for the site of the Pioneer Health Centre precisely because it housed a mixed population largely employed in London and relatively well off, since it would be impossible to conduct research into health among people who had not enough to eat. In Kent where we lived, the population was also relatively well off. When the war began and I travelled round England looking for a farm, I saw the poverty of the agricultural population for myself, but at this time it was chiefly from the Left Book Club that I learned of the condition of vast numbers of the British population, just as it was from these books that we knew what was going on in Germany. If this account quotes largely from other people, it is because my own experience was almost entirely confined to reading, although we joined the local Labour Party and went to meetings.

From the Left Book Club one gained a graphic account of what trying to live on £25 a year really meant. The most important book was a report entitled *Food, Health and Income* by Sir John Boyd Orr. I quote Strachey on it:

> Sir John Boyd Orr and his colleagues are public servants.* Hence we may say that in 1936 the British government announced that 10 per cent of the British people were getting inadequate quantities of every kind of food, and that a further 20 per cent got inadequate quantities of all the body-building and health-preserving foods. Thus 13,500,000, 30 per cent of the population, are very seriously under-nourished.†

Strachey then quotes Orr as saying that the number of children in the lower income groups is very large, and as supplying figures

* The report had been commissioned by official bodies such as the Rowett Institute and the Market Supply Committee.
† John Strachey, *The Theory and Practice of Socialism*, Gollancz (Left Book Club edition, 1937), p. 325.

which enable him to summarize as follows: 'Thus it seems probable that one-half of the children of one of the two richest capitalist communities in the world, which has developed an extraordinary capacity for wealth production, cannot get an adequate supply of the most elementary of all human necessities, food.' These figures were supported by *Poverty and Progress*, an investigation done by B. Seebohm Rowntree into the population of York, neither a distressed area nor a slum city. This investigation showed that 31 per cent of the working-class population and 18 per cent of the total population were living in poverty.

More than any other writer, George Orwell had the power to humanize these figures. He visited many of the people they describe and he had an ability quite unusual at the time to treat them, without patronage, as equals and friends. In addition, he was able, as most people of his background would not have been, to spend quite long periods in the appalling squalor in which the extremely poor lived. In *The Road to Wigan Pier* he brings alive what poverty of this kind really meant.

We knew, of course, that there were two million unemployed. Sometimes when we motored through the northern towns to Witherslack, we used to see the unemployed men standing in rows in front of their houses, and we wondered why they did that. Orwell describes the conditions they lived in and when one knows that often large families lived in houses consisting of two rooms up and one down, with a five-foot-wide alcove under the stairs serving as larder, scullery and coal hole, and a lavatory often fifty yards away behind the house, one realizes that the men had to stand outside while the women did the cleaning. Orwell wrote:

> One of [the three] rooms is a living-room, and as it probably measures about a dozen feet square and contains, besides the kitchen range and the sink, a table, some chairs and a dresser, there is no room for a bed. So there are eight or ten people sleeping in two small rooms, probably in at most four beds. If some of these people are adults and have to go to work, so much the worse. In one house, I remember, three grown-up girls shared the same bed and all went to work at different hours, each disturbing the others when she got up or came in; in another house a young miner working on the night shift slept by day in a narrow bed in which another member of the family slept by night.*

* George Orwell, *The Road to Wigan Pier*, pp. 57–8.

It is not necessary to quote Orwell extensively on under-nourishment, although he deals with it convincingly, because of the figures quoted above, but he wrote with irresistible persuasion of the lot of unemployed workers and their families. Thus speaking of the basis of the diet of an unemployed worker's family, which he says consists of white bread and margarine, corned beef, sugared tea and potatoes, he asks: 'Would it not be better if they spent more money on wholesome things like oranges and wholemeal bread?'* and then continues:

Yes, it would, but the point is that no ordinary human being is ever going to do such a thing. The ordinary human being would rather starve than live on brown bread and raw carrots. And the peculiar evil is this, that the less money you have, the less inclined you feel to spend it on wholesome food. A millionaire may enjoy breakfasting off orange juice and Ryvita biscuits; an unemployed man doesn't. ... When you are unemployed, which is to say when you are underfed, harassed, bored and miserable, you don't *want* to eat dull wholesome food. You want something a little bit 'tasty'.†

With these words Orwell opened up a breadth of understanding to which I had had no access before. I was also much influenced by an article which, although I have been unable to find it recently, I attribute with some confidence to him. This was called 'My Favourite Strike', and concerned a strike for the right to get drunk when not at work. Like many members of the middle classes, I had been brought up to regard all strikes as evil, strikers as the enemy. Orwell touched the imagination.

Strachey begins *The Theory and Practice of Socialism* with an analysis of the faults of the capitalist system of production for profit – what today might be called a free-market economy. Ready at hand he found the report on a National Survey of Potential Product Capacity, the authors of which had been appointed by the American government with the limited purpose of discovering the real productive capacity of American industry and agriculture, without reference to any particular system. Strachey says that the authors of the report had interpreted their terms of reference to mean that they should attempt to discover what was the capacity of the American productive system to satisfy the needs of the American people. This naturally involved ascertaining what were the needs

* George Orwell, *The Road to Wigan Pier*, p. 95.
† *Ibid.*

of the American people, which he says did not seem difficult, because in 1933, when the investigation started, the American people were short of a great many prime necessities such as food, clothes and housing.

Taking the example of housing, fifteen and a half million new dwellings were needed to satisfy the American people's need. Having explained that, the question then was: Would there be enough productive resources left over, *after the equally urgent immediate needs of the American people had been satisfied*, to enable them to build 1,550,000 dwellings a year for ten years? Strachey went on:

> Let us take a particular example. One of the productive resources needed for building 1,550,000 dwellings a year is structural steel. Would there be, the NSPPC authors enquired, enough structural steel left over from other equally urgent work for the job? At once we are led to ask whether all the uses which were made of the available structural steel were as urgent as building dwellings. Now in 1929 a very high proportion of America's output of structural steel was used to build skyscrapers, mainly intended for offices. And the authors of the NSPPC report could not help noticing that what the American people seemed to need was not office skyscrapers, but dwellings. A substantial proportion of the American people were ... housed in the most wretched kinds of run-down, tumbledown, insanitary and overcrowded slums and shacks. And on the other hand, nothing was more notorious than that nobody needed more office accommodation. For a high proportion of the recently built skyscrapers stood empty, while those that had filled up with tenants had done so by emptying the surrounding office accommodation of theirs.[*]

My intention in quoting Strachey at length on this subject is to show that, given any knowledge of the conditions of the poorer classes in Britain at that time, one was bound to find his argument convincing. What today's economists would make of the argument, I am too ignorant to know. Yet Strachey is writing of conditions after the stock market crash of 1929, and even a right-wing economist would have a job to prove it entirely irrelevant to the present time, which in May 1990 gave rise to an article in the *Independent* under the headline 'Big Bang, Crash – and Wallop' :† 'The Big Bang blew the lid on office development. The crash brought everyone

---

* John Strachey, *The Theory and Practice of Socialism*, p. 30.
† The Big Bang was the computerizing of the Stock Exchange, the crash the drop in share values of 1987.

back to earth. Now the metropolis is reeling under wallops of empty buildings. One acerbic observer goes as far as to suggest that half the proposed office schemes should be switched to housing – a total of around 500 sites.'

Strachey makes one other point which is worth repeating. In Britain and in America, the lives of all except the securely rich were dominated in the 1930s as much by the fear of want as by want itself. He is speaking of the managerial and professional classes and owner-producers, such as farmers. It is true that a high degree of unemployment affects everyone. I remember being told by Harry Waugh, who was then managing director of one of the biggest wine merchants in England, that in the thirties he took money at the gate of the greyhound racing course at Wembley, because he was unable to get any other job. When Jack left the Pioneer Health Centre, despite a double first from Cambridge and his experience of work in Lloyds Bank as well as his work at Peckham, we were extremely nervous that he might not get a job. In the end he did, but through the old boy network. Because of the fear of losing jobs, employers could treat their employees outrageously, and men with wives and children to support were forced to put up with it. I saw this for myself when, for a short time between my two marriages, I worked in a motorcar showroom.

I sometimes discussed these things with Oliver Stanley, who then held Cabinet rank. He would reply that the difficulty was that, if one meddled with the economy, one might easily succeed in making things worse. Although he would not have put it like this, he was thinking of what is nowadays called 'the trickle-down effect'. He believed, as so many people do and did, that the profits of the very rich are necessary to the well-being of everyone else.

Yet, if Strachey's analysis of the failures of the capitalist system is persuasive even today, his description of the alternative is breath-taking. He believed, I think, as all Marxists did, that the 'inner contradictions' of capitalism would lead to a gradual pauperization of the masses, and ultimately to the collapse of the whole system. And he believed that, now that a system of planned production was in force on over 'one-sixth of the world's surface ... ' the best men and women of every class ... will come to the conclusion that they cannot find a worthy purpose for their lives except by participation in the organized movement to change the world'.

Strachey relied to a large extent on Sidney and Beatrice Webb's *Soviet Communism: A New Civilization*. Neither the Webbs nor Strachey knew then that human nature is so evil that, all over the world, any economic system which relies on a central planning authority has led almost automatically to prison camps, torture, corruption and death. Even so, all three seem to have been a bit naive. Thus, after saying that every capitalist government is today faced with the urgent problem of finding a market even for those goods its half-stifled productive system produces, while only the Soviet government enjoys the illimitable market provided by its own population, Strachey adds: 'For it has taken good care to equip the population with the necessary purchasing power,' and goes on to quote the Webbs:

Who can compute the effect of the ever-widening desire for two or three rooms per family, instead of the one, or much less than one, with which nine-tenths of the population of tsarist Russia contented itself; of the never satisfied clamour for more clothing and better; of the ever-rising standards expected in public health and public education; of the demand for more hospitals and maternity centres, with an almost illimitable increase in the nurses and doctors serving all the villages between the Baltic and the Pacific; of the desire for more schools and libraries, with endlessly more teachers and professors and textbooks and scientific apparatus, over one-sixth of the entire land-surface of the globe?

And the Webbs finish this glowing account by saying:

Meanwhile, no one can fail to recognize that, in 1935, there is vastly greater plenty, in the cities and in the villages, than there has been at any time in previous Russian history. The shops and stores are now abundantly supplied, ration cards have been one after another abolished, and the total retail sales are going up by leaps and bounds.

No one can appreciate the spirit of the 1930s, which in the long term was to move mountains, unless they realize that not only Strachey and the Webbs believed all this stuff, but their innumerable readers did too. The mixture of the true, appalling poverty in Britain and the United States, and the false success of the Soviet system created a vast body of opinion which believed urgently in the necessity for change.

I do not think Jack and I would ever have joined the Communist Party, because we are not wild enough; but the matter was settled conclusively for us when we went to dinner with a Communist friend to meet a Communist lawyer and writer on politics. When we left, we agreed immediately that he cared absolutely nothing for the truth and that our host had never challenged his statements. Members of the local Labour Party, as also its leaders, were always fairly sound on the Communists. 'You can't trust them,' one of them said to us. 'In the end they'll always let you down.' But we did join the Popular Front, which to their everlasting credit did not include the leaders of the Labour Party, but was an attempt to create an alliance between all left-of-centre parties, including the Communists.

Only two things spoiled our lives in those days. The first was the necessity to have servants. In spite of the unemployment figures, except in large houses which offered both prestige and a life of their own, servants were not easy to get, and yet they were an essential part of middle-class life. For us it was absolutely necessary to have a cook, a housemaid and a nanny or mother's help for our children. These women were fed and housed and kept warm, but they were paid, if my memory is correct, something like £28 a year. At our level of affluence we could hardly afford all this and by the time war was declared we had a bank overdraft which, although not very big, was not negligible. Yet I never thought of managing with less; I did not think about it at all except when someone left, when I felt anxious about replacing her. Since I could neither cook nor iron nor sew, and had not the slightest idea of how a bath was cleaned or of any of the other household chores, I relied, as my mother and father had (even when he was living on the loan from Mr Conran), on others.

In England at the time, the food in large country houses was as good as anywhere in the world, a mixture of English and French cooking; everywhere else it was execrable. The cooks employed by people like myself were neither trained nor particularly interested. It was not until the war forced us all to learn to look after ourselves, and Elizabeth David came along to educate the whole nation, that food in England reached a standard which would have been acceptable in any other European country.

However, what chiefly spoiled our lives was Germany. It is customary to say that the German people too often shut their eyes to what was happening after the rise of Hitler and the Nazis. The same was at least as true in Britain, where most people resolutely refused to know about it. This was not an option for members of the Left Book Club, who in books like Douglas Reed's *The Burning of the Reichstag* and G. E. R. Gedye's *Fallen Bastions* were forced to learn it all.

Jack and I also had certain personal experiences. A young German doctor named Anni Noll came to work at the Pioneer Health Centre. She had left Germany because she had received an order not to treat Jews. This, she said, meant that if a Jew was injured in a car accident outside her front door, she could do nothing for him. Unable to accept this, she came to England.

Then we brought over a Czech girl, Freda, as a servant, and later Dr and Mrs Mandelbaum, two German Jews related to a friend of ours, came as our guests. Dr Mandelbaum had been in a con-centration camp, although he was a man of about sixty. He said that at this time – mid-1939 – it was not too bad if you could manage not to draw attention to yourself. 'Sometimes we had to stand in lines outside for twenty-four hours. It was all right for those who could manage to do this. But if anyone stumbled, or fell due to cold or fatigue, the Nazi guards fell upon him.'

All these people, particularly Freda, were terribly unhappy. In our unimaginative way, we had expected, not gratitude but some degree of elation at having escaped the horrors of Nazi occupation. But they had left their homes and everything they knew in life and come to a country where they knew no one, and were dependent on strangers. Freda was stony with misery and a great source of unhappiness to us. However, she soon developed a neurotic illness and departed to hospital.

Because he was working for a road transport firm, Jack auto-matically joined Movement Control, a section of the Royal Engin-eers, when the Army asked for volunteers for the reserve force. Movement Control was responsible for the movement of everyone else, and as a result landed everywhere in advance. Jack was called up on 1 September 1939 and war was declared on the third. He went to France a week or two later, and, except for a short period after the fall of France and another before D-Day, he was abroad for the whole of the war.

PART II

···

War

6

....

Learning to Farm

W e had two children by the time Jack left for the war; Thomas
was born in 1936 and Rose in 1937. We also had a nanny,
so that I could have done some sort of local war work, if I had been
willing to leave them to her; but I was not, and, although this
narrative is little concerned with their lives, I would never have left
them. This made my life boring as well as sad after Jack had gone.

He was the first to bring up the idea that I should buy a farm. As
early as 18 September 1939 he wrote:

> The more I think about things, the more I think if we ever get
> back again and settled down, we'd better seriously try to take up
> farming. I know that I don't really want anything from life but
> to be with you and the children and work together at home, and
> I can't see what else we can work at. Think about it seriously.
> ... Have a talk with Peter [Cazalet] about the whole thing. There
> is no doubt that land is a good thing to buy at this particular
> moment, and you might get some land-army experience or some
> actual experience with Peter. I suppose you're still finding too
> little to do, and it might be something to go for.

It was true that I had too little to do and I seem to have immediately considered his suggestion. I was already aware, however, that
the fact I knew nothing whatever about farming might turn out to
be the least of my disabilities. Farmers are unpopular with many
people today because their drive towards ever-increasing efficiency
brings with it certain agricultural practices the general public dis-

likes. Yet, in spite of the diminished economy, ours is a fair, well-ordered land, green in aspect, drained and watered, with well-kept buildings and modern cottages.

In 1939, although Britain was still one of the two richest nations in the world, her agricultural land, like the streets of Wigan, proclaimed the almost complete impoverishment not merely of the local population but of the nation's assets. The neglect of the countryside then was a matter of far greater concern than, for instance, the annual burning of straw.

I have written of this before, while the facts were still close enough for my account to be accurate. Since it is all so long ago that I cannot trust my memory for detail, I propose to quote what I wrote earlier.

Speaking of staying with the Oliver Stanleys at Witherslack, I wrote:

> The graces of the country-house society in England were almost entirely private ones, and hardly extended beyond the confines of the garden. Around lay the farms, impoverished and under-capitalized. Cottages and buildings fell into disrepair for the unquestioned reason that it was not a paying proposition to maintain them. By the time I travelled round England looking for a farm at the beginning of the Second World War, the desolation was complete. There were whole villages in which there was not a single plough, not a single water-tap and no drains. [There were standpipes in the street where the villagers drew water in buckets.] On the farms the buildings were falling down, the thatch caved in and smelling of must, the bricks and rubble overgrown with nettles. There were no fences, no roads and no water. Often the stock of several hundred acres would be a few milking cows, lying in short standings, continually slapping their tails against flies, and a few hens scratching about in the rick-yard. The derelict appearance of the farmyards was often increased by the hulks of American cars. The only implement the farmers ever seemed to own was a hay-sweep, and this they drove with someone's cast-off car because they could not afford a tractor.

(In 1939, referring to the subsidy of £2 an acre to farmers ploughing up grassland, Professor Sir George Stapledon wrote that this would cause more experimenting on the lands of Britain than had taken place during the last fifteen years. But he also said: 'It is to be feared that in many districts, and indeed in just those where

48

the ploughing up would be capable of doing the maximum amount of good, relatively little, or next to nothing, will be done just because the farmers are incapable of ploughing, have no ploughs, and because tractors are not in the districts in question.')*

When I got the letter from Jack suggesting I should buy a farm, I did not discuss it with Peter Cazalet, because, although he owned many hundred of acres, his only real love was his racing stable, and his farms were only slightly above the condition of the surrounding land. I knew without asking him that his view would be that to buy a farm, and without any knowledge of how to farm it, was the most certain route to losing money one could think of, and I went instead to see another friend, Buck De La Warr.

The ninth Earl De La Warr, a notable eccentric himself, was the child of two eccentrics, and, looking back on his achievements, I think that, in relation to many of his contemporaries, he was underrated. His father was a spendthrift who was said to have left the upkeep of several mistresses to Buck, as well as two derelict estates. His mother, who was the greatest influence in his childhood, was a Theosophist and a close friend of Annie Besant. Buck was brought up by her in the role of acolyte to Krishna Murti; but, when the Indian mystic and philosopher rejected the claims made for him by the Theosophists, Buck was able to do the same. As a result of his mother's beliefs, he was nevertheless a pacifist in 1914, when he served on a minesweeper, and later he joined the Labour Party, virtually alone among contemporaries in his own class to do so. I think he always resented his upbringing because it set him apart from other people, particularly from those who would naturally have been his friends. In 1931 he followed Ramsay Mac-Donald into the coalition National Government as a member of the National Labour Party, and at the time of which I write he was President of the Board of Education.

His father died in 1912 and left him an estate of about a thousand acres in a condition so neglected, I am told, that in those days it was impossible to ride a horse across it because of the molehills. In 1933 Buck came into contact with Sir George Stapledon, the guru of the agricultural revolution about to take place. Since both he and the systems he introduced will be often referred to, some account of both may be necessary. Stapledon was Professor of Agricultural Botany at the University College of Wales, Aberystwyth, and Director of the Welsh Plant Breeding Station. In this

---

* George Stapledon, *The Plough-Up Policy and Ley Farming*, Faber & Faber (1939).

latter capacity he bred the grasses which made the rotational system of ley farming possible, and he spared no pains in preaching the gospel to the farmers. Put at its simplest, ley farming consisted in ploughing up the old and worn-out permanent pastures and treating grass as a rotational crop. Almost all systems of farming are based on it today, and in those days the saying was that it made it possible to carry four head of stock where only one was carried before.

The excellent thing about Buck was that he was so dashing in his outlook that he adopted Stapledon's views with enthusiasm and put them into practice on his farms. By the time war began he had reclaimed hundreds of acres, built farm buildings and cottages, and, quite unusually, he was making a profit. All this had been achieved during the exact period when the land and buildings of even the richest landlords were often completely neglected, and the crisis in agriculture visible to the eye.

I went to see Buck immediately after I got the letter from Jack, and I think the fact that I was ultimately successful in farming was largely because I was in so early : before the wartime mood caused many other people to follow my lead, before the price of land and cattle spiralled.

Buck soon produced a civil servant from the Ministry of Agriculture who gave me advice as to where to look for a farm. (I may as well say here that since all the advice one received was based on the conditions of the past and these were about to change completely, much of it seems either wrong or pointless today.) This man gave an opinion which is now incomprehensible. Yet it served to start me off and, accompanied by Lucy Crocker, who had been an important member of the Pioneer Health Centre staff, I was soon driving round on the search for a farm. We started on the borders of Essex and Hertfordshire, and I described our experiences in a letter to Jack :

> From the Wood House
> 8.11.39

Lucy and I had another completely wasted morning. I must say the English countryside is very queer. There are so many decayed and rather morbid little villages and so many shut in and weird people. Lucy said this morning it was just like one little private madhouse after another and this is just what I had been thinking. ... I was very surprised because I don't think Kent or Sussex is like this but Lucy says it is the same everywhere, that if you walk anywhere in England and Wales you meet it all the time. We found out one thing which is the reason so many farms round here have these revolting little villas on them is that the farmers have sold all the farmhouses to people who want old Tudor weekend cottages. It is really rather awful because it completely spoils the whole character not only of the farms but of farming and it is really a disgrace that agriculture should have been allowed to fall to a level where the farmers had to do this, though in many cases if they were clever they must have got as much for the house as they would have for the house and farm.*

All this was very putting off and I never could decide whether I really intended to buy a farm until I actually did so. Still, I continued to behave as though I meant it. Just before Christmas I fell in love with a farm on the Wiltshire downs and Buck said that after Christmas his agent, Mr Pewsey, should come and look at it for me.

A good many other difficulties had to be surmounted. Although I had for a long time owned horses and dogs, I knew nothing about farming, and, apart from a few landowners with tenants and a home farm, I did not know any farmers. I could not just go to an auction and buy a farm.

It was fairly clear that I should have to go to a college or farm institute. The main difficulty was the children, whom I could not simply leave, but this problem was very quickly solved in a way that could not have happened before the war. A friend of ours, Mary Dunn, moved by the spirit which would soon move hundreds of people besides our two selves – roughly that, with the long-term future so ill-defined, one felt a necessity to do something worth doing and was prepared to take risks one would not have dreamed of in peacetime – had already bought a farm at Lavendon near Northampton with a house big enough for more than one family. Her farm was near Moulton Farm Institute, one of the two best in England. Sometime in January 1940 I moved myself, my two children and their nanny to stay with Mary at Castle Farm, Lavendon.

Mary Dunn was the daughter of the Earl of Rosslyn, like Buck's father a reprobate and impoverished peer. In her youth she was one of the most attractive of what was still called London society, while recently she has had renewed fame with the revelation that John Betjeman apparently wished to marry her. Bevis Hillier,

---

* *Plus ça change* ... Farmers still sell farmhouses, but now it is because having joined several farms they do not need all the houses.

Betjeman's biographer, quotes the writer Daphne Fielding as saying: 'She looked like a pretty and impertinent schoolgirl dressed up in her mother's clothes. She could get away with almost anything through her charm, and was always forgiven.' And she added: 'There was often plenty to forgive.'

Mary had as much charm, more zest and more appetite for life than almost anyone I have ever met, and she lived on her wits. She never had any desire to be a great hostess, as several of her contemporaries were, but she did want to go to the opera, to the theatre, to all the parties, and to have horses to ride. Until she married Philip Dunn, she succeeded in doing almost everything she wanted to do by a confident, irrepressible and sufficiently engaging determination to cadge. She knew everyone who could supply free seats for the opera or a free mount, who had a country house or a villa in the South of France, and she simply trusted them to look after her. After she married Philip, she was able, for instance, to buy Castle Farm, Lavendon, but he kept her on a fairly tight rein in her personal expenditure.

I did not know her well until I married Jack, who was one of her friends; then I lunched with her once at a house in Regent's Park when we were both heavily pregnant with babies whose birth was overdue – she with her second child, I with my first. After lunch she drove me round Regent's Park in an open Bentley at reckless speed, in the hope that this might induce birth. 'If you could choose when to have it,' she asked me on our return, 'would you choose next Monday or take a chance?' I chose next Monday but she, true to form, took her chance.

My child was born punctually on the following Monday and Mary visited me in the nursing home where, following the habit of those days, I would be confined to bed for several weeks. She was magnificently pregnant and she wore a printed silk dress, high-heeled shoes and a large picture hat. The baby she carried with such panache was born about ten days later and is known to the public today as Nell Dunn.

On the night I arrived at Castle Farm, Mary welcomed me with a splendid dinner and a bottle of wine and I felt happy almost for the first time since the war had begun. Part of our conversation that night is worth repeating, since it illustrates the principles by which Mary lived. At the beginning of the war she had gone to stay with Peggy Dunne, a friend of hers and of mine who had a house, stables and land in Warwickshire, and taken with her two children, a nanny and two horses. She had refused to pay Peggy more than

£6 a week for this lot because she said it was all she could afford. Peggy had therefore insisted to me that I should not pay Mary more than £4 a week for myself, my two children and nanny. However, I felt unable to do that, and I offered Mary £6 a week, which she refused to take. 'I have far more money than you have,' she said. 'I'll take four.'

One other thing was decided that night. Another friend of mine, Coney (Antonia) Jarvis, who was married to Ralph Jarvis, heir to Doddington Manor, an Elizabethan house near Lincoln with a good deal of land, thought that she could do worse than spend the war learning something about farming while Ralph was in France. I arranged with Mary that she too should come to stay and go to the Farm Institute with us.

Coney was a tall and very striking Nordic blonde, the daughter of that Charlie Mead who appears in the letters of Conrad Russell. She was a very great friend of mine, and we were both (modestly) immortalized by Evelyn Waugh in *Unconditional Surrender*, where Everard Spruce's two secretaries are named Frankie and Coney.* Soon I was writing to Jack as follows:

> You have no idea how much I love Mary. She hasn't got the solidity of Coney but she is the sweetest character I have ever met – unpossessive, unaggressive, uncompetitive, tolerant, sweet-tempered, always gay & friendly & unsuspicious and ready to enjoy things. Leaving you out of it I have never (possible exception Tortor) before stayed any length of time with anyone & liked them more & more every day. Coney for instance is really nice & would be a better person to marry but she is far more possessive & ungenerous, rather strikingly critical about everything which belongs to anyone else or that anyone else does (I rather guess Ralph is like that too & they encourage each other) & takes an awful lot for granted without making tremendous efforts in return. I am not complaining of Coney because I expect everyone to have their faults but, except for being irresponsible, Mary really has none.

When I arrived at Lavendon, Mary had been the proud owner of a farm for two weeks and had been attending the Farm Institute for about the same time. Her conversation was so lavishly sprinkled with references to stores, foddering, lime efficiency, soil analyses

---

* Evelyn Waugh, *Unconditional Surrender*, Chapman & Hall (1961). See also Frances Donaldson, *Evelyn Waugh: Portrait of a Country Neighbour*, Weidenfeld & Nicolson (1968), pp. 113–14.

and so on that I despaired of ever catching up. However, she admitted that she had already made one or two bloomers in class, and when pressed for details said that on one occasion when the lecturer had been emphasizing the necessity of making sure, when buying a dairy bull, that it had a good milk record, she had remarked that she failed to see how a bull could have a good milk record.

Coney and I enrolled without difficulty at the Farm Institute which we tried to attend every morning. In January and February 1940 snow lay so thickly and so frozen on the ground that one could walk round Mary's farm, crossing from one field to another over the top of the hedges. Moulton was about ten miles away and in those days anti-freeze had not yet been invented. Nine days out of ten the car began to boil after we had gone a few miles, and we had to drive by alternately running the engine until it boiled and then turning it off and waiting until the water had thawed out. We were almost invariably late, but on the days when the veterinary surgeon, who came from outside, missed his lectures because of the state of the roads, we hoped it might stand to our credit that we at least were there.

The standard of teaching was appalling, as lectures consisted chiefly of material read out of a book at dictation speed. The point in going to the Institute turned out to be almost nothing we could learn directly but the relationship we formed with Mr Stewart, the director, Mr Lindsay, his assistant, and Miss Strang, who was in charge of both dairying and hens; although, to be fair, students living in did practical work which must have had more point. Mr Stewart, Mr Lindsay and Miss Strang also led the Agricultural Advisory Service for Northampton. In order to promote and keep these relationships, we attended the lectures regularly; at least, Coney and I did. In the following narrative a man named Cecil Evans will constantly be referred to. He managed farms for Peggy Dunne and when Mary and I started farming, he helped us. He had apparently already advised Mary to get rid of the bailiff who was running the farm when she bought it.

From Lavendon
15.2.40

I will tell about life on the farm. Mary had a terrific row with Lawrence (the sacked bailiff) about two days after she sacked him. Cecil Evans was with her and Lawrence, who is I think a bit mad, suddenly laid about them & called them both everything he could think of. So on Cecil's advice Mary kicked him off the farm with a month's money & told him not to come back. This leaves Mary bailiffless but thoroughly happy as she is now busy running things herself.

She is very sweet but completely without discrimination. She doesn't go to the college any more because she has too much to do. But she does mainly all the wrong things. It is difficult to describe but you know her & can probably imagine it. For instance, her cows were being fed all wrong & we got the right rations written out by the people at the college. Well they are right and they are good & if Mary would give orders & possibly watch them carried out once or twice the whole thing would be first class. Instead of which she goes mad with excitement, gets Coney & me up at 6.30 in the morning & we all rush out & mix the food ourselves. Result we get mixed up in the amounts, give one cow twice too much & two others half enough & leave all the men standing round saying 'If you'll excuse me, my lady. . . .' Actually it suits everyone. Because Mary enjoys herself absolutely madly, though struck to the earth by every mistake, and Coney & I don't in the least mind making fools of ourselves in front of Mary's men whereas we wouldn't dream of doing the same thing on our own farms.

Everything we learn at the college is very scientific & when they sent out Mary's ration sheet it didn't obey the rules. Coney & I worked out the sum to see if it was correct (in starch equivalent and protein equivalent which are now everyday terms to us) and finding it wrong we tackled Mr Stewart about it yesterday. He was very much amused and asked us what was wrong & we told him correctly. He said of course he knew it was wrong but he was making the best, i.e. cheapest, use of the foods Mary had. All this sort of thing is quite fun & we all enjoy it but so far I am not making any practical progress towards being a farmer. I can't tell good hay from bad. I can't tell a fat sheep from a thin. I can't tell a good milker from a bad. . . .

[*Lavendon, undated*]

There are three good people at the college, Mr Stewart, Mr Lindsay and Miss Strang. Then there are three others who take various subjects. They all lecture fast & badly & contradict themselves & they all really resent any questions or attempts to find out something about their subject. Two of them get really rude if anyone asks more than one question. They seem to prefer complete apathy in the students so that they can spout their lecture and go away & not be worried with really teaching anything. It is an odd point of view but they all seem to have it so I wouldn't be surprised if it isn't quite common among bad teachers.

Lawrence, Mary's ex-bailiff, is still in possession of his cottage but is due to go this Saturday. We all had a pretty shrewd idea that he didn't mean to go but Mary was too frightened of him to go & find out (he is really a maniac and called her a silly bitch & various other pretty names which broke her nerve). . . . So tonight I went down & said I had just come to find out what time he was going on Saturday as Mary had a new man coming on Monday and wanted to put the furniture in. This wasn't particularly brave of me – though Mary was impressed – because I was pretty certain he couldn't be worse than a bit rude to me as I would just take the line that it was nothing to do with me & would tell Mary what he had to say.

Well sure enough he has absolutely no intention of going. So now we are busy finding out whether we are legally on safe ground to throw him out & if so we are jolly well going to – bag and baggage.

We all take rather a self-pitying line about how hard it is not to have any men about to deal with this sort of thing, but as a matter of fact we are thrilled by the whole thing and longing to bounce him out on his bottom.

I no longer remember exactly what happened, but I have no doubt we bounced him out on his bottom. In those days the law was much in favour of landlords, who could bounce anyone out whenever they felt like it. The story of Lawrence does nevertheless give an example of what we were up against in trying to find a bailiff. The owners of large estates normally employed farm managers, a more educated and more reliable order ; the bailiff had usually risen from the ranks of farm labourers. The minimum agricultural wage was thirty-five shillings a week, and this set the standard for those on higher wages. Men with ability and experience were not attracted to agriculture, and those who did work in it were more or less forced to cheat their employers in order to live. In all my letters to Jack there is much emphasis on honesty. 'Cecil Evans is absolutely honest' ; 'Mr Stewart says he is honest' ; and so on.

When in spring the snow finally cleared, I asked Buck to let Mr Pewsey come with me to see the Wiltshire farm I wanted to buy, but he explained that because of the weather they were so far behind with the work that it would be many weeks before Mr

Pewsey could be spared. When I told Mr Stewart this, he said he would come with me himself. He was as good as his word, and, as he thought the Wiltshire farm would need more money than I possessed, he actually saw several farms with me. This chance had the result that he, Mr Lindsay and Miss Strang all became closely involved in my affairs ; and as I stood on the brink of the agricultural revolution in which science and engineering would take over from Farmer Giles, this was of inestimable benefit. When Cecil Evans told me that there was a good farm – Gipsy Hall – for sale at Wilmcote, Mr Stewart came with me to see it.

Wilmcote is famous for the house in which Mary Arden, Shakespeare's mother, lived, but apart from this it has few attractions. Passing Mary Arden's House, you arrive at a T-junction, where if you turned left in those days you soon came into the open country. But if you turned right you passed on the left an endless line of recently built houses and bungalows of the kind then referred to as ribbon road development. On the other side there was a long line of nineteenth-century stone cottages, and then the gate to Gipsy Hall. For some reason connected with the lavish past, Wilmcote, although only a few miles from Stratford-on-Avon, was given its own railway station and this was to prove a great asset, particularly when friends from London came to stay.

When you first turn in the gate at Gipsy Hall there is an inviting prospect, since a long drive runs the full length of a fifteen-acre field. At the end of the field is a second gate, and it was after we passed through this that the prospect changed. Immediately in front was an orchard and to the left of that some new Dutch barns at the entrance to a square yard with farm buildings on three sides and a pond on the left. Behind the pond were more Dutch barns and, in the far right-hand corner, the house.

This place had no pretensions to be anything grander than an agricultural holding with a serviceable but plain house, built in the latter part of the last century. What made it unattractive, however, was not the simplicity but the mud. All round the farmyard the mud lay wet and thick on the ground; and in fact, except at midsummer, one did not go out of the house at Gipsy Hall except in gumboots. The mud was an indication that the land might be wet and heavy and indeed this was true, but Mr Stewart thought, quite correctly, that it was surprisingly well-drained.* What made

---

* I have only recently learned that the whole acreage had been quarried for stone which would surely account for the drainage.

it unlike almost any other farm that I had seen, and certainly any that I could afford, was not only the extent and splendour of the Dutch barns but the fact that it had been extremely well farmed, and looked marvellously well. After the snow and frost the fields were strong with winter wheat, the spring crops were going in and the grassland looked reasonably productive.

On the day when we went to see Gipsy Hall Mr Stewart and I had tea with Clyde Higgs, an extremely forceful character who was ultimately to have a great effect on my life. He had large farms with milking herds which supplied most of Stratford-on-Avon with milk, and was an important local character. He was horrified when he heard from Mr Stewart that I was considering buying Gipsy Hall, which he described as a wet hole unfit for a woman to farm. But Gipsy Hall was easier than it looked, and Mr Stewart was undisturbed by Clyde Higgs's vehemence. When we went home it was with some idea that I might bid for the farm.

7

....

Gipsy Hall

Gipsy Hall was a holding of 375 acres and it was for sale for £8,500. I had recently sent Jack an estimate of how much money we had, which read as follows:

£11,000   securities with Lloyds Bank.
£900   in Annesley Trust.
£1,750   possible from Dave [a friend in whose business we had invested money].
£5,000   with Julian [a friend to whom Jack had lent money to buy a partnership in a firm of stockbrokers. This had been many years before and Julian was thought to be a rich man.]

We also had the Wood House but we did not want to sell this, so this left a total of something over £18,000. I had been told that one needed in addition to the purchase price something between £15 and £20 per acre working capital.

I made an offer of £8,000 for Gipsy Hall – just over £20 an acre – and it was accepted. This was not the end of the matter, however, because I was immediately offered £10,000 for it, which left the position at least temporarily open.

Three things tempted me to sell. The first was that Julian had some secret drain on his money and actually could not pay back our £5,000. In the very long run we got back a good deal of what he owed, but at that time we received absolutely nothing. This meant that, although I could still just about buy and stock Gipsy Hall, I should probably need a mortgage to make it work.

59

The second great difficulty was that, apart from a very small cottage in the middle of the farm, Gipsy Hall had only one house. It was thought that at the price I had paid I could afford to build some cottages, but this would obviously take time and meanwhile, since the bailiff would live in the farmhouse, there was nowhere for me and the children. The third reason was that the farm was without any of the attractions either I or any of my friends had been accustomed to. By the beginning of April I had not yet decided and I wrote to Jack as follows:

5.4.40

As to the farm itself I still think in spite of all these fears that it would be a good buy in many ways. No one will ever say the Donaldsons have bought a lovely farm but you know it wouldn't help us much if they did & we were losing a packet on it. And I have really begun to believe that short of a miracle you can't have everything. The lovely farms are apt to belong to other people of our class & consequently with our views on aesthetic matters, who paid too much because of the beauty of the place, let it go downhill & now want to get out at a profit because they have put in electric light & an Aga cooker. This farm is so near the borderline of unattractiveness & that is what worries me about your not having seen it. To me it is not unattractive. I like its workmanlikeness & when I am there, though I don't love it like I loved Bilbury [the Wiltshire farm], I have quite a cosy feeling about it & am not repelled & ashamed by the idea of owning it.

But it is a complete toss-up whether you will feel like that too or whether you will wish it was a bit nicer. Of course, one thing is that you are really much better at liking sensible things than I am. I *say* I want a good farm and don't mind about the house but it isn't true, but you say it and mean it.

This was quite true. I am a nervous snob with not exactly a desire to show off, but a great desire not to seem ignorant or foolish; whereas Jack has none of these ignoble feelings. The situation was immediately complicated by the fact that a farm which adjoined Gipsy Hall was up for sale and Cecil Evans thought it might suit me better. The choice between the attractive and the practical is best explained in the following letter to Jack:

Lavendon 9.5.40

We went to see the farm adjoining GH farm. Peggy & Mary came. It is without exception the prettiest & most charming place I have seen. It is right off the road in a little sort of hamlet & both the houses are charming – so much so that one would have difficulty in deciding which to live in. The country is also very pretty, much more so than GH. Those are the good points. The bad are that the land needs heavy stocking, draining thoroughly everywhere & the whole lot ploughed up. There are, with the exception of one Dutch barn & another ordinary barn, no buildings to speak of. The electric light is a mile off &, though there is plenty of water about, it is not laid on either to the fields or to either of the houses. There is no arable land except about 30 acres ploughed recently & just now being sown with barley. You would have nothing to feed your stock on next winter and therefore could not keep any. You would have to stock it with stores this summer, sell them off this autumn & wait until next year to begin any serious stocking.

I was very tempted because it is so lovely. Peggy & Mary were of course very pro, & Cecil thought it was impossible to advise as one was a certainty (as far as anything is) & the other a bit of a gamble which would bring no returns for 2 years at any rate but that on the whole he would have a go for the 2nd farm, accepting the offer for GH. . . .

When I got back I rang Mr Stewart up & went to see him. He & Miss Strang had been in that neighbourhood lately & had gone to see Gipsy Hall. She had been much impressed and thought it a good proposition & very cheap. . . . Mr S. thought I should not sell. He said we must decide whether we wanted a commercial proposition or a country house & if the former GH at the price was the best bet. He thought draining wet land might run one into anything – crops might go wrong with wireworm, store cattle were too dear to buy to be worth going in for the summer & therefore there would be no returns at all this year. He & Miss Strang were both full of plans for going ahead with milk & poultry at GH. . . . And so I am going to tell Cecil absolutely definitely we won't sell & go right ahead with making a fortune.

They were both quite definite we should not sell. They said the interest in farms was increasing in a staggering way now & that having got a good one it would be folly to part with it.

But, although I wrote that I would go ahead and make a fortune, I hesitated for a short time longer for a reason I kept to myself. There was Smith. Smith was the bailiff and the person responsible for that excellent state of the farm which alone made Gipsy Hall a possible proposition. Everyone took it for granted I must keep him on. Cecil thought him quite irreplaceable, and even Mr Stewart, who did not go as far as that, thought it very important to have a man who knew the farm. Cecil, when questioned on the point, felt sure he was entirely honest. It was here I had my doubts. There was nothing about this rather attractive Welshman, clearly at the moment on his best behaviour, which suggested to me great openness or honesty; and he was clearly very strong. I thought life could be unpleasant if one failed to get on with him.

I brought to my new task a mixture of unjustified confidence and consuming anxiety. I was confident that in the long run I should succeed in this undertaking and I find from reading *Approach to Farming* that, when a neighbouring farmer advised me not to milk at Gipsy Hall because it was too heavy and wet, I bet him that within four years my herd would hold the leading milk record for the county. (I do not think I succeeded in making good this boast, because it was almost impossible for a herd of Ayrshires to beat the best Friesians, but I got somewhere very near it.) Yet, conscious of my extreme ignorance of most of the matters I had to deal with, such as whether the corn merchant was cheating me over price, I worried incessantly and unnecessarily. By the following year I simply dealt with the most reputable merchant and took the price he gave.

Over the larger matters, I had a very comforting if superstitious theory that I should always run into the expert I needed at any given moment. This was encouraged by the fact that the Ministry of Agriculture had taken over two farms, Dodwell and Drayton, not far away from Gipsy Hall, in order to carry out experiments with ley farming on heavy clay, and by the news that in charge of these experiments was none other than the great man himself, Sir George Stapledon. When Jack came back from France on 18 June and had three days' leave, we went with Cecil Evans to visit him, believing we had an appointment. This turned out not to be true, but when Sir George, initially rather cross at being accosted by unexpected strangers, found that Jack was just back from France, he invited us to come back and have tea in a barn that afternoon. When he heard we came from Gipsy Hall, he said: 'I am told my education is not completed until I have seen the wheat at Gipsy Hall.'

In the barn we met Lady Stapledon, who telephoned me the next day and suggested that, if, as I had said, the guest house I was then living in was too expensive, I might consider the one where they were living temporarily, which was much cheaper. At this time I still had a nanny and I moved with her and the children at once.

As a result, I dined with the Stapledons almost every night for some weeks and by the end of that time we had become intimate friends. Thus I added to my close advisers Sir George Stapledon himself and Lady Stapledon – in letters referred to as Stapes and Dorrie – Mr Wilkes, Stapledon's technical colleague, and Mr William Davis, second in command at Aberystwyth and on the Warwickshire farms.

But one cannot live or thrive on advice alone, and the first two years at Gipsy Hall were very rough – much rougher than I remembered until I re-read the letters I wrote to Jack at the time, and there was much cause for anxiety. In the first place if I left Smith, the bailiff, living in the farmhouse, as everyone said I should, I had nowhere to live myself. Owing to Julian's defection I was extremely short of cash, and it was only after much discussion with Jack – now stationed at Darlington after the evacuation of France – that I took a lease on one of the ribbon-development houses near Gipsy Hall at a rent of a pound a week. I moved in the minimum of furniture from the Wood House, and during the whole of my period there I put down no carpets. I remember that when Frank and Elizabeth Longford came to lunch on their way somewhere, Frank was much impressed by my lifestyle.

The house I took was opposite the Eighteen Cottages, which were the exact agricultural equivalents of George Orwell's Wigan houses. They had one room down, with I think some sort of scullery behind, and two up; they had neither water – which was got from a standpipe on the road – nor drainage, while the lavatories were at the back. In the Eighteen Cottages lived Nora, who came to do everything for us – look after the children, cook and clean – as well as her brother-in-law and sister, Mr and Mrs Higley, who became very much devoted to my children. Also in the Eighteens lived the Highman family. Highman was at first the tractor driver, but in the course of time I promoted him to foreman. He was one of the most splendid men I have ever met and without him I could never have succeeded. When I first went to Gipsy Hall, I raised his wages from thirty-five to fifty shillings a week. The curious thing is that, although we worked together for seven years, I do not know his Christian name.

There was plenty to worry about in the summer of 1940. My intention was to have a milking herd, but since I had no milking plant I had to stock the pastures with a mixture of beef stores (young cattle bought to grow and then sold to be fattened) and sheep. This was disastrous, partly because there was a drought all summer and the cattle did not improve, but chiefly because the government's policy, which was to plough up grassland and grow wheat and secondly to encourage the production of milk rather than meat, meant that beef cattle bought in the spring could be sold only with the greatest difficulty and without profit in the autumn. Practically every farmer I knew had been caught in this trap, but I nevertheless regarded it as a personal failing, although comforting myself with the knowledge that beef were for me a temporary expedient until I was ready to milk.

However, the real trouble was Smith, the bailiff. When I recently read the letters I wrote to Jack, I realize that in buying a farm and expecting someone else to run it but also to allow me to play an active part, I was asking the impossible. I quote from a letter I wrote to Jack much later about Smith's successor:

30.1.41

Rather a curious thing happened tonight. You know I don't always & entirely get on with Carling. Don't assume more than I mean. I couldn't like him more & he has every reason for liking me. But there is a slight undercurrent of suspicions & jealousies between us which makes our relationship in some ways the same as my relationship with a nanny, however good. I hate having to take an opposing line with him because I am never sure we shall get through it without badly annoying each other.

Well, the milking is not properly done. Quite apart from the fact that the cows are not stripped after the machine, which they have got to be ... the whole performance is most incredibly slapdash & slovenly.* I went in today for the first time for a week or two & found Thomas still doing it alone although the new & highly paid head cowman has now been here nearly a month. He made no attempt at all to wash the cows, which is one worse than his usual flick over; if the machine fell off he shoved it back without cleaning it, & he whisked up and down at a speed which suggested he was in for a race, rather than attempting to do a decent job of work. It is all quite serious because at this rate we shall lose our accredited licence which means 5/- today & will mean correspondingly more as our production goes up.

(The point of quoting this letter is to illustrate my relationship with the bailiff, but I cannot pass those paragraphs without regis-

---

* In those days the last milk was still drawn by hand which required a good milkèr. Soon it was discovered that it could be done equally well by pulling the machine down on the cow's udder.

tering the incredulity I feel when I read them today. I find it impossible to believe that, either on my farm or on any other, milk to be sold to the public was ever produced in this way, or that Carling should not have spent enough time in the milking shed to prevent it. However, to continue :)

So I had to send for Carling & have it out. I decided while doing it to force the issue over the stripping which has been a slight argument between us for some time. ... I put it as nicely as I could but quite firmly & elicited the following. Thomas has fallen in love with a married woman since when he has gone to hell & lost all interest & in any case has volunteered for the RAF, so will I suppose be going sooner or later. Bibby, the new man, knows his job, but he and Carling can't hit it off – I suspect the same sort of undercurrents between them as between Carling & me – & secondly Bibby is both anxious about Carling bossing him and at the same time not really the type of a head man, as he cannot, or at any rate has not, organized the work properly. Carling not only agrees with my criticisms but endorses them heartily & is equally worried about it. I don't know what we shall do. It looks like trouble all round & more advertisements for men. But the whole thing amuses me as it fits in with my latest theory, originally formed after reading your comments about lack of confidence among your brother officers. Almost nobody has your sort of confidence & it is the lack of it which causes almost all the trouble in the world. In the case of Carling & me I fear that he will a) take advantage of my lack of knowledge & b) of my being a woman, & consequently try to swing things over on me. While he fears that I will take advantage of my ultimate power to give an order to swing things over on him. If we could both get rid of our fear all would be well, because neither of us will do what the other fears unless the other does what he fears. Carling & Bibby are in the same position & so I believe are 75 per cent of the world.

This letter was written in 1941 and concerned Carling, who was a very nice man. The problem in 1940 was Smith, who was not. The first complaints against him were that he discussed nothing with me and allowed me no function on the farm. 'It does seem to me', I wrote to Jack, then in Darlington, 'that there is really not much point in living this excessively uncomfortable and rootless life unless it is really made worth it by the farm.'

The question of what to do about Smith was very much complicated by the fact that the farm was in such good order. At this stage in the war the people who came to walk round it were all men, and I learned in my thirty years of farming that men are naturally less analytical and less suspicious than women and in consequence bad judges of character. Almost the only mistakes I ever made in taking on someone for an important job were when he was highly recommended by some man.

Yesterday [I wrote to Jack] the Stapledons and Wilkes came over Gipsy Hall. I think they were surprised, not so much by the crops which they had heard about, but at the pastures and the general state of the farm, and when I told Wilkes what we had paid he said we had begged it and I think he really meant this because when I said about the house difficulties he said that at the price we had paid we could easily afford to build a decent house and still have a reasonably cheap farm. His point of view is quite definite that we should be mad to get rid of Smith.

This was the advice I received from everyone, except Mr Stewart.

I discussed it for hours with the Stapledons last night. She is entirely on my side and for getting rid of him. Stapes is more cautious and objective. His attitude is roughly this : Smith will make you a lot of money but I quite see you will not learn to be a farmer. Do you really want to be a farmer? This is a striking question. Do we really want to be farmers? Enough not only to risk losing a good deal of money by getting rid of Smith, but more important enough not to believe that on a long view we will lose money by getting rid of Smith?...

Stapes said : Nobody but you can really know or judge what you are likely or capable of doing. But if you are either not sure or not prepared to give your whole time then you will never get a better man than Smith and you will be lucky if you get as good.

However, as the summer passed it became evident that Smith was not trying. Sheep were sent unfit to the market and the ricks were not thatched. He was away a lot and it was known that he was looking for a farm. (He was already too late to achieve this ambition. Farms were selling at prices which rose every day, and were becoming almost impossible to rent.) Then everything was made worse by a lot of unnecessary fuss about the threshing of the wheat. Usually, corn can be threshed during the winter, but the Gipsy Hall wheat was thought to be good enough to be sold at a much higher price for seed, and Smith had not merely to be endured but sucked up to in order to get the threshing done in time. He was often rude and I was very frightened of him. In the end, after much worry, it turned out that there was a glut of seed wheat and the price was not much higher than for milling.

Then one day I counted the sheep. This is not entirely easy to do. A good shepherd does it as some people are said to read, taking in a page almost at a glance; but sheep move all the time and the inexperienced are apt to wonder whether they counted that little lot in the corner and start all over again. However, I counted them several times and each time I made them short by twenty-three. I think it had never occurred to Smith either that I knew how many there ought to be or that I would count them.

I brought the matter up with him only in the most preliminary way. He was immediately pretty bloody rude. I asked him if any had died. He said he didn't know – some had but he didn't know how many. When pushed a little further he shouted at me & asked why he should know any more than I should. I made the obvious retort that I paid him to know & left the matter at that.

I dealt with this matter by asking Mr Margetts, the local land agent and surveyor, to do an apparently routine valuation of the stock on the farm. On the morning he was to arrive Smith was dressed to go out. When I remonstrated with him, he merely said he had an important appointment. 'The sheep will have to be accounted for some time,' I said, and he immediately went into the house and changed his clothes. Taken by surprise, he accounted for the loss of twenty-three sheep by deaths – five dipping, six shearing and so on. When he said this he became liable to a criminal charge.

I asked Highman whether many sheep had died on the farm and he answered that he thought he had heard one died dipping. Then I went to see a solicitor to ask him whether this was a case for the police. He thought at first that I could not prove anything, but I pointed out that if twenty-three sheep had died the bodies would not have been easy to dispose of and in the ordinary course of events would have been buried somewhere on the farm. At this he rang the police and, without giving names, gave the facts and asked them if they would prosecute if names were given. After making the same objection as he had and receiving the same answer, the reply was that they would. I wrote to Jack:

I think left to myself I just might have done it, but the Stapledons urged me not to – on the grounds that the waste of nervous energy it would sooner or later involve simply wasn't worth it & that if the police gaoled him and the Wyatts were involved [two brothers who had left without notice] and got gaoled too the feeling in the village might go either way & I might have difficulty with men. ... Any way Stapes hated the idea & was very keen I shouldn't. So I have done absolutely nothing.

I think by now Smith was already under notice because Carling came soon after. In any case he left immediately. One unexpected event seems worth recording. When I was away or if I was short of cash, Smith sometimes paid the weekly wages; at that time, I owed him £24 on this account. When I was settling up his own wage and various other things, I asked him what more I owed him.

'Nothing,' he replied.

'Are you sure?'

'Quite sure,' he said.

In this way he repaid something like half the value of the missing sheep, whether out of gratitude that I had not prosecuted him or out of fear that I still might, I could not decide.

8

....

Approach to Farming

In the spring of 1941 I wrote a book, one of the very few I have written without persuasion from someone else. My book about the British Council was commissioned by the Director General, and one about the Royal Opera House by the chairman of the board. *The Marconi Scandal* was pressed on me by my husband who became interested in it after an argument with Evelyn Waugh. All the rest were commissioned by publishers; and, since publishers' suggestions for books are often unexpectedly dotty, this is not a prolific source of ideas.

Once when I explained this to Rebecca West, she waved a hand and said, 'Ah, passive,' but noticing that I took slight offence at this remark, explained that none was intended; there were merely two kinds of temperament. I have no idea whether this is true or not, nor do I know how much my own attitude was induced by my father, who believed it an impertinence to attempt something requiring talent unless this burgeoned out of one, and was therefore merciless to any conceits in my youth. Certainly I have for most of my life felt that writing was a secret and shameful occupation, a presumptuous piece of affectation which it was necessary to keep from one's friends, so that when someone telephoned me in the morning (the only time I am able to write) and said 'Are you busy?' I instinctively denied it and spent too much of my working time in idle gossip, rather than reveal the nature of my task.

For all these reasons I have never regarded myself as a professional writer, although I have written thirteen books, and earned considerable sums of money, and although it is the only thing for which I have any natural talent. I have spent years of my life trying to excel at riding, tennis or golf; and, because I am interested in style, have in each appeared more promising than in fact I was. Only as a writer did I succeed without appalling effort. Yet, although I am superficially fairly confident, my neurotic fears are such that when I am writing I wake in the night with a start of fear, convinced that I cannot do it. Even now I dislike very much the fact that wherever I go people ask me what I am writing. I know that it is well intended, really a politeness, but I have an aversion to discussing it.

However, my first book, *Approach to Farming*, was a very jolly affair and held none of these terrors. I composed it as I walked round the farm during the day and wrote it down at night. It was very short and very enthusiastic, and was the story of my endeavours to become a farmer up to date. Smith does not appear in it, although I think he may have been in an early version because I was advised by my publisher to consider the laws of libel. I did not, of course, believe the book had any future when I was writing it, which may be why I enjoyed it so much.

I began by showing it to certain intellectually difficult friends, including Sir George Stapledon, and when they all praised it, I sent it to Jack's brother-in-law, Richard de la Mare. Dick was the son of Walter de la Mare and he was a director of Faber & Faber (he later became chairman). Many friends of his were friends of mine, and rumour soon had it that he did not like the book. However, Geoffrey Faber, then chairman, was very enthusiastic and Dick pretended to be when he wrote to tell me they would publish it.

He offered me 10 per cent on the first 2,000 copies and 15 per cent after that, with an advance of £25. He asked for some alterations and these had to be completed and delivered by July in order that the book should come out early in October 1941. How times have changed!

It was actually published on 9 October which is Jack's birthday, and I took the children to stay with Dick and my sister-in-law Katta (Catherine) for the event. While I was there I wrote two letters to Jack, the first of which, though not relevant to this subject, is relevant to my life.

Yesterday I was taken by Katta to pick blackberries for the Women's Institute. Three other lights of Much Hadham came with us. I must say it would be a terrible thing to settle by accident in Much Hadham. There is an enormous society of a dullness &

lack of originality not to be believed. But they are all quite innocently genial & friendly, so that if one took a house they wd expect one to join in & wd suspect one, I suppose, of the most horrible motives if one refused. One of the 3 women has a husband in Egypt. He is an RE & is on some job too secret for her to know what it is. She is a tall, gaunt, hideous woman with a leathery complexion & a hook nose. She is one of those really nice English country women whom one cannot conceive why anyone marries, tho' they often are married. The sex appeal part appears to be completely lacking, tho' apparently it isn't. She is very unhappy & she spoke to me as a kindred spirit, with complete intimacy as though she had known me for ages. I think I replied in the same spirit. She said she couldn't really imagine how she had got as far as she had. She had always thought she wd be dotty by now. Originally she had thought the idea of his being at a camp in England was too horrible to be borne. She said no one who hadn't had the experience cd understand anything about it & that made one so lonely. And she said she was getting old & bitter & when other people's husbands came home on leave she could hardly pretend any more to be pleased. She said at one point, 'But I am used to going about alone now.' And I knew that for her, that was almost the saddest thing, like an insult, a humiliation. I thought then I am luckier in that respect if in no other. I have got past that. I go about quite naturally & confidently by myself. But I know how she feels because just at the beginning I felt like that. I don't know what the moral of all this is or why I tell it to you. I think it's just that all over England women are suffering like this & I think it is devastating. But nobody cares or even remembers them & the war will go on for years yet. . . .

I spent the day of publication in London and wrote to Jack the next day:

Walter de la Mare has been here for the night. I got on very well with him. I know this by all the ordinary tests & also with certainty because when he left he said good-bye to me twice. The first time he said, 'I hope we shall meet again soon. I shd like to see your farm.' And the second time he said, 'I must say good-bye again. It was lovely to have a talk.'

I must break off here to tell you another odd & to me pleasing coincidence. Yesterday I went to London & I went to Dick's office to travel down with him in the evening. I was shown into the waiting room where his father was also waiting. So we went into

Dick's room together. Dick came forward with a book in each hand & said, 'I've got a book for both of you.' They were the first advance copy of my book & the first advance copy of a new one of his. I liked that. Walter suddenly said to me after dinner when we were discussing the two books: 'Are you able to talk about your book alright?' I said, without taking thought, 'I had a period when I squirmed if anyone mentioned it. Now I've got that under control. Is that what you mean?' Believe it or not, it was what he meant. So what I had always regarded as an unpleasant & neurotic idiocy suddenly became in some way a qualification of some sort of integrity & any way a guarantee of some sort of sensibility & a passport to his friendship. He said he always had it with every book & never got over it. ... Later he asked the company generally whether they ever felt depressed in the mornings. I replied, 'Always.' I could see that he was relieved at sharing in some way something he was vaguely ashamed of. However this was not quite so romantic as we eventually boiled it down to cigarette smoking. ...

There is a Norwegian girl, wife of an English doctor, very pretty, very nice, & fairly intelligent. At dinner Walter de la Mare & I were discussing the fact that we still found it difficult to hate the Germans. We had all sorts of other emotions about them – boredom, irritation, contempt etc. but for some reason not hate. She suddenly started almost to abuse us in that passionate way foreigners have – saying if our homes were broken up & our friends killed etc we shd soon hate them. I said: 'I haven't seen my husband for nearly a year, you know.' The effect was tremendous & I felt rather ashamed. She is fairly newly married & adores her husband & she went down like a pricked balloon. I felt almost indecent, but I don't think it was indecent. People who talk like that are really accusing other people of a complete lack of imagination & I don't think one ought to accuse Walter de la Mare of that.

The book is lovely. It is green with the name in white & a white panel on one side with my name in green. Only the white isn't white but pale green.

I never saw Walter de la Mare again. Perhaps I ought to have asked him to see the farm, but I do not think he would have come. Although, as I have said, I do not care for it now, *Approach to Farming* was an immediate and, for a book on farming, fairly widespread success. My memories had suggested that it was reviewed only in local or farming papers, but this must be because it was not reviewed in the *Sunday Times* or the *Observer*. In addition to all the farming papers, praise from which was probably the most informed and therefore in some ways the most pleasing, it was reviewed in the *Times Literary Supplement, Time and Tide, Daily Sketch, Punch, Manchester Evening News, Oxford Weekly Review, Oxford Mail, Listener* and *Country Life*. The first review to appear was in the *Birmingham Post*. I wrote to Jack:

> It is a very good one, and I think might be wonderful from a selling point of view. Although there is a review of a book by A.E.W. Mason & another by Quentin Reynolds, who is the latest American newspaper & broadcasting star and one of the most popular people in England at the moment, I am given pride of place and also the longest review. I was in London this morning. Both the Times & Hatchards have got it displayed in their windows & Molly was in Birmingham yesterday & it was displayed in a bookshop there.

I had all the pleasures which go with the success of an early book, letters every day at breakfast and much local fame. Only one thing spoiled it: quite soon no one could buy it. 'Carling came in,' I wrote to Jack, '& said that all the merchants whom he sees in Stratford have told him that they had tried & tried unsuccessfully to buy A to F. He said as a result the few copies that there were were being lent around and therefore the others would never buy it.' And later: 'For some reason I have sunk into depression. I think it may be because no one seems able to buy *Approach to Farming*. Hannah & Rob [Hudson, then Minister of Agriculture] and Buck have all tried & failed. I suppose it is something to do with wartime difficulties.'

These letters were written in October and the trouble was probably due not only to wartime difficulties, but to the unexpected success of the book, which neither booksellers nor publishers were prepared for. What is impossible from this distance to understand is a letter from Dick's secretary written on 22 November saying they had been out of stock for a fortnight and 'there is every likelihood that a reprint will be necessary before long'; and another from Dick written four days later saying it was odds-on they would decide to reprint immediately. If the shops had been full of the book, one could understand this hesitation, but since it was unobtainable I think if I had known enough I should have been very cross. In the end they reprinted five times, always a bit too late. These impressions were not big and I think the total sales were about 10,000, although they might have been much bigger if people had been able to buy the book. In principle one could not complain since, unaided by the war, a book about farming would not have sold at all.

The success of *Approach to Farming* led to my being asked to broadcast. The first time I went to London to join in a programme with George Haynes, then director of the National Council for Social Services, and Clough Williams Ellis, the architect and landowner, who designed and built the village of Portmeirion on his own land in Wales. At this time the BBC used the most appalling technique. Everything was written down and read on the programme. In spite of that an incredible amount of time was spent on it. I wrote to Jack:

> We worked from 3 to 8 on the script and then went down to their basement cafeteria to have a drink. .... The one drink turned into 2 and then supper. .... Sunday G.H. and I finished the script and Monday morning we started to rehearse. I was incredibly bad to begin with, & Alford [the producer] was vicious – exaggerated imitations and so on. However, he kept me at it all day but by the time I got to the mike I had no idea whether I was making any sense or not. You see, he rehearsed me well and hard, but one day isn't really enough. After all in the theatre you have three weeks. You have to go slow and emphasize more than you would think.

It was exactly this emphasizing, which was also pressed on me by the producers at Birmingham, where I went quite often, which finally ended my career as a broadcaster. The emphasis was apt to fall indifferently on the right or the wrong word, and I imagine was not unlike the speech of some of the commentators on Channel Four today. This so horrified the only producer I ever met who understood the job that, having employed me once, he never asked me again.

Clough Williams Ellis's wife was a Strachey. 'Sister to John,' I wrote to Jack, 'rather awful and incredibly Strachey.' Nevertheless, Mrs Williams Ellis said one thing which I have remembered all my life. Talking about writing, she said: 'One must never say "It's a fine day", one must succeed in showing it.' This is a good precept, although she chose a bad example to explain it, because it is not the day but character or situation which should reveal itself by indirect means.

9

....

Clyde Higgs Gives Advice

After the Carlings came everything went very well on the farm. We stood at that time on the edge of an agricultural revolution and Carling, who had been at Moulton, understood this. He was a very good-looking and well-educated man and in every way a change from Smith. Mrs Carling, who had the smooth pink cheeks of a milkmaid, was really nice and in addition an expert in the management of hens.

I wrote to Jack in February of 1941 : 'The farm is going very well. Carling is very efficient. All the beans have failed which means sowing spring ones but all the wheat looks good and Mr Stewart was stunned by the beauty of the ploughing which has been done.' The praise for the ploughing belonged to Highman, the hero of this part of my life. Then in May I wrote: 'Mr Stewart was here on Sunday. He says he has seen no wheat like ours and no oats like one field of ours. How's that?' And again in May I wrote: 'Just come in from going round the farm with the War Committee. It made them sit up. They implored me to take over the derelict land next door, but I said only if they financed it. When they left they thanked me for a "tonic" & admitted the farm looked even better than last year. They said they had seen nothing like it anywhere, and valued it at £35 an acre, i.e. 75% more than we paid.' This was particularly satisfactory because the War Committee had been told by gossips that the farm was going down and were invest-igating. They had powers which they could use if they found

75

anything wrong. The yields at Gipsy Hall were never quite as good as expected, because the wheat grew a lot of straw.

The children too were doing well. I found a most splendid girl called Molly Hands to teach them, and gave her instructions to let them play on the street with the village children. They were intensely happy but they acquired a Birmingham accent, than which there is nothing worse in the world. This never mattered to Rose, who grew out of it as soon as necessary, but Thomas suffered when he went, at about eight, to Summerfields school in Oxford, where the headmaster was a snob and could not like him because of his accent.

I was the only person who was dissatisfied. Carling was no less determined than Smith had been to run the farm himself and, in order to do this, to cut me out. I wrote to Jack:

I am in a furious temper today. Molly and I always like to work on the farm but except for the dreary jobs like hoeing and thistle cutting it somehow happens that we never do. Whenever we say to Carling 'Can we help?' there is always some reason why it would be much better if we didn't. Every day now there are appeals on the wireless for more women to join things and do munitions and both Molly and I are beginning to feel that unless we work all day on the farm [the children always came with us or stayed with Mrs Higley and Nora] there is no justification for our arrangements as they stand. She at least ought to join something and I at least ought to let her go. I have never been able to pin on Carling the fact that he is deliberately trying to stop us joining in but he is certainly incredibly stupid about using us. This morning I said to him that Molly and I were going to work today and we would either stook or go on the cart. He said they weren't going to stook and he wasn't sure what he was going to do until he saw whether the soldiers came. (We sometimes use one or two for harvesting.) He had got on a poker face and he said he would let me know later in the day. As I went down on my bike I saw the cart and three men go down to the field.

So I fetched Molly and we just went down there and I got on to the cart and she pitched on to it.* We got on very well and every time Carling, who was driving the tractor, came down with an empty cart to take away the loaded, there was our cart loaded up and ready, so nobody could say we were holding them up.

* I do not remember what happened to the three men, but I think Molly and I worked alone.

However, the third time he came he brought two soldiers with him which meant that there was nothing left for us to do. So, as I am very brave, I walked straight up to him and asked him why he had brought them. He said he'd got a lighter job he wanted us to do. So I said, 'We don't want a lighter job. We don't find this heavy, we enjoy it, and as the cart's always ready I assume we are doing it all right.' So he said he wanted us to restook some oats which had fallen down and were getting wet. 'If you don't do it, the men will have to.' I thought it undignified to go on having an obvious barny in front of the men, so I said all right we would do it. But I was furious. The oats did need doing but I was convinced that he would never have asked us to do it if we hadn't been doing this, because he never asks us to do anything. ... Anyway he won the first round and I am not sure what the next move is going to be. But it's going to be something because I refuse to pay soldiers to do work I can perfectly well do myself. And Molly will have to leave if this goes on.

This matter to some extent solved itself through our extreme shortage of labour.

Today [I wrote to Jack] I have done the hardest day's work of my life. I either go on the cart and load the sheaves that are pitched up or else as a change I pitch it. But our wheat is so heavy I can only just pitch it. The potential argument with Carling as to whether we should work or not has dissolved into thin air as we are so short-handed he cannot afford to ignore me. In fact he is reduced to asking us rather shamefacedly if we think we can stick it all day as they can't do without us. We do it all day and every day and it is part of our lives but it is much more your sort of thing than mine. You would be very jealous of my hands if you could see them – they are really horny now.

My memory of Carling is of liking him very much, although I knew I had had difficulties. I had quite forgotten all the detail until I read these letters, and I remember Mrs Carling as delightful. Carling was extremely ambitious and he saw in me some kind of a menace to his authority. I think he would have behaved differently if I had been a man.

I also forced my way into the milking parlour and again through shortage of labour was often asked to relieve the second cowman. I must say here that, although skill and experience is needed to look after the health of animals, to know when hay is fit to carry, and to plough a field, most farming jobs turned out to need none at all.

In the days of hand milking I suppose there was something which had to be learned, but in putting a machine on a cow and taking it off there is none. The skill here lies in the feeding of the cows, and that, as I would later prove, is an intellectual problem of an inconsiderable kind, although requiring a certain perfectionism in practice. It may be better to know the cows one from another and in about three weeks I did. In very large herds they are marked with a number.

Some time in the winter of 1942 I was asked to take part in a radio series and Clyde Higgs volunteered to help me with the script. It may be remembered that on the day Mr Stewart and I first saw Gipsy Hall we had gone to tea with Clyde Higgs and he had said it was a wet hole unfit for a lady to farm. I had seen him on various occasions since then, once at Sir George Stapledon's when he had congratulated me on settling down so near the great man, because, he said, I should need him. He was a deliberately rough character but not without charm; I liked him. On this occasion, after we had discussed the broadcast, we walked round his farm and then came in to tea. I quote now from *Four Years' Harvest* which was written soon after:

> He started to ask me a great many very searching and, as far as I could see, purposeless questions about my life. Was I writing another book or some articles? Was I reading anything then? He asked me questions too about the farm. Was my bailiff a good man? How much did I pay him? How much did I pay my tractor driver? Had I got a good cowman? Having satisfied himself on all these points he settled down in his chair and remarked in a slightly grumbling tone:
> 'Well, you're not the girl I thought you were. In my opinion you'll never do any good until you get rid of that man of yours.'
> 'What do you mean?' I asked. ...
> 'Well,' he said, 'what's the point of it? What do you think you're doing sitting down there in the village with a bailiff in the farmhouse running the farm?' ['What is the point of my living this exceedingly uncomfortable life in a district where I know no one, unless I have some real function on the farm?' I had written to Jack, so when Mr Higgs said this, I took it on board at once, but I was not immediately prepared to admit it.]
> 'What do you mean?' I asked. 'I know practically nothing about farming.'
> 'Well, you've been nearly two years on a farm.'

'I know,' I replied. 'But I haven't learned much since I left Moulton. I have a theoretical understanding of the subject and I have been responsible for the policy at Gipsy Hall. But one doesn't learn much from one's own men, and my bailiff has always been there to make the detailed decisions.'

I was actually tremendously excited but I continued to make objections.

'It's no use,' I said. 'I don't know anything about it. I shouldn't even be sure when the corn was ripe enough to cut.'

'You cut wheat,' Higgs replied, 'when the grain is hard. You can bite it to find out. You cut oats when you squeeze it and find the milk has gone out of it. And you cut barley when the heads have dropped.'

I smiled a little ruefully at this fireside farming, but I must admit that I have since found these methods work out all right. In any case, one has only to make these decisions once or twice in any harvest, because after the first day or two the problem is to cut as much as you can before it is overripe. [At this time we still cut with the binder, but these remarks are probably just as true with the combine.]*

Looking back on this visit, I think, as I thought then, that in the matter of advice I owe more to Mr Higgs than to anyone else I have ever met. I knew at once that I would do what he suggested and I wrote immediately to Jack to tell him so; but I also knew it could not be done quickly.

Almost immediately two rather frightening things occurred. The first was that Carling got to hear of all this.

It turned out [I wrote to Jack] that whoever had told him had known complete details such as that it was Clyde Higgs who suggested it to me. I had told no one in the district except Molly who swears she had told no one and whom I believe. So the only explanation short of magic is that Nora reads my letters to you and then rushes off and tells anyone concerned what she has found out. I find this impossible to believe.

At this distance I find it also impossible to believe I could have been so naive. Obviously the person who spread the talk was Clyde Higgs himself.

Anyway, it did no immediate harm. The Carlings were both anxious to stay and I certainly was in no hurry to get rid of them

* Frances Donaldson, *Four Years' Harvest*, Faber & Faber (1945).

and the matter was settled with promises of good behaviour on both sides. However, much worse was to come:

Today we have suffered a severe loss and a grave setback: Joe Newlands has given notice. He is the only man on the farm who understands stacking and thatching, he is the carter and the shepherd and my favourite man. Both Carling and I are very gravely shaken. Haymaking begins next week and harvest is not far off. We are completely hamstrung by having no cottage in which to put a man and a complete shortage of local labour. It is not worth trying to get the cottage Joe will vacate. [Joe's was an Orwell-type cottage of which I said in *Four Years' Harvest* that the only water for a hundred yards was that which poured off the walls.] Two or three months ago his landlord gave him notice. This was pure bluff as he hadn't the slightest chance of getting him out. I explained this carefully to Joe at the time but I knew then that he didn't believe me and I recognized that I was up against all the pathetic insecurity and ignorance of the past. This proved to be true and the little man has been looking for a job with a cottage ever since. He has done it very badly and given a week's notice at the beginning of haymaking, but I forgive him because I realize that he could not know that if he had told me two months ago that he was looking for a job, I wouldn't have said, 'Well, take a week's notice then.' It sends a wave of insecurity over the farm. People look at each other gravely and say they wouldn't be surprised if Highman wouldn't soon like a change and so on. The most serious thing for me is that it does away with any chance of my being able to do without Carling until two cottages are actually built on the farm. I could never weather a crisis like this without Carling and without a cottage in which to put a new man, supposing Highman left with Carling.

Reading this letter today it astounds me that, with all the experts I collected to advise me, they allowed me to buy a farm of nearly 400 acres which had, apart from a cottage three fields away on the canal bank, only one house. On reflection, I think it was because they were used to pre-war conditions when there were plenty of men and all willing to live in the only cottages that then existed. However, I learn from this letter that I had by now taken steps to build two cottages, something I ought to have done when I bought the farm. There was some trouble about this because, although I got permission to build without difficulty, there was no way of getting the materials. Then I met a property man who was building houses in the district and he said he would build these two for me. They could not be ready, however, for at least a year.

In the meantime, I was forced to sack the cowman. On 31 July I wrote to Jack:

> Samples of everyone's milk are tested by the Medical Officer of Health every so often. There are two tests, one is called the Methylene blue test and is for bacteria which may be present for a number of reasons and is difficult to trace. The other is for bacillus coli which can only be present in the milk if the dung or urine has got in, i.e. through dirty production. It is not only rather a disgrace to have a dirty test but also you lose your TT and Accredited licences if you have too many. We have had three dirty tests and the last two have been bacillus coli. I have threatened and implored and done everything I could and now we have had the third I have just said I won't have Hall in the milking shed any more but will do it myself. He is a slovenly slut and doesn't make any pretence of trying to produce clean milk, and I am fed up with it. I have said I will pay him the same money to work on the land for 2 months if he will stay, but otherwise he can get out with a week's notice. It will mean I shall have to get up before 6 (which, until the extra hour comes off, is before 4) because I shall have to get the cows in myself and this takes half an hour, but it will be a good opportunity to get a lot of experience while Carling is still here to advise me.

Then on 6 August I wrote:

> I haven't written for three days but I am now head cowman and the alarm wakes me at 5.30 and I rush out to fetch the cows. As a result I am so crying tired in the evening, when I usually write, that I haven't had the energy. With the double summer time it really means that one is getting up at 3.30 which is practically the same as doing a night shift. I hope I shall adjust to it and finally not get too tired. It is all going very well and I am convinced that I am in every way a better cowman than Hall. Not only is the shed spotless throughout the milking but the cows are up 5 gallons. That can't be counted to me as they have been moved to a field with more keep, but as Carling predicted they would go down it is at least satisfactory.

Sometime during the summer I telephoned Clyde Higgs. There was a telephone in the farmhouse but not in the house I inhabited and I asked his help in getting one installed.

'Certainly not,' he replied. 'If you want a telephone, you can move in beside it.'

Nor was it all bad luck because at this point Pat appeared. O.J. Pattison was the agricultural organizer for the district. He came from a farming family and had both the instinctive knowledge of old Farmer Giles and an education in the latest scientific approach. He won my heart when he first visited Gipsy Hall by pointing at my best cow immediately on entering a field and saying: 'I bet you wish they were all like that one.'

He came to see me several times and I soon learned that he was bored with his job and had made up his mind to take a farm of his own. I asked him at once whether he would consider acting as an adviser to me, and this was immediately agreed. I wrote at the time:

> For me it made everything easy. All along, although I had been perfectly serious in my intentions, I had been uneasy. When the gossip of the Warwickshire markets [that there would soon be a good farm for sale] was repeated to me I had minded because I knew that it was most probably right. I had faced with fear the fact that I should be entirely alone on the bad days, those days when everything goes wrong and everybody leaves at once and there is no one even to discuss it with. I was afraid, too, that I should not learn by my mistakes. I should know when I had made a mistake in cultivation, but I should not necessarily learn how to avoid it in the future. I had none of the advantages of discussion on the market-place, which is the main school of every farmer, because I am the wrong sex. I knew very few farmers and I was incapable of buying or selling my own stock. All that I wanted Pat to do was to come over once a week and tell me what I was doing wrong and why, to buy and sell for me and above all to be at the end of a telephone, so that in moments of greatest despair an sos could be sent out.

Only one problem remained. Mr Stewart had been so definite that a man must live in the farmhouse to be available when things went wrong. I discussed this with Pat, who took the view that in life you had to take some risks, and I could have a landgirl living in the house with me who could be sent down to the village on a bicycle. In addition, if I moved into the farmhouse it left the house I was living in free for a farm worker. This account leaves out the enormous importance of Highman. I made him foreman and I could not have got on without him. He could never be persuaded to tell me what to do, but since he could not bear to have anything done wrong, when (sometimes deliberately in order to get his opinion) I gave him an order he did not want to carry out, he always said what he thought I should do.

Clyde Higgs got Carling a job with the War Committee who had the idea of running a farm institute. The farm institute part fell through and then Mr Stewart got him a job managing the largest estate in Northamptonshire. Here he remained for the rest of his life. I had a letter from his wife the other day in which she told me the management of a large estate had always been his ambition, and so I do not think he would have stayed with me very long in any case.

10

....

A Farmer

21 Sept 1942

Note the date – now I am a FARMER, though you wouldn't think
it to see me, because I look like nothing so much as a housewife
rather inefficiently moving house.

All my friends had begged me to spend some money on the
farmhouse, saying I had lived too long like a pig and it was bad
for morale. One of the difficulties was that one had to give clothes
coupons for the material for curtains, chair covers and so on. I
consulted a friend, Hannah Hudson, wife of the Minister of Agriculture, whom I thought had the best taste and knew everyone. She
took me first to see John Fowler of Colefax and Fowler and, because
I was with her, he took a great deal of trouble. He made curtains
for my sitting room of dark green blackout material (no coupons)
relieved with a fringe of alternating dark and light green silk. He
also managed to sell me three extremely pretty oil lamps (there was
no electricity at Gipsy Hall at that time). Then Hannah took me to
see a Mr Cole who made wallpapers in an attic somewhere roughly
behind the shop which today bears his name. There was in those
days something so unusual about these wallpapers that he had to
send a man down to Gipsy Hall to put them on the walls, since he
said the local builder could not do it. I had them all over the house
and wrote to Jack:

> The wallpaper on the landing and stairs is lovely and the bath-
> room is going to be the best we ever had, except for one thing

which is that I could only get one piece of lino in London and that was the shiny oilcloth type with a hateful black marbly effect on white. I put in a new bath and when I got here I found the lavatory was an absolute bugger and took half an hour to fill, which is really impossible with me and two children and two landgirls. So I bought (£7.10/-) a new one with a modern low cistern and now it works a treat. The paint is white all over the house and it is wallpaper everywhere – white backgrounds with patterns on. The downstairs ones and the landing and bathroom are really lovely. . . .

And later:

You can never imagine how pretty this house is. It is quite incredible that such a dingy place can be so completely trans-formed. . . . Anni [Noll] said it was like a house that had had pernicious anaemia and was suddenly cured.

26.9.42

God knows when I last wrote to you. – For days I couldn't even find a pen. . . . I don't know where to begin. But I suppose the most important thing is the farm. I think it's going to be o.k. I thought before that the first week would be a nightmare trying to decide what everyone ought to do, etc. It's quite easy with the tractor drivers and the stock people because they just do routine work but what, I wondered, did people like Oakley (the deaf and dumb) do before breakfast and on days when there was no obvious gang work like hoeing or harvesting. However, it doesn't arise. The difficulty is to find enough people to do all the thousands of little jobs that need doing. . . .

I must describe the staff. First of all, Highman is super as a foreman – at least for me. He is a man without an inferiority complex and you know how rare that is. He's never touchy and never obstructive and he's quite obviously out for the best. So that if he disagrees with me or advances some reason why I shouldn't do something, I never suspect an ulterior motive. Then he turns out to be awfully good at a lot of things. When Carling used to earmark the pigs, he did it with two men and fiddled about discussing which way the numbers should go for hours. Highman did it this week with one girl and a speed and precision which was a treat to watch. He's obviously mad keen to make a success of it and looks awfully eager and happy and is sweet to everyone. His faults probably are that he doesn't think ahead, isn't used to organisation and may not be forceful enough with the men, but I think I can supply all that. I'm giving him £4 a week and paying his cottage. Then there's Cyril Wheeldon, age eighteen, rather lacking in force but quite a pleasant little cowman and a very useful relief tractor driver. Both he and Highman have been ploughing by moonlight up to about nine o'clock. ... Then there's Oakley, the deaf and dumb.* Then on Monday Sharp starts. He's nice and intelligent and I expect him to be first class at tractor work and reasonably good with cows. ... But he's got our house and he doesn't want to take a lodger and I think everyone is going to be jealous and cross. Nora is already. ... That's all the men, but, including me, there are five women, and Pattison calls it the Nunnery and Oakley has been heard to announce that he's sick of this bloody Women's Institute.

The pre-war estimate of the labour necessary on a farm was three men per hundred acres, but that was in the days when the plough was largely disused. It was said at the time of which I write that this should be increased to four men per hundred acres. We had roughly one man and one and a half girls per hundred acres. In addition, I had failed to find a cowman and was still responsible for the milking myself. This situation was relieved by the farm sale. In August I had written to Jack:

Terrific excitements. Pattison (whom I now call Pat) arrived yesterday to go through the cows and decide which we would cull. He was so horrible about nearly all of them that I was reduced to despair. The trouble is not only that the bad ones are so bad, but that the good ones are not really awfully good. Then we suddenly decided to have a farm sale to get rid of all of them except about ten or so and buy better ones with the money. I had decided already to get rid of the sheep for the moment, as we have ploughed up so much, and the hens will have to go as without Mrs Carling there is no one to look after them, and I want to simplify all these small things to start with. So we will have a wonderful farm sale and we shan't stand to lose anything because Pattison will post six men round the ring to buy in anything which doesn't fetch enough. Isn't it exciting? I have been longing to get rid of all these beastly cows for ages.

Today I do not know why the cows were so beastly, but at the beginning of the war no one realized how very fast and how

* Oakley is always described as 'the deaf and dumb' and I think he was. He seems to have had some method of making himself understood, but I no longer remember it.

far prices would go up. One was supposed to buy good cows for yesterday's money and never succeeded in doing so.

I had a conversation with Clyde Higgs. He is very cross with me a) for selling the cows after [on his advice] they have passed the agglutination test and b) for engaging Pattison. About a) I didn't tell him the real reason which is that they are such damn bad milkers. But on thinking it over I shall tomorrow as I think he is less dangerous if I tell him the truth than if he finds it out later from the Carlings, as he surely will, because he thinks he is my chief adviser and I confide everything in him. About b) I knew he would be furious, again because he is my chief adviser, and the interesting thing is that Pattison, who sees him nearly every day, hadn't got the guts to tell him himself.

The sale took place on 10 October and we made a profit on everything.

The gross total was £2,029. But auctioneer's fees and advertising have to come off that. The nicest thing is that it was done absolutely slap-up in every way. Pattison was argumentative and extremely irritating, cancelling every order I gave and taking all the men on his job and leaving me with one girl for all I had to do, but I must say he brought it off. We had a great bit of luck in that a super cowman whom I have engaged to come here in the spring when the cottages are built was on his holiday and he came and got the cows ready. Pattison had spent about two days doing the same thing for the sheep and they looked wonderful. ... On top of all this, the house was just ready in time. It is too pretty for words. I had lashings of food and tea and beer and I even secured a bottle of gin and I did it slap-up like a party and asked everyone in. Anni [Noll] had been all last week and done the flowers and the whole house looked out of the class of anything anyone had ever seen. It put Gipsy Hall on the map in quite a different way. People kept saying to me they couldn't believe I had done all that in two years, and I had to refrain from saying two weeks, you mean. It was great fun in retrospect and I am awfully proud and pleased but it was dreadfully hard and nearly killed us all and it only came off by the skin of its teeth. The sale was at two and I had asked lots of people to come early for drinks and food, but by quarter to one I was still trailing round in a pair of dungarees with no buttons on one side showing my underclothes and a filthy face and in absolute panic because there were still six cows which hadn't been tied up and no one knew at all where the sheep were and the calves hadn't been separated. It all just worked, but it wasn't really fun at the time. Everyone was too tired and too cross to enjoy it.

Some time in 1942 Dick de la Mare wrote asking me to write a sequel to *Approach to Farming*. I had the greatest difficulty in doing this and I now understand why. If you work at physical labour for about fourteen hours a day, no thoughts occur unconnected with what you are actually doing and nothing stands out in memory. On 14 October I wrote to Jack:

It is very odd, but since I have been so very busy, I can't think what I should write to you about. I realize now that my letters have always been about people and what they said and did or else about my thoughts. But nowadays I never see any people and I haven't time to think. I can't describe the things which happen on the farm because too many happen for it to be possible to discriminate. The cottages are going to be dreadful but you mustn't mind, at least not more than I do, because they are going to make the efficient running of this farm a possibility. I have been lucky in running into Shellabear [the property man]. Everyone says that, even with permission, it is really impossible to get the materials for building now.

In the same letter I wrote:

The farm is going very well, and there is no doubt I did the right thing. It is incredibly hard, but immense fun. Highman is a miracle. ... Pat argued with me about making him foreman and thought he wouldn't be good enough, but now he thinks him one of the best men he has ever known. He is so nice and easy to get on with and never obstructive or trying to get out of things and no inferiority complex. ... Then Cyril Wheeldon has blossomed so much since I had the farm. I gave him a rise and I had to give him responsibility because there was no one else and he has risen to it like a bird. Then I have a girl tractor driver, a thing Carling would never have, and between them and me the two tractors never stop even at meal-times and if it only won't rain we shall finish the drilling earlier than Carling ever did with 30 acres more than he had.

Nevertheless, the work was too hard and by the end of the winter we were all fed up. We had only about twenty cows, but Pat (who said the farm was understocked and, when the War Committee had asked me to plough up thirty extra acres, had persuaded me to offer thirty-five, while left alone I would have tried to settle for fifteen) also bought bullocks and sheep to eat the food we had grown for the cows we had sold. We already had a herd of breeding sows which I had bought from Moulton. I wrote to Jack in March:

I can truthfully say two things. One, since Carling left on 21 Sept there has not been one single day which has not been an urgent one. Urgent in a way one expects seasonally, but which perpetually is almost killing. Always there is the fact that, if you don't get that done today you can't get that done tomorrow and then in the middle the fox takes three hens which you have known for months must happen if you didn't get the hen-house mended and now the door must be locked after the horse has gone. So all the men do that instead of doing any of the urgent things. And so on, *every* single day.

The hardest thing on this farm is this: Highman, who is almost without exception the nicest man I have ever met, has absolutely no drive at all. Nor can he manage the men. Therefore I have not only to supply the drive but also to be constantly on the alert to circumvent Highman circumventing me out of sheer good nature. For instance, Metcalfe [cowman about to get the sack] is a lazy bugger and always trying to get other people to do his jobs. At one time he had the whole farm staff dancing round twenty miserable cows on at least two days a week. Then I put my foot down and said no member of the farm staff was to do anything for him without my permission. Nevertheless, I can't stop Highman. He has Nanny's quality of always doing anything he thinks needs doing [Jack's nanny who visited us often]. But it is no good in a foreman. I will go out in the afternoon leaving Highman to mend a drill I want to use the next day. When I get back I'll find he hasn't touched the drill because Metcalfe's calves were so badly in need of litter. Then my whole week's programme is buggered up.

I must explain that today one man can and often does milk between 100 and 120 cows, although I doubt if he looks after the young stock. In those days it took two men or a man and a girl to milk about forty cows and Metcalfe at this time had only about twenty. As far as I can make out, the only change since then is in a different placing of the milking stands and the understanding that it can be done. In my day we had only just left hand-milking behind and the possibilities of the milking machine were not understood.

Everything was made worse because at this time I had to spend many hours at sales trying to buy cows on a market where the price rose every day. And in October the ordinary work was added to by four acres of peas I had grown on land which had previously failed to roots. 'It would have been a good gamble,' I wrote to Jack, 'but I can't get any pickers. We can't really do it ourselves and it is customary to have it done by casual female labour, but this bloody village won't turn out, so it is a flop.'

I went on picking with the few I could muster and, although at least a third of the crop was left behind, we made a good profit out of it. Once I took Rose, then aged five, with me to help.

Now I must tell you about Rose this morning. She really was so sweet. We went up together to pull pea plants for the cows. She worked very hard, but she began to get bored and she kept saying, 'I don't really like pulling peas. Of course I know it wins the war, but it makes my hands so cold.' Or, 'Thomas is so naughty. He won't do anything he doesn't want to do and although pea-picking is beastly it does help to win the war.'

The other day, I said to Rose, 'Do you remember picking peas at Gipsy Hall?' and she replied, 'Yes. It made my hands so cold.'

Now about the children. Before we were up here, I used to be fairly careful about letting them get in the men's way. So they never had much fun on the farm, and didn't get many tractor rides, etc. Now I never bother about them and in spite of the bog of mud they are having a splendid time. They have bought a rabbit which they feed and clean out without being prompted, which is unusual in children. They always go out into the fields when there is a job like mangold pulling. Today the men were threshing and Thomas was there all afternoon. He had got High-man's penknife and was cutting string to tie round the sacks.

The threshing was the worst thing; even the men found this exhausting. One of the girls was called Sheila Rees-Mogg and she, like me, was a natural sergeant major, while like me she was used to dogs and horses and naturally good with animals. I wrote to Jack:

I have had rather a beautiful day, though, as I am exhausted and both my eyes are entirely closed with dust, it wouldn't be many people's idea of pleasure. I've been feeding the [threshing] drum for two solid days and halfway through the first day I got the hang of it. The man feeding the drum is the most important because he sets the pace for those in front of him dealing with straw and sacks. It has always been done by Oakley, the deaf and dumb, who is quite incredibly bad and our threshing standards are about half as good as they ought to be. Since Carling left, I have tried every possible combination to get the drum better fed, but never got it any faster and always produced endless rows with Oakley. Then I suddenly realized that, if you made practically no effort but let the suction do the work and only kept it going smoothly so the drum didn't get bunged and the suction cease to work, you went at double the pace. I can now truthfully say that, although I'm not near the class of those who do it well, I could give every man on this farm a ten-sack start and beat him. So I am immoderately proud of myself. Also it is the vantage point for giving black looks to people who are not working hard and therefore the right place for the boss. Of course, I am a fearful prefect by nature, and I remind myself of when I was at school. Sheila is a tremendously hard worker and I am very apt to keep changing her to any place which is holding us up, thereby speeding it up and administering an indirect reproof to the one she changes with. Whenever I do it, I think of myself when I was an intolerant, pompous and humourless captain of games. . . . It's very bad for my character and gives me too much sense of leadership and power of the wrong, black-look kind. Luckily, I only do it now and then and landgirls really are the end and fall into housemaidy gossip on all the most unsuitable occasions.

There was no electricity at Gipsy Hall and no heating; the water was pumped by a ram which took seventy-five gallons to pump twenty-five and so sometimes there was no water. Because of the hardness of the work, and more particularly because of the lack of petrol, the isolation at that time was almost complete.

I don't think I have ever described to you the formidable nature of GH meals. We nearly always have two landgirls living in the house, and Nora, who is rough and rude and by turns sulky or out to entertain with dull stories about what she said to the butcher. Then there are the children who quarrel incessantly and usually make scenes about their food. My method of enduring all this is to withdraw from it. I'm told I very often have to be addressed three times before I even hear it.

However, apart from the cows, which were still a difficulty, everything went very well. The bullocks, which were fed on the food we had grown for the cows we were unable to buy, were graded A when they went on the market, a thing rarely achieved in those days. I wrote to Jack:

There were a lot of jokes at the market on the lines of 'There must have been a bit of black marketing in feeding stuffs here', and one complete stranger came up to Pat and said, 'Did you have something to do with these bullocks? They are the best I've seen on Stratford Market for many a long day. ... Pat told me exactly what to do, but these bullocks were looked after entirely by a landgirl under me and no man had anything to do with them and as it is a man's game I am proud of that. Of course, Pat is jolly useful in more ways than one. He bought the bullocks and told us how to feed them and, as he knows everyone on the market, everyone came to look at them and GH is getting known as a good farm. I absolutely loved it.

Yet I think now that these bullocks should not have been on the farm. People were always buying me bullocks, but these were the only ones that did really well and even then we should probably have made more profit by selling the food that they ate. Here is something else I wrote at the time:

There was one particularly awful period when flu set in on the farm and Sheila, Cyril, Oakley and I were left alone to do everything. The muck was still not spread and it was getting late for the ploughing, so Sheila and I decided that come what might Cyril and Oakley should get on with the spreading. We devised a scheme whereby Sheila pulped the mangolds while I did the milking. Then I left Cyril to do the washing up, and Sheila and I fed concentrates and hay to the calves and dry cows, concentrates followed by mangolds, followed by hay to the bullocks, tore down the fields and fed the sheep, came back and fed the pigs and poultry, all before breakfast. This left the outliers to feed and all the mucking out to do during the morning, and triumphantly we sent Cyril and Oakley out to the fields.*

What is so difficult to explain today is why we had all this stock, particularly considering the difficulties. We needed eggs for ourselves and we occasionally killed a pig, but we could have done this without the pedigree herd which, on the advice of Mr Stewart, I kept. We might have had a few sheep to graze after the cows in the summer, but there was absolutely no case for the bullocks.

* Donaldson, *Four Years' Harvest*, p. 52.

Today, I think, most farmers specialize and prevent all this frittering of labour.

'The farm looks really well,' I wrote in the spring, 'has been graded A, and is always admired. Few people give me the credit they ought to, because farmers are mean-minded and hate new boys who are bumptious, but those that do really do. And I know in my heart I deserve it too.' Nevertheless, we were all worn out and thoroughly fed up. It was the only time in my life when I woke up tired in the mornings and none of us could have gone on at this pace much longer.

11

....

Four Years' Harvest

In the early part of 1943 everything seemed to change for the better. There were many reasons for this: the first being a sheepdog bitch named Meg, who came from Northumberland. Pat had been trying to get me one for some time and he fetched Meg from Leamington Station and took her to his farm, where he put her in a loose box for the night. The next morning she was gone, having scraped under a very small hole in the bottom of the door. Her loyalty and imagination were immediately established by her later being found on the railway line heading north. Most dogs prefer men because they are snobs and recognize the boss; just a few prefer women and Meg was one of these. When she came to Gipsy Hall she settled down at once, disdainfully rejecting the status of a pet by always refusing to come into the house. When I went in she lay down just outside until I came out again and then she followed me everywhere. I wrote to Jack:

> I've got a trained sheepdog, a bitch. I wonder if you have any idea what a pleasure this could be. I've been trying to get one for months (it's ridiculous not to have one with all this stock), but they are terribly difficult to come by. This one – Meg – has saved me about ten days' walking in the two days she's been here. Normally, when we move the sheep or round them up it takes me and at least two others, swotting round every corner of the field, yelling strange war cries and then running like hell to head off lots that have doubled back. Now I go by myself and stand in

a gate and Meg does the rest. Apart from the work, there is a great pleasure in it. She is a very pretty bitch and one's affection for a working dog is always of a quite different order from that of an ordinary dog.

At this time there was actually some doubt about who Meg belonged to. Pat had been trying to get a dog for himself as well as one for me, and when he presently said he had far more sheep than I had and must have Meg, I could only let her go, although I rather resented it. One day I went over to see Pat, driving a converted van with what we called 'a flat platform' which was hollow underneath so that one could store stuff. I was greeted enthusiastically by Meg, who stayed outside as usual when we went in to tea. When I got out of the van in the yard at Gipsy Hall, she jumped out from under the flat platform.

'I am tremendously sorry,' I said to Pat on the telephone, 'but I brought home a stowaway.' That was the end of the matter.

That summer I learned when to carry hay. On 6 July I wrote to Jack:

Goodness knows when I last wrote to you. We seem to have been carrying hay forever. Like many other great agricultural secrets, the moment when hay is fit seems to me pretty easy to determine. I've been dreading hay for eight months because I knew nothing about it whatever, Carling having been very secretive, and I thought I wouldn't know what to do. The first two fields Pat had to come racing round to advise but now at the end of three weeks I should be prepared to back my judgement against anyone around here except Pat.

The most important thing, however, was the advent of the combine harvester, and in *Four Years' Harvest* I wrote about it:

A combine harvester cuts the corn and threshes out the grain all in one operation, and as you haul the sacks off the field you appear to have finished the last of the processes which are the part of the producer. But normally this is not so. The grain comes moist from the combine and in that condition it will not keep. It has to be dried. The drying equipment is big and expensive and very few farmers have the acreage to justify the installation. [No longer true.] Since it was hoped to encourage the use of combines, the Ministry of Food had agreed to build an enormous dryer in Stratford-on-Avon to take grain from the farms nearby. So seriously is the necessity to dry corn taken, that the War Committee had refused to allocate a combine to any farmer who could not state definitely how he proposed to get his corn dried. But in the case of farmers near Stratford, the Ministry's dryer had been accepted in fulfilment of this obligation.

In the early spring and summer it became clear that there was some danger the dryer would not be ready in time. No one could say that it would not be, because it had now become a state secret, and, although farmers had been circularized about it, it now seemed there was some loss of patriotism in even mentioning it. [Faber's editors passed all these 'its' and the two 'nows'.] I, for one, was distraught. I have explained how we had taken on the harvesting of an extra thirty acres of wheat with infinitely less labour. I saw no possibility that we could do it this time by ordinary means. Apart from this, I was utterly determined not to start the winter with about a hundred and fifty tons of wheat to thresh. Thirdly, I had engaged the services of a contractor. ...

Nothing happened for several months of nightmare apprehension, then a circular was sent round by the chief executive officer of the county, saying that the Ministry of Food was hoping to make alternative arrangements and adding: 'In the event of their failing to do so before 28 July, I shall be glad if you will kindly get in touch with me.'*

Now this was silly talk. If one had waited until 28 July and still heard nothing, the corn would be ripe for the combine and it would be too late to do anything for oneself. I had what I described then as information from an 'unimpeachable source' (which could only have been Rob Hudson, the Minister of Agriculture) that the Ministry of Food had given a promise to the Ministry of Agriculture that in the event of the dryers not being ready, they would as a last resort take over all the grain from the farmers concerned, and unlike many farmers I got some sleep at night.

It was all solved in the simplest way. Corn merchants all had dryers, which in earlier seasons had been used for foreign grain. This year they were all empty and only too glad to take the British wheat; it was also a very hot year and it turned out that much of the grain did not need drying. Why we could not have been told this earlier was never explained.

The combine itself worked here with miraculous ease, and I regarded it with devotion and awe. For it came in the guise of a

---

* Donaldson, *Four Years' Harvest*, p. 71.

saviour, the only thing that could have made another winter at Gipsy Hall endurable.

'No stooking,' I used to say to myself, as the sacks were brought off the field, 'no carrying, no stacking, no thatching and no *threshing.*'*

Almost equally important, about this time the two cottages were finished. In my eyes they were slightly more distinguished than they might have been because, for the sake of economy, they were given flat roofs. I did not gain as much out of them as I had expected, because, when I moved Highman into one of them, it was no longer possible to induce anyone to live in the cottage he left. However, I had, with the house I had lived in myself, two others and when I advertised excellent cottages for a head cowman and a tractor driver, I had dozens of men to choose from. For the first time since I had been at Gipsy Hall, I had acquired the numbers which any experienced farmer on my acreage would have insisted upon.

The new tractor driver I do not remember, but the cowman was Price. I have said earlier that there is no difficulty in feeding and milking a herd of cows; all one needs is a certain degree of perfectionism. Nevertheless, as with children's nannies, some people add magic. Price was one of these. By the end of the year the cows were averaging three gallons a head. (I am not sure how good that is today, because, with proven bulls standing at the AI centres, the general level of cows must be much improved, but in those days, for an Ayrshire herd, it was exceptional.) We had many heifers calving at this time and soon were milking forty cows, averaging three and a half gallons. I think I am right in saying we soon showed in the rankings of the best herds in the county. Price was almost certainly rather extravagant with feeding stuffs, but, after nearly three years of mismanagement or doing it myself, he stood next to Highman in my esteem and affection. And in fact he had transformed the farm. I paid him £4 10s a week, but when the agricultural wage went up five shillings I put him up to £5.

In the winter of 1943–4 I wrote *Four Years' Harvest*. This book was recommended by the Book Society and seems to me now to be much better written than *Approach to Farming*, possibly because at the time I did not like it so much. In terms of sales it did nearly as well, although again it was out of print for months. I notice nowadays that almost everyone who writes only one book (of memoirs or something of the sort) complains bitterly about its presentation

* Donaldson, *Four Years' Harvest*, p. 74.

by the publishers. Possibly because I had such a drubbing with my first two books, I never complain because I regard it as a waste of time. I learned then that, after putting heart and soul into the writing of a book, one has produced one of several hundred of the publisher's output, and it is a useless expenditure of spirit to expect the kind of attention the inexperienced hope for.

Four Years' Harvest contains a rather good analysis of the agricultural situation and the ingrained attitude of farmers, followed by what today seems a particularly silly plan for the future, advocating nationalization of the land. At the time this was much admired by some people, and, published first as an article in *The Countryman* (editor Robertson Scott), it produced letters of congratulations from several pundits, including one from C.S. Orwin, director of the Agricultural Research Institute and a fellow and the estates bursar of Balliol College.

So I might be said to have succeeded beyond my dreams. The two books ensured me a celebrity status, even though in a very restricted circle, and the farm was an acknowledged success. When Rob Hudson, the Minister of Agriculture, visited us, he said afterwards to his wife Hannah that on most farms either the arable was good or the stock, but that at Gipsy Hall both were good.

However, 1944 was spoiled for me by the tragedy of Leonora Cazalet's unexpected death. She had gone into the London Clinic for a small operation because she wished to have a third child and had failed to conceive. During the night after the operation – which was of a kind, I believe, soon abandoned – she died. I have never forgotten her and even now often think of her, and sometimes dream of her, as I do of Freddy, my father, but seldom anyone else.

At the beginning of 1944 I went to stay with Frank Sykes, a very good farmer with a widely known name, who later managed the Queen's farms at Windsor, and whom I had met through the Cazalets. When I told him that I had made a profit in my first two years, although only a small one (£200 in the first year and £600 in the second), he told me that these results were 'phenomenal'. However, any danger of euphoria was kept in control by the facts. I wrote to Jack at the end of 1943:

I'm just one shade off actual tears all day. You know we haven't had any hot water since July. Some days we have no water and other days we just have cold water. It's frozen quite hard four nights running and it's freezing now. The house has no heating of any sort and only the boiler for the bath kept it liveable in last year.

I no longer remember what had gone wrong to make things as bad as that, but it forced me to spend a considerable sum to have electricity brought on to the farm, which made for greater efficiency as well as hot water for a bath.

And if hubris did lurk anywhere in the background, Nemesis was not far behind, and appeared in the matter of the accounts. I should, perhaps, in any case say something about money.

Quite soon it had become apparent that we had bought Gipsy Hall without sufficient capital to stock it. This had not been recognized by my advisers at the time because no one had anticipated the degree of inflation in farms, farm stock and implements which began to take place immediately. In fact, I could not have survived the first year or two without Peggy Dunne. She always lent me money when I needed it, on one occasion agreeing to a loan of £1,000 (multiply by about twenty) over the telephone. However, when I borrowed I always had wheat in the barns to be threshed and bullocks to be sold with which to pay her back. Secondly, I was always absolutely confident of making a big profit in the third year, and increasing it in the years to come. My accounts were done by Burgis & Bullock, Mr Burgis attending to them himself, after looking at my books and finding I used the double entry system I had learned at Moulton. (He said he knew only one other farmer who did this and that was Clyde Higgs.)

On 31 August 1944 I wrote to Jack:

I've just had a shattering blow. I went to the accountants this morning ... to clear up certain points. Nothing is certain yet [but] I said to the man (who wasn't Burgis himself who usually does our accounts because he is on holiday): 'Have you arrived at any figure yet?' He said: 'Yes, but it's perfectly ridiculous and I think these items I want to see you about will help to alter it.' I said: 'What is the figure?' and he said: 'Five [pounds] and eleven pence.'

When Mr Burgis came back he went into the accounts himself, and certain adjustments might have been made. However, as I put it to Jack, I was frightfully sick at this figure, though I shouldn't have been much better pleased at making a profit of £200. It appeared that the takings had been exceptionally good and the profit somehow frittered away, a fact which no one could explain.

There seem to be three main reasons. One, our valuations are generally too low. This doesn't contribute enormously because they've been too low in each year. Two, they are down. That really means that we took it in extra milk instead of keeping it in oats and beans, etc. A.G. Street wrote an article in which he said that, if a man [producing milk] had his books done at Michaelmas and made a profit of £1,000, if they were done again at Lady Day, he would find that he had lost it. This is an argument that at the present price of all commodities milking doesn't pay, so that oats and beans valued at £1,000 could be completely lost when converted into milk. The third and by far the major reason seems to be ordinary extravagance. The takings seem to be all that can be desired. They are in fact £8,240. This is a figure of about £21 per acre and Burgis says that is actually high. He also said that on that turnover it would be reasonable to expect a profit of about £800 which is in fact exactly what I did expect.

Various reasons were given and some adjustments made to improve the position, but I was inconsolable.

'I think I can best explain what I feel by saying that if I was working for an employer, I should hand in my resignation,' I wrote to Jack. And later in the same letter:

Of course, I was brought up wrong. Except that I take this so much more seriously, it isn't really any different from the fact that we always overspent our income by £500 and never could see how or where it was possible to cut. The thing I didn't realize was that it wasn't enough to earn as much as another farmer, I'd also got to have the same outlook on expenditure as another farmer. Then of course we've had a house and butter and eggs and all the rest of the list (cars, petrol, men to fix anything that wouldn't work and to fetch and carry) and we certainly wouldn't have as much if the money had been invested in any other way. ... But all those are really only arguments for you. They don't help me much. The truth is I am suffering a blow to my inordinate pride. And it may be a very good thing. Still I don't like it.

Mr Burgis had been fairly comforting because he thought the whole thing was ridiculous and that there was something wrong in the valuations. However, he said we would not be able to tell anything more until we got next year's accounts and saw how they compared. So for a year I had to live with it. Then I wrote to Jack: 'The farm profit, after you have paid me a salary of £90, is £1,814, which means that if you had been farming it yourself and not paying this salary it would have been £1,900. This is on the usual basis of low valuations and everything possible charged against profit.'

During the whole of our farming career of nearly thirty years, Jack and I never again made a loss, although we did not show very big profits. After the experience of 1943–4 we gave up expecting the accounts to tell us anything of interest or value except what we had to pay in tax – seldom very much since the books were done, legitimately, with nothing in mind except the necessity to keep this down.

However, the way we had been brought up continued to tell against us. When I told Hugh Gaitskell at Kingsbridge, the last farm we owned, what we had started with and what we had then, he said we had lost a lot of money and not in the least kept up with inflation. This was no doubt true, but we had educated Thomas at Eton and Cambridge and Rose at Cheltenham Ladies' College and Oxford. Kate (born after the war) was sent to Cranborne Chase. We also entertained a great deal at weekends. During the course of nearly thirty years we twice moved farms. All this expenditure might have been covered if we had chosen the right moment to do this, but we never did. We sold Burden Court Farm in Gloucestershire for £50,000 and two years later it was worth £200,000, and we sold Kingsbridge Farm in Buckinghamshire again for £50,000 and in the course of a very few years it was worth about £800,000.

Jack came home in August 1945 and, like so many after the First World War, he felt he would be happy forever as a farmer. We stayed at Gipsy Hall until 1948, and during that time we built two more cottages, exactly when or why neither of us can remember. Jack says that I did this while he was away, but that is hardly possible, partly because there is no mention of it in my letters or in his, but also because I could not have got the building materials. I think they were built just after the war, because even by the autumn of 1944 we seem to have been once more in trouble for labour. Two of my best landgirls left, one to a better job and the other to be nearer her family, and for some reason, possibly because we had begun to look forward to the end of the war, I had difficulty in replacing them. Even if I had succeeded, I could have given them lodgings only by having them in my own house, which for the same reason I was anxious not to do. It would have spoiled everything when Jack came home for us to be permanently accompanied by two landgirls. But the main trouble, as I have already explained, was because we undertook too many things. My recollection is that I enjoyed farming during the war, and only Jack's prolonged absence made me unhappy. However, no one reading my letters to him would think this. I wrote to him in the autumn of 1944:

> You've no idea how utterly wearing and boring farming can be. At the moment, for instance, there is the rest of the wheat to combine. That takes Highman and one boy. There are the potatoes to be got up which takes the biggest gang one can get. [Prisoners of war were sent onto farms by now.] There is the sugar beet to be lifted – can't start on that for the moment, anyway. There is silage to be made which takes a whole gang. There is 70 acres to plough. All these things should really be done before autumn and winter rain make them impossible. In addition, there are a thousand and one delaying jobs like weighing sacks and getting them off to the station and grinding food for the cows, etc., which also have to be done. ... I'm tired and bored and I want to stay in bed and read a book. ...

At the time I write (autumn 1990), I have recently paid a visit to Gipsy Hall, the first since I left it just over forty years ago. Alan Brookes, whose grandfather bought the farm for his daughter and son-in-law, very kindly showed us round and explained how he farms today. (Farmers are in a bad way at the moment because of over-production and a projected drop in the subsidy of 30 per cent over ten years.)

The farm looked rather lovely because Alan has got rid of several hedges so that one sees a rolling vista which was invisible in my day. Also, I thought, like some other places, it seems actually improved by the loss of a great many hedgerow elms in the hurricane of 1987, which gives it a parklike look. Equally important, good roads have been made round the house and buildings.

Alan keeps thirty pedigree Charolais cows and has ten in-calf heifers, also forty commercial cows whose progeny he rears for beef. These are a Charolais cross on Herefords and even, he told me, on the descendants of some of the Ayrshire cows I left behind. He also keeps 350 breeding ewes. He tells me that beef has paid for the last ten years, providing the bull produces fast-growing stock. Charolais are very popular. He has no land 'set aside' and very little plough, and he grows enough cereals only to feed his own stock.* Much of the work is done by contractors and he has comparatively few implements. This is current practice on all except the biggest farms because, as Alan rightly said, it is impractical to invest, for instance,

---

* Because of over-production, the Government pays farmers £80 an acre to set land aside, that is not to farm it.

£70,000 in a combine harvester which works only a few weeks in the year.

Most astonishing of all the changes since my day is that his entire farm staff consists of two single men who live in the village. Jack and I like to feel we improve the places we live in, and for forty years I have believed I improved Gipsy Hall by leaving behind adequate housing for the staff. Now three of the cottages are let and Alan proposes to turn the fourth into a holiday cottage.*

In 1940 I paid £20 an acre for Gipsy Hall, a sum which would today be more like £400, allowing for inflation. Yet now it is valued at nearer £2,000 an acre.

---

* He tells me that the cottages were used until they got rid of the dairy herd in 1969 after many of the barns burned down. In a speech to the House of Lords immediately following our visit to Gipsy Hall, Lord Mackie of Benshie said that farmers were in a very bad way, and he went on: 'When I went to farm at Benshie forty-five years ago, I put in a day, and we had twelve full-time men on the farm. ... Today, I believe there are three men on that farm. On Saturday, while out shooting, I met an enormously efficient young man who was farming 600 acres with one man. I reckon that he will survive.' However, Lord Mackie said that small farmers with up to 200 acres could not make the kind of living they had a right to expect 'given the prices that we can afford or that should exist given the great advances in agriculture'. He said there will be opportunities for people who are competent and who have money. However, that will be no good for the countryside. When I was at Gipsy Hall, I asked Alan what happened when someone had flu and he replied: 'They can't.'

12

··

War 1940–1943

During year 1940 the real war began and many of my letters were on that theme. I give them here as a whole rather than as they occurred in order not constantly to interrupt the theme of my farming career. Today they read like a stereotype of how the English are supposed to feel and behave in a war; but the excerpts are exactly as written and I give them for what they are worth. Before the fall of France, Jack was at a railway yard near Amiens, but at the time of Dunkirk he was south of the river Seine and eventually came home from Cherbourg. He was stationed first at Derby, then at Darlington, but early in November he went to the Middle East. He was in Sicily during the Allied attack and returned to England in time to go to France for the invasion. He was almost always up with the armies as he had to move them and their equipment.

Lavendon 11.5.40

I can't really write letters properly any more. I suppose one will get used to it, but at the moment it seems idle to write you local gossip now that the war has really started. I spend most of the day on my knees looking up places on a large map of France which lies on the floor. All those with no personal stake in the present business think it is a good thing. Opens everything up etc., etc. I think they are probably right. Even in the present gloom I was able to raise a resounding cheer for the resignation of Mr Chamberlain. I wonder if by any chance you listened in to him.

Lavendon 13.5.1940

There were no letters this morning & I am sure you must have written on Wednesday or Thursday so I suppose one must assume that we can't have a postal service now we are fighting a war. That probably means you are not getting my letters either, but I will go on writing as they will probably turn up in a bunch one day.

I find life intolerably gloomy & tiresome & where at the beginning everyone felt the war as a direct blow, now most people who are not personally concerned have settled back to their usual more or less carefree life & are not very much more concerned about the present phase than they were about Finland. Coney is coming back today & I am immensely looking forward to this because it will be great to have another person in the house who has the same point of view as oneself.

22.5.1940

I can't really write to you because I daren't even think of you. I don't know where you are or what has happened to you. But just in case the posts still work, this is just to tell you we are all right.

Lavendon 25.5.40

I haven't been able to write to you for a few days because my fear has been so great. But if you are somewhere where letters will eventually reach, you will expect to hear from me.

Lavendon 29.5.40

I got a letter from you today dated 22nd & posted on the 24th. I leave for the Institute before the post arrives & it will give you some idea of what I have been feeling during the last 10 days if I tell you that Mary put through 3 telephone calls to try & get hold of me to tell me the letter was there, though she knew I would be back at lunch time. The days I feared most for you were the 20th & 21st. .... Your letter is a very funny one & I could not resist reading most of it to Mary & we both shrieked with laughter. It is so immensely casual & says so fearfully little &, received in this devastating tension, unrelieved by having a job to do which has some bearing on the present events, it reads exactly like a letter from someone who is having a rather exciting holiday, say in the Pyrenees or sailing. You are immensely matter of fact & apparently at that time anyway have absolutely no idea of the sort of scenes which one's imagination creates for one when one is sitting impotently in England. Of course it is quite different for you, but here an announcer on the wireless says in parenthesis & quite casually that the Germans have dropped bombs & parachutists on hundreds of railway junctions. The subject is never referred to again & no more light is shed on it. But one knows one will hear no news of any sort, possibly for a month. Unless a wireless announcer one day casually announces to you that bombs & parachutists have been dropped on the Buckingham–Northampton border, you will never know what the last 10 days have been like for me. .... What was rather heavenly about your letter was your casual attitude that as you were very tired you would write me all details the next day – exactly as though one could count on a normal post as well as everything else. It is very endearing to find you so unmoved. Ralph's attitude on the telephone was much the same & it gives one a kick to know that people who have actually been through some of it are so unperturbed.

The whole of my present attitude is based on the assumption that you are the south side of the gap & it is really rather heartless to be even temporarily relieved when one thinks of the people in the north. But now it has really begun I find that all one's emotions are used up for oneself & one has nothing left to spare for other people.

Lavendon 12 June 1940

I feel so tremendously guilty because all your letters & field cards say you don't hear from me & of course it is because for several days I didn't write to you. I would try to explain why this happened, but it is the sort of thing one could never really discuss until this war is over & we are one day together again. Of course, during that week or two one did get an impression here that was in fact worse than the actual happenings. There was for instance an article in the NS&N which said that the whole of Northern France was razed to the ground under which lay unnumbered & unknown dead & that the worst of H.G. Wells' prophecies had understated the present situation. I have since seen people who have returned & who say that there never was any foundation for this sort of account & so I suppose it was written by a Fifth Columnist or one of those masochist idiots of the Left. But you can imagine the sort of effect it had on me. And I had a vague & superstitious feeling that to write to you was to assume too much & to court disaster. [Once when I asked Coney if she prayed about Ralph, she replied, 'Oh no. I wouldn't take a risk like that.']

Train to London. 4 June 1940

First of all I agree & acknowledge all your plans in the event of complete chaos. But have you kept a note because they are quite long & complicated & you will not remember for long. Secondly I agree all you say about England. I think I have already written it to you. Thirdly I agree that for both of us, if it should happen that we were asked to take a risk, England & the war must come before everything. ... Then I have exactly the same feeling as you about not being able to endure the idea of the bloody Boche humiliating England. Also I am not frightened. I wouldn't say this to anyone but you because one can't really tell in advance how one will feel & it may be just boasting. ...

The morale here was not too hot for a day or 2 but never really bad. We are all frightened of what the French may do. ... Here we have all been so tremendously revived by the behaviour of the BEF, RAF & Navy. It is the first time for 10 years the English have attempted the difficult (almost impossible) & brought it off & it gives one a different feeling about England. ...

I think we shall get through & I am glad that in the end I have kept the farm for us & all the difficulties have made me love every blade of it. And you have no idea what a warm little feeling one can have for cattle which one has paid for. ...

I met 3 BEF officers last night including Gordon Lennox. They were simply heavenly. So pleased with themselves & their men. Did you hear about the Labour Corps who were given one good officer & some rifles & held Arras for days? These three said whenever you saw a tin hat you felt safe for a minute until you lost the bloody thing. But they said it was the damnedest lie to say the Germans were not good soldiers. They were very funny about the Belgians who they said were never anything but an intolerable nuisance & very fast bicyclists in the wrong direction. They said they met Belgian officers driving out of Belgium when they went in.

The English are sweet today. All the BEF who are back smile broadly at everyone they see & in this carriage are 4 other people, one soldier who may be BEF & we are all offering each other cigarettes etc. We are all barricaded up on the roads & I have been stopped 7 times for my identity card.

At the end of June 1940 Jack returned to England and, although he was in Darlington, letters about the war largely ceased. Two written then seem worth quoting:

24 November 1940

I went to Coventry. It is rather difficult to describe it because it both is & isn't what one had expected. The papers said the whole of the middle of the town was flat. Well, it is & it isn't. Whole areas are completely flat, but round them you can drive in quite ordinary streets with rather damaged buildings all round. The Cathedral is demolished except that a lot of the outside walls and the spire stand. There is no water or gas at all, some electric light but no power. Everything was chaos on the organization side. I spent the whole day buttering slices of bread which I did at about twice the speed of anyone else present, which was not surprising as some of them seemed to have been doing it for 24 hours on end. I had no conversation with the people being fed but some of the bread cutters were just ordinary Coventry women. I must say they were extraordinary. They were quite cheerful and full of dull jokes which I suppose only the English make, but which are very good in this sort of time. For instance, when one of the women said she was going home for half an hour one of the others said: 'Now don't you go having a hot bath & a good lie down.' In order to appreciate this, one has to realize we couldn't even get a glass of water to drink & that this woman hadn't had an ordinary night's sleep for ten days. We asked them about the morale of the people. They all said it was wonderful. They said the only thing which got any of them down was when the papers said it had not stopped production, because, apart from the general chaos & lack of power, several of the factories did not exist at all any more. I do think it's silly. It just makes people distrust all official reports.

On the way home the most odd thing happened. A soldier and his wife stopped me for a lift. I said something about having come from Coventry & the man said, 'Oh, we're Coventry people, but my wife left because of the bombing.' Then she said from the back in a perfectly ordinary voice: 'We lost two of our children. The third was buried, but they got her out all right.' They both spoke in such ordinary voices that I thought they could not be talking about something which had happened recently, so I said, 'This was some time ago, you mean?' & they said: 'Oh no, in the big raid last Friday.' This was all they said about it and we might have been talking about the price of eggs. Is it the result of shock, or what? It seemed to me absolutely terrifying.

Apparently there has been a certain amount of trouble in Coventry amongst the workers – not strikes or anything with a political motive but just general slackness because they earned so much money at the beginning of the Bevin push & so didn't want any more; also a certain amount of bad morale because so many unattractive characters had been drafted in to do the work & had been billeted on all of them. All just the squalid & sordid side of human nature & it is so odd that the same people are so awfully fine when something really hits them. It makes me think that every now & then the world has to be shaken up when it is getting too slothful. It is rather like the Flood or Sodom & Gomorrah.

21.12.40

Peter [Cazalet] was very gloomy. He has got a battery made up partly of men from Chester, partly of men from other batteries & partly of new recruits. He says they are the dregs of the earth. Many of them can't read or write properly, a good many have VD, they desert in hundreds, not permanently but for 2 or 3 days at a time, which means an appalling lot of trouble hauling them back & confining them to barracks. And they all *cry* all the time. He says he has even got officers who cry & out of the whole lot of his officers only Nitty [Anthony Mildmay] and one other are any good at all. He swears there is nothing unusual about this battery. He says all the later ones are like this. As a result he is very gloomy.

I asked Victor [Cazalet] who was there last night if anyone in the government was any good. He said Sir J. Anderson and Hugh Dalton did their jobs well. He referred to Bevin & Morrison with the most bitter contempt as 'those awful windbags'.

13.3.1941

Ernest Bevin has just announced the conscription of women, beginning with the 20's and 21's. This won't affect me, I suppose, as I am both a mother and a farmer. But I am wondering if it may eventually affect either Molly or Nora. I am going to make Molly do a lot of farm work all summer, so as to be able to call her a part-time farm-worker.

22.3.1941

I may soon have to give up smoking. I should have had to some time ago but for Mrs Wheeldon keeping me a special supply and today I hear she has absolutely none in her shop. There are no luxuries now. Hardly any sweets or cigarettes, no fruit at all at the moment, no cheese, only 8 oz of jam a month, no gumboots (mine have started to let the water in) and so on with almost everything you want.

10.4.1941

We had more bombs on the farm again last night – this time in the field where the roots were last year which is getting a bit close [to the village and our house rather than to the farmhouse]. They made enormous craters and mucked up about an acre. I don't know how I am going to get the holes filled up again. When they fell it was pretty noisy and woke me up. I wondered where they were and placed them just right. So I went across that field this morning on my way to the farm. The first thing I saw was exactly like a well only about half the diameter. I went up to it and started peering down it and only then realized what it was. So it was lucky it didn't explode there and then. I think it is almost certainly a dud because it was just slung overboard with the other two by an aeroplane in a hurry and they both went off at once so I suppose this one was meant for Coventry which has had it very bad two nights running. They say the casualties were as bad as last time and they got the Daimler works. . . . Apparently the chief bomb officer came while Carling and I were both away and said that if the bomb didn't go off by 2 o'clock (which it didn't) it probably wouldn't go off at all. But if it didn't, no one must go into the field or work it until the bomb had been removed, and they were too busy to remove it for 6 weeks. Well, this field is 18 acres and has been manured all over and prepared for roots. In six weeks it will be too late. Hell and damnation.

Another remark the bomb officer made was that he thought it was not an accident, but that they were aiming at the buildings which he says would shine in the moonlight and should be camouflaged. I haven't any money to have them camouflaged. I don't suppose it could be done under £150, but on the other hand I suppose one has some responsibility to the whole village.

14.4.1941

I forgot to tell you about the bomb. It exploded after all at 10 p.m. last night. So the field is ours again, even if spoiled by three enormous craters. They are big ones apparently, everyone who knows about craters says so.

13.5.1941

Birmingham yesterday. A great deal of damage has been done since we were there. The bottom of New Street is more or less non-existent. The Midland Hotel is completely out of action though not on the ground. The street behind the station is more or less demolished from one end to the other. Everywhere you go you see burnt and demolished buildings.

I must tell you about the lunch we had because it will give you an idea of food now. We could have fish or meat or rabbit (this was at the Queen's which you know is the most expensive and best). I chose the rabbit because it was done with mushrooms and sounded nice. Of course I ought to have known better at this time of year and you couldn't even cut it much less eat it. Mummy had the lamb, which was all right. She wanted a dark sherry but could only get light. They produced a tray of sweets to choose from. There was stewed rhubarb, an open flan and a tart. 'What is in the flan ?' 'Rhubarb.' 'What is in the tart ?' 'Rhubarb.' 'What is the mixed fruit salad ?' 'Rhubarb and tinned plums.' We went back for tea and saw the first attractive-looking cakes we had seen for months. Some of them were cream buns made with vegetable cream, but the rest were rhubarb flan cut into squares. I asked for cigarettes, not because I thought I'd get some but just to see. The waiter said they hadn't seen a packet for five days. The position is that you can get them in your own shop if you are lucky or have a pull, but otherwise you haven't a chance of buying them anywhere. I also hear they have begun to favour men. I am told that in factories and in shops in towns they keep them for men and won't sell them to women. Don't you think that's monstrous ?

29.6.41

Russia has now been at war for one week. So she seems to be holding them, although it is almost impossible to know what is happening. If she does succeed in keeping them out of Russia it will be the most sensational slap in the face for all and sundry.

3.8.1941

Yesterday I went over to the Stapledons where Buck [De La Warr] is staying. He said he hoped it [the resistance of Russia] would not lead to too much optimism in England and everyone thinking the war was over. This gave me an opportunity I have been waiting for for some weeks. I said I thought it was a pity that all the leaders of opinion in England were so anxious to squash optimism of which in my opinion there is not nearly enough. I said, 'What is overlooked is this: because this is a people's war and anyone may get bombed any day, it doesn't alter the fact that no cabinet minister and no newspaper editor is living in one room in the house of someone they hate and who hates them, because they have been bombed out of their own, or, having two children, do not wish to be bombed out of their own. Nor have the wives of cabinet ministers or newspaper editors any direct experience of living while their husbands are in the Middle East. So they think it is a good idea to keep telling people who, in this war as in every other, are the ones who are really taking hell, that they've got to go on taking it for at least another two years. Whereas the best chance is to let them have some glimmer of hope that it might be only for another six months or so.' This was very enjoyable because it really made a great impression and shook Buck a bit. I hope he will repeat it to some of the other wiseacres who see that no day passes without the newspapers and the BBC reiterating that there isn't any hope at all for at least two years, which they repeat in a schoolmasterly way to keep the children good and not because they really believe it themselves. We were drinking burgundy which had been slightly mulled owing to being heated by an electric stove so I was in really good form by then, and maybe not making quite the impression I thought I was.

1.7.1941

Do you realize that the meat ration lasts only two days? There are no eggs, fish has been plentiful but now that it is controlled I suppose it will disappear, no fruit, practically no cheese or jam, no cakes, rationed bacon, practically no chicken. The only thing that remains plentiful is green vegetables. Before they were controlled there were plenty of tomatoes at anything from 4/- to 6/- a lb [pre-war price about 10p], but now they have all disappeared. Most pubs close three days a week for lack of beer and cigarettes are like gold.

22.8.1941

Yesterday ten soldiers came to fill in the bomb craters. The position is that I pay the army and we are paid by the war insurance, but nobody pays anything till after the war. One of the ten was a corporal. When he had settled nine men to work he came back to the farmhouse because he said there were some forms to be filled in. These turned out to be forms that should have been signed in the evening agreeing the number of hours they had worked. Then he messed about talking to Mrs Carling. Molly and I went down the fields and on our way we met one of the soldiers coming up. He asked if we had seen the corporal and we said we thought he was at the farmhouse. He said: 'Well, if you see him, tell him I've gone to the village to get some fags.' This should have left eight men working there, but when we got there there were only seven. I suppose the eighth had had a sudden desire for some sweets. All seven were leaning on their spades talking. In the afternoon we went down again and there were eight men there. Three were working and the other five leaning on their spades. On our way back later in the afternoon we met the corporal and one man coming down. I went up to him and said, 'I want to see that paper I signed this morning.' He said, 'Why?' I said: 'Because I'll sign for seven men this morning and eight this afternoon, but if you've got ten down for either I'll cancel my signature.' He said, 'Why?' So I told him in well chosen but quite moderate language why. So he said, 'Well, you see, I'm sort of here to supervise. I'm not supposed to work.' So I said: 'Well I don't pay for supervision, especially supervision done at the other end of the farm while the men lean on their spades. ...' This did a bit of good and after that a little, a very little work was done. It doesn't matter very much because in the end it's the war insurance that pays. ... Perhaps they behave better in other countries, but all the farmers who are having them for harvesting report the same kind of behaviour and what's the use of a man with two stripes, who I imagine is equivalent to at least a foreman, if one of the men can say, 'If you see him tell him I've gone to get some fags.'

The Post Office people are also an enigma. I posted the proofs of *Approach to Farming* by airmail. I asked, 'Is it possible to send a parcel by airmail?' 'No.' Luckily I know the drill. 'Well, what is the maximum weight one can send by airmail?' 'Four pounds.' 'Well, will you weigh this?' It weighed eleven ounces. So I said, 'Well, I'll send it airmail.' 'It will cost you a small fortune.' It actually cost £1 7s 6d which I thought might have been worse. But isn't the whole thing odd? It happens every time. They always deny that you can do anything you want to do, but if you know the form and continue to press them, it always turns out that you *can* do it. Then they always comment on what a lot it's going to cost.

9.10.1941

You say you suppose I have really given up smoking. This gave Molly and Nora a good laugh. After making the lives of the household a nightmare for about three weeks, I have returned to my usual habits. The shortages vary from time to time. The present one is matches which can't be had for love or money.

27.10.41

I find it difficult to say anything about the war to you because, although I think your optimism is hopelessly wrong, I think it so very right and clever of you to be optimistic as it gets you through. But if you talked like that here you would simply be laughed at. No one talks in terms of less than years and Buck said one should say 'If' not 'When'. American aid has been such a frost – however, who knows? No one has been right about anything yet so they may just as easily be wrong about this.

8.12.1941

I have just got back from a week-end with Oliver and Maureen. ... I told him that both you and Coney, writing from Lisbon, were much more optimistic than is the fashion here. He merely shook his head.

The letter of 7 November 1943 was written from Fairlawne, where I was staying with the Cazalets. Both Peter Cazalet and Anthony Mildmay had transferred from Anti-Aircraft to the Welsh Guards which had not yet been sent abroad.

I got very quickly into roaring form and I said to Peter, 'This is the first time I've been in good form for two years', and he said, 'I don't believe it. I think you've been practising every day', and we all thought all our jokes were wonderful and so on. And it was awfully lucky it went that way because apparently Peter and Anthony have to put up with a shade of sourness from wives whose husbands have been away for a long time. For instance, with Peter in the Chair at a meeting at Shipbourne, Mrs Joynson gets up and says: 'Wouldn't it be better as *nearly all* the people it concerns are *overseas* to leave the matter until they come home?' about some piffling thing that no one cares about any way. Peter had said, 'The test of Frankie is whether she is sour or not.' And of course by nature I'm awfully sour, but I don't really keep it up and I do get nice and drunk.

21.11.43

First of all about Tom [Oswald] Mosley. He has been let out and

114

his wife because he is ill, and with that the country that remained unmoved by Spain, Munich, Darlan, the fate of the International Brigadiers and the fate of the Jews has risen as a man to show what democracy is by signing protests in an attempt to get him put back again. Now I think that's very seriously distressing and I want to know what you think. ... Mosley was always a joke and everyone knew it, in spite of the fact that he did annoy a few Communists by marching through the City and beating them up. There was only one moment when he ever aspired to be anything more than a joke and that was when a German invasion was feared. Then he was put in gaol and quite right too. Now he is ill and has no organization and is no longer a menace and is let out. And in any country which believes 'IT COULDN'T HAPPEN HERE' quite right too. But not at all. There's the biggest and most united dust-up I ever remember about anything.

24.12.43

I had such fun yesterday. Irving Berlin's *Army Show* was in Birmingham. It's the only thing I've really wanted to see for years. It was only two weeks in London and impossible to get into. So I wrote four weeks ago for seats in Birmingham. The theatre didn't even bother to answer. I had promised to take Pat and when we didn't get seats we decided to go just the same and go to a cinema and do our Christmas shopping. I saw Irving cross the hall at the Queen's where we had lunch. I hadn't seen him for seventeen years but he was always a heavenly little man so I wrote him a note. He was divine. He's one of the most modest and lovable people I have ever met. Anyway, without any fuss or bother or throwing himself about, he put practically the whole American Army on to getting two seats and then in the middle of the show it seemed we'd got into some that were already sold and he came through the pass door himself to settle the argument.

This is a really bad description of one of the proudest moments in my life. Irving sang 'Oh! How I Hate To Get Up In The Morning' and at that time we were standing against the wall on the side of the stalls. When he had finished he came according to my letter 'through the pass door', although in my memory he came over the bridge. Certainly he walked up the centre of the stalls, found the theatre manager and pointed to us. Soon after we were moved back into seats.

PART III

*Farming
in
Peace*

13

....

Burden Court Farm

Sometime in the spring of 1947 we saw an advertisement for a farm for sale on the Cotswolds, which, it was said, had panoramic views. We thought that even an estate agent's office could not use this phrase if there was no view at all and we decided to go and see it.

What neither Jack nor I can remember is why we stayed at Gipsy Hall so long. In all our wartime letters we had agreed that if, when he came home, he decided to join me as a farmer, we would have to have a more attractive farm and farmhouse. Yet we not only stayed there for two years, but, as I have already said, built more cottages; in addition, I am quite certain that we did not try to find another farm until we saw this advertisement.

On the day we visited Burden Court Farm at Tresham, near Wotton-under-Edge, it was in thick fog. It was 600 feet above sea level and was sometimes in fog when the rest of the country was clear but equally often in full sunshine when the rest was in fog. We could not see the view but we believed in it, because in both the field in front of the house and that at the far end of the farm there was a sheer drop to valley land beneath. Legend has it that we made an offer there and then without actually seeing the panorama, but I think we must have gone once more first.

We offered £16,000 for 500 acres, of which about a hundred was second-class land in the valley, and soon we drove over to an estate agent's office to sign the contract. On our way back to Gipsy Hall we were both in a state of hysterical gloom. The estate agent had seemed so clearly dishonest that we thought we had walked into some trap, either by paying too much or, worse still, by overlooking some obvious crab. As it turned out, someone had been done, but it was not us.

This farm had been an outlier on the estate of Robin Hale, a descendant of Sir Matthew Hale (1609–76), Lord Chief Justice, born and buried at Alderley, the next village to Tresham, where Robin now lived. The *Dictionary of National Biography* expends eight pages on Sir Matthew Hale, ending with the information that he had inherited his estate which has then remained in 'possession of posterity to the present day'. It seems probable therefore that Burden Court had once been part of Sir Matthew's property.

Robin Hale had spent most of his life in New Zealand, returning when he inherited the house and estate at Alderley. Because of death duties, for the first time in the history of this family, he had been forced to sell some of the outlying land. The tenant of Burden Court, whose name I have forgotten, arguing that he had lived there all his life and that the good condition of the farm was entirely due to his activities, persuaded Robin that he should pay a price much below its market value. (The law by now ensured that this would in any case have been lower than if offered with vacant possession, because Robin could sell it only with a sitting tenant.) Robin felt the force of his tenant's argument and sold the farm well below its market value, some said for £8,000; whereupon it was immediately put on the market at slightly below the right price, since the farmer was anxious to get out before Robin came to hear of all this.

We were not so lucky with the sale of Gipsy Hall. We believed it to be worth £21,000 and we were advised to have an auction. When the great day came, Mr Margetts, the auctioneer, took bids from all over the hall but withdrew the farm just below the reserve.

'Who was the highest bidder?' I asked him.

'There were no bids,' he replied.

This was an unpleasant experience, and, when selling houses, which we often do, we have always since refused an auction. However, the next day, or soon after, Alan Brookes's grandfather offered £17,000 and we accepted. The following day we were offered £18,000, but at that time a seller's word was his bond.

I do not propose to go into much detail about the actual farming of Burden Court. I have already indicated that with a good advisory service and experience of horses and dogs, farming is not really difficult in the way that old Farmer Giles made one believe when I

ABOVE LEFT *My mother and my father, Freddy Lonsdale*

ABOVE RIGHT *Daphne du Maurier*

RIGHT *P. G. Wodehouse in his library*

The Wood House (by Walter Gropius)

ABOVE *Leonora Cazalet*

RIGHT *Mary Dunn*

ABOVE *The house at Gipsy Hall*

BELOW *Thomas and Rose at Gipsy Hall*

ABOVE *The author with Highman at Gipsy Hall*

The author with Meg at Gipsy Hall

My daughter Kate

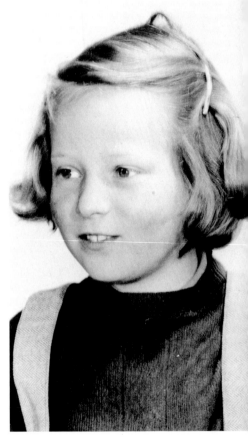

ABOVE *Kingsbridge*

LEFT *Evelyn and Laura Waugh (hat by Donaldson)*

BELOW *Susan and Tony Crosland at Kingsbridge*

ABOVE *Hugh Gaitskell*

ABOVE RIGHT *Tony Crosland and Roy Jenkins listening to a speech by Denis Healey*

BELOW **Denis and Edna Healey with Tim and Cressida**

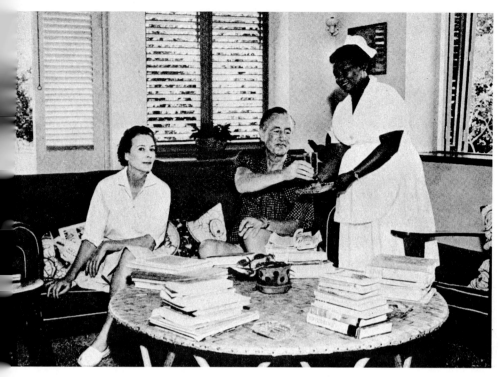

ABOVE *Ian and Ann Fleming at Golden Eye, with Violet*

Jack, as the Queen's representative, handing insignia of honorary knighthood to conductor Bernard Haitink

ABOVE *The author with Jack at North Mays*

The whole family: Thomas is sitting on the arm of the chair, Kate on the arm of the sofa. Rose is standing centre back.

first took it on; although at that time it was still quite difficult to make money. Both Jack and I are duffers when it comes to machinery and indeed have blank minds to its intricacies, so we had to have a good tractor driver. But we had no foreman at Burden Court and only young and inexperienced cowmen who took their orders from me. Jack went in for hens in folds and, when we had ewes, looked after them in company with a man called Jack Dickenson. We had four good cottages and never had much problem over labour. I think I am right in saying that our dairy herd reached an average of 1,200 gallons. Since we constantly sought their advice, we were quite soon the pride and joy of the Agricultural Service (then headed by W.E. Jones, afterwards Sir Emrys and chief adviser to the Ministry of Agriculture, and Derek Barber, afterwards Sir Derek and chairman of the Countryside Commission and later of the Royal Society for the Protection of Birds).

We stayed at Burden Court for thirteen years and then moved to Kingsbridge in Buckinghamshire, a much smaller farm which we bought from Aidan Crawley. We had three reasons: one, our two eldest children had finished their education and we did not need so much money; two, Jack had developed so many outside interests that I found myself too often alone getting the cows out of the corn; and three (by far the most important), we had taken on extra land rented from our neighbour George Fairweather, and doubled the size of the dairy herd. Because I found the work too much, we engaged a farm manager, a Scot who had been farming all his life. He instantly seized the affections of our sheepdog who followed him everywhere; he was a wonderful judge of cattle and could catch an old ewe by the leg as she passed him while continuing to talk to me; but he lacked that particularity which had distinguished our own efforts. In no time the milk yield was down to an average of 800 gallons, and the land was growing couch. We could not retract so we decided to get out.

I have nothing more of interest to say about farming in Gloucestershire; my knowledge of it is now quite out of date. More interesting, I think, were the inhabitants, since neither wars nor agricultural revolutions seemed to have changed them since Sir Matthew Hale's day. The Duke of Beaufort ruled in the manner of an archduke of a small principality. By some accounts a bad landlord, he nevertheless was supreme and much revered throughout the land. He was almost invariably addressed as Master by members of the middle and upper classes, an address which actually referred to the fact that he was Master of Hounds, but nevertheless showed deference to his position, a special courtesy in the speech of even his closest friends.

We never had the opportunity to address him in this or any other way, because, although the majority of our friends were Tories and included several Ministers of the Crown, the fact that we were members of the Labour Party made us pariahs in Gloucestershire society. We were nicknamed 'the Vyshinskys' and during the whole time we lived there – thirteen years – the only people we knew were Charlie and Joanie Harford, who lived in a large, ramshackle Georgian house and were much beloved; Ian Scott, who farmed across the road at Saddlewood; to his honour Derek Gunston, a retired Tory MP who had voted against Munich, and his wife Gardenia; Evelyn Waugh, who in spite of certain necessary pretences, cared less for people's politics than for their ability to entertain him; Laura, his wife; Hiram Haig Winterbottom; and Eny Strutt, who, at eighty-odd and riddled with arthritis, caring even less than Evelyn about politics, entertained regularly at the weekends. In her house I first met Sir Alan (Tommy) Lascelles, who as erstwhile secretary to the Prince of Wales contributed, although never directly, to the book I would later write. We were too busy to mind our ostracism much, but our children had no friends and in holiday seasons, when the roads were full of parents and children on their way to parties, they read their books at home.

But if the upper classes were insensible to the changes wrought by two world wars, the villagers were peasants, who seemed not to have advanced since their ancestors worked for Sir Matthew Hale. I think I am right in saying we put in the first bathroom in the village, and certainly water was drawn from a standpipe except in the several farmhouses. Most prominent in our lives was Mrs Tuck, whom we inherited from our predecessors and who did the housework. She was due in nine months to receive the old age pension and she said she would stay with us only during the intervening time to help us to settle down. However, during the thirteen years we lived at Burden Court, the mornings when she failed to appear at an elastic 8.30 might be counted on the fingers of one hand.

Since Mrs Tuck and her brother Bill were among the last survivors of the generations who for hundreds of years had lived in this small village in the valley, without piped water or drains, radio or television, telephones or cars (neither Bill nor Mrs Tuck had ever been to Gloucester or Cheltenham, both about twenty miles away), as much as anyone I have ever met they deserve some memorial here.

122

If I had known Mrs Tuck would be with us so long, I might never have taken her on. I am a snob about appearances, and Mrs Tuck was like some glorious old she-elephant devised in the brain of a rural George Belcher. The immensity and the variety of the curves of her figure were not those of the human body, and she must have measured something like forty inches across the beam. She wore, winter and summer, a dark but excessively shabby cotton dress with a cardigan, and, beneath the skirts of this inappropriate garment, she twisted her stockings into a neat roll below her knees. When she bent over to do some chore, even the least conventional of our guests were startled into a pop-eyed disbelief. Her face was red and strong-featured except for her eyes which were small, blue and deep-set behind prominent cheekbones. Her teeth were mostly still with her but they had a sunken appearance, and her hair had both the unnatural frizz of a new and bad permanent wave and the colour of years of dyeing allowed, in the weariness and resignation of old age, to grow out, dead and tow-like. Mrs Tuck had achieved these effects without the aid of artifice.

I could never have got rid of her even if I had wished to, because in all that village there was never anyone to take her place. But I never wished to. My embarrassment and my desire to keep up appearances, even the pride it might be proper to take in my household arrangements, were overcome by Mrs Tuck's unusual charms.

When we first went to Burden Court, both Old Bill and Mrs Tuck worked at Saddlewood, the farm of our neighbour, Ian Scott – Old Bill all day and Mrs Tuck in the afternoons after she had finished in our house. Ian told us that four or five years before, when he first came to Saddlewood, he had decided that he could not employ either of them. He might have taken them on and paid them what he thought their labour worth if he had been allowed to, but, at the minimum agricultural wage, they were both too old and too unskilled in modern practice to be of any use to him. So, when he engaged the other men on the farm, he had to tell Old Bill and Mrs Tuck that he did not want them.

They were both very kind to him about this, as country people usually are if you explain to them that you are doing something because you cannot afford to do otherwise, since they find this human and understandable and their sympathies are aroused. So they did their best to help him out. When he said he could not take them on because he could not afford their wages, Mrs Tuck told him the price she had had to pay for her meat that week, a commentary on the mad times in which we live. And when he explained that he was not allowed to offer them less than the minimum wage, she said: 'Aw! Shut up!' by which she meant 'Oh! Go on' or 'Whatever next?'

Ian felt a little mean after this interview, but he knew that Mrs Tuck could get plenty of housework if she wanted it, and that Old Bill could earn a living walling on piecework for the neighbouring farmers. So he soon forgot about them.

On the morning that he first took over the farm, he went down to the yard at 7.30 to give orders to the five men he had engaged, and found to his surprise that six awaited him. From the end of the row Old Bill smiled at him, a sweet and shy smile.

When Ian had given his orders to each of the other five men, he sent them about their business and then he turned to Bill. Bill told him there was a great 'shore' in the wall of the field he had earmarked for the sheep, through which they would be bound to get out, and he suggested he best go down and mend it. Ian lost his nerve, dithered and let him do it. He decided he must take time to consider this problem.

He was still considering it that afternoon when he turned into the stables to look at his pony and found Mrs Tuck mucking out. She said good afternoon to him in a pleasant, welcoming way, but without effusion or subservience, and Ian knew he was a beaten man. He understood enough of the countryside to know that, although he had just paid good money for Saddlewood, Bill and Mrs Tuck had worked there all their lives, and their old, flat feet and misshapen bodies had acquired rights in its service which he could never contravene.

As it turned out, he never regretted Bill, for he had a local knowledge and a tireless and undistracted interest in his work which made up for his lack of the more modern skills. There was only one thing he did that Ian would have liked to change. When the weather was bad, he protected himself from it by a trick he learned as a boy. Taking four sacks, he forced holes through them, and, slotting them together with two pieces of string, he slung one pair over his shoulders to cover his chest and back and tied another pair around his waist to protect his legs.

'The damned old fool doesn't realize', Ian said ruefully, 'that nowadays it would cost no more to dress him in Savile Row. And I haven't the guts to tell him.'

He never, however, became completely reconciled to Mrs Tuck, for she was domineering. She knew exactly how everything should be done, how it always had been done, and it was not so much that she had a contempt for newfangled ways as that her opinion of the mental powers and the administrative ability of the boss was low.

'I do tell him,' she sighed when something went wrong. (This construction of speech, invariably used locally, was sometimes pronounced with the vowel dropped, thus: I d'tell him. Another Gloucestershire construction which never staled for us was their way with pronouns. Jack once asked a neighbour whether he might have the contract to cut his corn with our combine, and the farmer said he would think about it, because, he added reflectively: 'The last man, he sucked I in proper.')

I never objected to Mrs Tuck's tyrannical ways in my house. I am insufficiently houseproud, and too lost in gratitude to anyone who will do the housework to have room for views on method. When we first took over the farmhouse, my predecessor warned me that Mrs Tuck had one failing.

'She is a little light-fingered,' she said.

And she showed me how everything of value in her house and all the accumulations for the winter, such as apples and cheese, were locked against these depredatory fingers.

This is an instance of the black power of words. As a family, we are incurably untidy and lax about our personal possessions, and it is impossible for us to lock up anything, because if we do we can never find the key. It took us a very short while to find out that Mrs Tuck was the soul of honour. Money taken out of Jack's pockets and left on his chest of drawers might be put into a neat pile, but not one penny of it was otherwise touched. All our handkerchiefs and stockings (goods which had a peculiar attraction for Mrs Tuck, we had been told) returned every week from being washed, and my earrings, which, when they hurt me, were thrust into unexpected places, were retrieved from under the cushions of a chair and handed back. Yet when we first went to Burden Court, nothing big or small was ever missing, either in the house or even in the farmyard behind it, without the men winking at each other and remarking with a jocose and happy certainty: 'Ah! We do know where that be gone.'

On these hills in Gloucestershire nearly all the farm men, many of the farmers and occasionally a member of the middle class shared a strange physical trait. They spoke in high castrato voices. No one ever explained this, but it must surely be a freak result of soil or climate, since it is heard only here, though in men whose back-grounds are in other ways dissimilar. One soon gets used to it and almost ceases to hear it, but when, on our first arrival, the men made these piping allegations against poor Mrs Tuck, it had a sinister effect.

If I had known as much of life as I do now, I would have guessed immediately from the archness of their glances and their beastly merry mien that they were merely making mischief; when they really believed that something had been stolen, their attitude was far more grave. They had adopted a theme supplied them by their last employer and embroidered it to enliven their eventless days; and soon after we got there these suggestions ceased to be made.

However, Mrs Tuck had one small weakness: she could not resist sweets. When the children were young and sweets were still rationed, we decided to keep this temptation out of her way; every night when we went to bed we hid the sweets at the back of a large, dark cupboard behind a screen of books and toys. It was only when we discovered that, on the occasions when we forgot to do this, Mrs Tuck herself, as she did the room next morning, restored them a little depleted to their hiding place, that we made up our minds to grudge her nothing. But by then we had also discovered that on the not infrequent evenings – for I am an absent-minded house-keeper – that we ran out of bread or sugar or something else essential, Billy, Mrs Tuck's son, would always come up from the village with enough to last till morning. The surplus from her kitchen garden found its way into our saucepans and her flowers decorated our house. We became ashamed of the lack of generosity which defines possessions between friends.

And Mrs Tuck's friendship was not so lightly won, nor given without due consideration. Once I had a Swiss girl of a rather lurid appearance living in my house as nanny to my youngest child, Kate. The village gossip, which swirled ceaselessly around, centred on this poor girl's head. The tales of what she did on her afternoons off, or when I turned my back or went to London, were so extreme that I decided to convey to the village, through Mrs Tuck, the threat that I would not indefinitely permit a member of my household to be so slandered without invoking the law. The point was lost on Mrs Tuck, as I had been afraid it might be.

''Tis her own fault,' she said severely. 'I do tell her.'

I waited nervously for some further revelation of Betty's unsuit-able conduct. It appeared that ever since she had first come to us she had attempted to make friends with the villagers, smiling as she passed them pushing Kate's pram, and sometimes even stopping to talk. If one would persist in being so friendly to people, how could one not expect that sooner or later terrible tales would be told about one?

"'Tis better not,' Mrs Tuck said. 'My own sister do live twenty yards from me, but 'tis ten years now since I did talk to her.'

However, it would be wrong to think that Mrs Tuck was incapable of the tender emotions. It was only that her approach to other people was more cautious and her idea of social intercourse more contained than is usual with the rest of us. During the last year or two of our time at Burden Court we acquired a farm manager to take some of the work off us. From certain signs which I observed, I realized that Mrs Tuck held this gentleman in affection and respect. Mr Kennedy was a Scot and a little dour himself, so I wondered what communication passed between these two people that their hearts were thus entwined. However, when Mr Kennedy went on holiday, Mrs Tuck confessed to me she missed him.

'You see,' she said, 'when he do walk up the village, we do wave to him.'

Our presence in the village altered much. We put in the first bathroom and the first boiler to heat the water in the tap; we were the first to observe the law relating to overtime, and we brought with us every kind of newfangled farm implement. But we exercised by far our greatest influence through the men we employed. We needed, for our agricultural undertakings, at least two skilled cowmen, a skilled mechanic and his assistant. We could not find these in the district, so we imported them from outside, and supplied the village not merely with families used to quite different ways, but with nearly all its bridegrooms during the time when we were there. In this time local thought, local ways, the whole civilization changed more than it had during the past two hundred years.

We, in our sentimental, town-bred way, sometimes regretted this. So we were glad that Mrs Tuck and Old Bill were still with us, representatives of the years now gone.

In those days there were fixed rules in relation to the work undertaken by the different sexes. The men went out to work each day to earn an income for the family, but it was the task of the women to supply their household with all the rest of its needs. One of these was wood for the winter. Nothing may be cut (this rule is occasionally infringed), but any pieces of wood blown down in storms or lying about are considered free to all, as mushrooms and blackberries are. All through the summer groups of women laboured up and down the part of our farm which lies in a valley, transporting this fallen wood, and it was the mark of the bachelor to be seen in their company. Sometimes they wheeled old, derelict prams or other improvised wheelbarrows, but the more stalwart amongst them carried great branches on their backs, like beasts of burden.

The advent of the foreigners from the outside world changed all this. Our men mocked at the villagers' notion of chivalry, while their women put on very superior airs. More important than this, our foreman took out the tractor and trailer on Sundays, and collecting on one afternoon more wood than could be gathered in a summer by the old-fashioned method, used the mechanical saw to cut it up. The young brides who married our cowmen sneered at their elders and sat ladylike minding their babies while contemplating a storehouse full of wood. So only Mrs Tuck and Old Bill, a bachelor, were left to remind us how this society had conducted itself through hundreds of years until we came.

All through the summer Bill came home through the fields from Saddlewood in the evening, collecting and bearing wood on his back, while Mrs Tuck went down the valley and returned flushed and breathless to compare her haul with his. For Mrs Tuck 'do speak' to Bill, and this, in regard to a circumstance I will presently relate, was a curious fact. They were each as strong as two ordinary people (though Mrs Tuck could be very delicate if I asked her to lift something heavy in the house), and the limbs of the trees they carried were a matter for astonishment to strangers to the village. Once, when our farm manager, Mr Kennedy, had been with us only a short time, as we walked round the farm together we passed a great elm tree which had blown down in a storm. As we passed, Mr Kennedy remarked with the grim humour he sometimes permitted himself: 'Mrs Tuck hasn't had that one yet.'

Bill's back garden had the appearance of the yard of a timber merchant, such was the quantity and variety of wood that stood there – enough to last most people a lifetime. For this humble task had for the old man all the charms the sophisticated find in more complex occupations – the fine exhilaration of a game of golf on a seaside course; the minute, close satisfactions of a stamp collection.

Old Bill was a collector by nature, and, because of this characteristic he, although previously regarded with much patronizing humour by the youth of the village, one day came to be raised to fame. It had long been said that he was a miser. When I first heard this it brought no picture to my mind except that of a mean and close old man. But Joyce, my afternoon daily, who came to Burden Court in the first place with us and then married our tractor driver, and who had an intelligence very different from that of most of the natives of these parts, assured me that this was not what was meant.

'If you pass his cottage at night,' she said, 'and look in through a chink in the curtain, you can see him counting his money on the table. Some of it is in pound notes, but there's a lot of gold. He keeps it in sacks under the boards of the floor.'

I was still unable to take this seriously, and for years we heard this story and treated it as we did most of the village gossip.

Then one morning, after we had been at Burden Court for six or seven years, three of our young employees came into our yard at 7.30 in a fine state of excitement. From where they lived, in order to reach the farm, they had to pass Bill's cottage, and Bill, who had several miles to walk to Saddlewood, left home half an hour before they did. On this particular morning, as they walked up the hill past his house, they saw a lorry standing in the road and three men enter the house and return again to the lorry. They stopped and questioned these men who said they were engaged on refuse collection, but it seemed an odd time of day for such work, and the farm workers were convinced they were thieves, robbing Bill of his miser's hoard. They suggested to Jack that he telephone the police, while they themselves went back to investigate.

Now it happens that Jack was unable to believe in thieves, and this natural disinclination had been reinforced by his need to defend himself against the men. Every time five sacks of barley stood where someone thought there should be six, or a recount of eggs showed two missing out of twenty dozen, or the petrol tank emptied itself unexpectedly fast, the men advanced suspicions founded on the lowest view of human behaviour. If Jack had paid attention to them, he would have spent too much of his time telephoning the police and then apologizing for a wild goose chase. So this morning he soothed them down, gave them their orders and sent them about their business.

It happened, however, that the business of two of them took them back down the village past Bill's cottage. The road was now deserted, but curiosity was strong, and they turned into the house.

The scene that met their eyes was satisfactory indeed, for they had not hoped for so much luck. The floorboards were up to reveal a deep dark hole in the earth beneath, and near the door there lay one sack, its mouth open to disclose that it was undoubtedly stuffed with banknotes. Elated, they returned to the farm, and then, unfortunately only then, Jack telephoned the police.

Now weeks of excitement followed for all of us. The police began by taking the one remaining sack to the police station. There they examined its contents. There were golden guineas as well as notes and the total amounted to £90. Then they interviewed Bill. They asked him how much he thought he had lost, but, getting no coherent reply, they changed their tactics and the following dialogue ensued.

'Do you think it could have been five hundred pounds?'

'Aar.'

'Could it have been eight hundred?'

'Aar.'

'A thousand?'

'Aar.'

'Fifteen hundred?'

'Aar.'

After that they gave up and no one has ever known exactly how much was stolen that day. But at this point Mrs Tuck threw some light on the matter. She remarked to me that she reckoned much of the money stolen had belonged to her; and when I asked her why, she explained that her father, from whom it appeared Bill had inherited his propensities, had collected money in this way all his life. When he died she reckoned that half of his fortune should have come to her, but Bill had taken the lot. She said she had never bothered about it, since, as Bill had no direct heir, in good time it would all come back to her children. Mrs Tuck's husband died just before she gave birth for the second time, to twins, and, with an earning power of eighteen shillings a week, she had brought up three children unaided. To those of us with knowledge of the ways of people blessed with a more fortunate environment, it seemed strange that Mrs Tuck, so particular in her choice of those to whom she do talk, should always have been on the gentlest terms with Bill.

Armed, however, with this further piece of knowledge we began to do the arithmetic. It was clear that Bill spent almost nothing. He bought one small piece of meat a week, but except for this he relied on bread or on meals sent in by his neighbours who were all generous in these ways. Apart from an old cap, coat and pair of trousers, he clothed himself only in Ian's sacks. If one allowed his father thirty or forty years of saving after his children had reached working age, and Bill himself about fifty-six, and then deducted only what it seemed likely had been spent, one reached a startling figure – for the rates of pay had risen steeply during all this time, particularly in the last decade. So large a figure in fact that we all felt cheated, as though we had been robbed ourselves; all, that is, except Jack, who took the rather remote view that it was a splendid thing, since money is only money when in circulation.

The police, who had been hampered in their investigations by Jack's dilatoriness on the telephone, nevertheless arrested all three thieves within the week. They were not, it appeared, professionals, but three young men who had been working on an electrical installation in a nearby village and had been tempted by the tales they had heard in the pub at nights. In spite of their amateur status, however, they had had time during the week to dispose of the money, and none of it has ever been seen again. Even Jack was a little shaken when he learned that quite a large proportion of it had been burned by the mother of one of the men, in an attempt to save her son from the law.

The three young men who worked for us and who had been involved in these proceedings lived together in a cottage we had turned into a hostel to house them. They were all single and one of them was a pupil, the son of a rich man, who had the unusual hobby of collecting vintage Rolls-Royce motor cars. Our pupil drove one of these, an early twentieth-century open car, painted yellow. Into this romantic vehicle half our farm staff now piled excitedly day after day, while Jack and I struggled unaided round the lambing ewes and did the milking. On the first of these occasions they were sent for by the police to see if they could recognize one of the thieves in an identity parade. When they returned, we were all waiting eagerly to question them. Two of the boys confessed to having been quite unable to distinguish among the line of men they had seen, but Arthur, a virile youth who owned a motor bike on which he scoured the countryside at night, had had a shot at it.

'You see,' he said, 'there were twelve men and I knew nine of them. So I thought the other three a reasonable bet.'

But the great day was when, after the suspects had been committed for trial, our party went to Gloucester, taking Old Bill with them, to give their evidence in court. Bill had never been to Gloucester before, and, as he heaved himself into the back of the yellow Rolls-Royce, he spoke to its owner.

'You won't lose I, will 'ee?' he pleaded.

The thieves all got prison sentences, but, since none of the money had been returned, the case ended on a note of anticlimax. All this time I had been worried about Bill. The excitement and attention had kept him going all these weeks, but it had seemed to me that when these glorious days were over, his life's work gone, he would have nothing left to live for. He was too old, I thought, to start all over again. So two or three weeks after the great case at Gloucester I was surprised to meet him striding along the road beneath the branch of a tree, straight in his back and with his head held high. The smile he gave me was as sweet as usual, but it seemed less shy.

''Tis cowld,' he said.

When I got back to the house I asked Joyce about him.

'What has happened to Bill? I thought all this would finish him. But he seems as bright as a button.'

'Well,' she replied, 'he got his picture in the paper.'

'What d'you mean?'

'Didn't you know?' she said. 'When he went to Gloucester they took his photograph, and next morning it was in the *Daily Mirror*. He's been as proud as punch ever since, showing it to everyone in the village.'

The next afternoon she brought the *Daily Mirror* to show me. It was a fine photograph, large and a good likeness. He was leaning back against the seat of the old Rolls-Royce and his face, between his cap and his grizzly beard, looked handsome.

I put the *Daily Mirror* down on the kitchen table, and I shrugged my shoulders at Joyce. On our computation it had cost Bill more than £4,000 to get his picture in the paper, but it had been cheap at the price.

14

··

Evelyn and Laura Waugh

In my book *Evelyn Waugh: Portrait of a Country Neighbour*, I defended Evelyn against the charge of snobbishness on the grounds that he chose his society in one group as rigorously as in any other; that he did not want to know a duke unless he was also amusing. Evelyn had a romantic attachment to the aristocratic virtues, but he had no use for those of the aristocracy who lacked them. 'He liked high spirits, extreme confidence, social ease, the rich, the beautiful and the brave – and these only for short periods.'*

These words were written not much more than twenty years ago, yet I realize they are no longer an adequate defence against a charge of snobbery. So out of fashion are the aristocratic virtues that even those who would naturally possess them have to avoid demonstrating them. Dukes may make derogatory remarks about us behind our backs, but to our faces they are extremely good fellows. Thus on present-day standards not only Evelyn but Freddy and I fall into the category of 'snob'. I mention this because it may go some way towards answering a question I was at that time often asked, and will presently try to answer. Although denying the suggestion that Evelyn was a snob in the sense of wanting to know someone who was not amusing but was nevertheless a duke, I wrote this:

It was his extremely narrow vision of the human race that made so many social occasions such a flop. Evelyn liked the smarter of

* Donaldson, *Evelyn Waugh: Portrait of a Country Neighbour*, p. 20.

133

the intellectuals, the more intellectual of the smart – no one else. No one else liked him. With all the more ordinary people of the world, but also with three-quarters of the most interesting, he was unable to establish any communication. This was the fact – impossible to explain, useless to excuse. His predilection for gossip had something to do with it, since as a basis for conversation gossip is viable only within a small circle.*

Looking back on it, one can also say that Evelyn was unable to behave well enough to be successful as a snob. My friend Tortor Gilmour once told me that the Queen (now Queen Elizabeth, the Queen Mother) admired his work and wanted to meet him. Presently a drinks party was fixed up at Tortor's flat, to which Jack and I were asked but to which, scenting trouble, we refused to go. Evelyn was frightfully excited and pleased to be asked, but when he came back he was openly deflated. He had expected a degree of splendour and Tortor's room was very small and on this occasion over-crowded. Uncomfortable and cross, Evelyn was seated in an arm-chair next to the Queen.

Lifting a glass of champagne, she addressed him with the words: 'What luxury.'

'*Luxury?*' he replied, and came home aware that he had dished his chances.

'What had you hoped for?' I asked him.

'Oh!' he replied. 'Luncheons in London and an invitation to Balmoral.'

Exactly because he was so open in his reply, one did not know how seriously he spoke.

Evelyn was always willing to meet people once, in the hope of alleviating his congenital boredom. When we first went to Gloucestershire, everyone who came to stay with us wanted to meet him, and to begin with we took our guests to drinks at Piers Court. On no single occasion was this less than a considerable embarrassment. Normally intelligent people were inexplicably struck dumb in his presence, not because he did not try enough, but possibly because he tried too much. Sometimes he made extra-ordinary mistakes, as when he explained to Harold Hobson that the Bodleian was 'our little library, you know', without giving any thought to the idea that Harold might have been at Oxford himself. But I think the chief trouble was his jokes.

His humour was always satirical, sometimes black and above all

* Donaldson, *Evelyn Waugh: Portrait of a Country Neighbour*, p. 20.

134

stylized. He was extremely funny, and, as with only two other people I have ever met, his command of language was so great that he spoke almost as well as he wrote. Yet one had to get used to him and I think it is true to say that, with the exception of Jack and me, all his friends were people he had known for a long time.

In any case, when our guests said they would like to meet Evelyn, we soon took to saying we thought he was away.

In the book I wrote about him I said there were two questions which, with different degrees of frankness, with more or less grace, we were constantly asked. One was, How can you like him so much? The other was, Why does he like you?

In answer to the first, I can only say that, looking back over my life from my advanced age, I think Evelyn was the most attractive man I ever met. In saying this, I do not speak of physical attraction, in which he was notably short, although he had a particularly charming voice. But he was the funniest, the most original, and, in his off-centre way, one of the most intellectually serious people I ever met; and, when he tried, infinitely seductive. He was also enormously educative and I personally think I owe much to the years in which we saw him often.

In the book I wrote, I remarked on the fact that so few of his friends had honoured him in obituary notices. I suggested the following as one of the reasons why this might be so:

> In his youth he made for himself by his wit, charm, his gaiety and his genius a large circle of boon companions. ... But as he went through life, with a stroke of the pen here, a flick of the tongue there, he divested himself of many of the friends of his youth. He was born with the trick of hurting most devilishly with half a dozen words. It was not, or so I think, because so many of his friends no longer loved Evelyn that they could not write about him, but because they were unable to believe that he could – uselessly and without apparent regret – impale the friendship of a lifetime upon one heartless sentence if he any longer cared for them. One cannot assume the right publicly to mourn a man if one feels rejected by him.

When I discussed this passage with Laura, his wife, she said that it was all rot. 'He could always get them back', she said, 'whenever he wanted to.'

I am aware that this is a *non sequitur* in relation to the paragraphs I had written, but I have always remembered what she said because I believe it to be true. The trouble with Evelyn was that when he

was bad he was horrid. It is easy to remember and circulate incidents involving outrageous behaviour; to pin charm on to paper and repeat jokes which involve knowledge of the circumstances in which they are made require some of the talent of a Boswell. No one who did not know Evelyn could understand how enchanting he could be and younger men writing about him are apt to miss this point. He is too often presented as merely cross and rude. Thus Noel Annan, in a book called *Our Age*, says he committed all the seven deadly sins except lust, and writes of him: 'Most prone to envy, gluttony and anger, far from sound on pride and covetousness ...'*
I saw a great deal of Evelyn towards the end of his life and I do not understand why Noel attributes to him either the first or the last. Evelyn was entirely aware of the quality of his own talent and he never seemed envious of writers who might be regarded as his peers; indeed, he was generous in his praise of Graham Greene, Anthony Powell, Henry Green. Again, when he was writing *Pinfold* he was sent the proofs or the manuscript of Muriel Spark's first novel *The Comforters*, in the hope that he would praise it. He was upset but only because her novel was on the same theme as his own, and he thought it the better of the two; yet he was unsparing in his praise of it. In the same way when Nancy Mitford wrote to him and said that Sybille Bedford's novel *The Legacy* had missed the attention of the critics, he immediately wrote an article for the *Spectator* ending, if memory serves, 'I salute a new talent.'

It might be thought that he envied people of higher rank, but I do not think that is true. As I have tried to explain, he admired them and he looked to them for amusement. He chose to ape not the aristocracy of his own day but that of preceding generations; having taken up a pose, he played it for all it was worth even when he knew it was unpopular.

Nor do I understand why Noel Annan attributes to him the sin of covetousness. I think he coveted, as we all do, more money and anything else that took his fancy, but not strongly or in any greatly sinful way. His sins were both more calamitous and more outside his control, and Noel is right to count among them accidie.

Chiefly one must emphasize the point that, although he could be bad-tempered and rude, he was not so *all the time*. More often he was funny and entrancing. This answers the first question, 'How can you like him so much?' During all the time we knew him he was never rude to us, seldom cross, although often in a fit of

* Noel Annan, *Our Age: Portrait of a Generation*, Weidenfeld & Nicolson (1990) p. 163.

depression from which it was usually easy to lift him. We were devoted to him.

This has much bearing on the second question, 'Why did he like you?' In his diary there is an entry for 10 June 1963 which reads: 'We cherish our friends not for their ability to amuse us but for ours to amuse them – a diminishing number in my case.'* And it is a fact that, although everyone is agreed on the quality of wit in his novels, in conversation his jokes were often taken seriously or flew by unnoticed. I suppose we had others of the qualities he insisted upon, Jack by birth and upbringing, although not by taste, since he is very versatile in his interests, and I from the Embassy Club days. Thus Jack had been a friend of Tom Mitford and of Emerald Cunard, and I put champagne behind my ears when it was spilled – for luck. 'Ah!' Evelyn said to that, 'Brought up in a nightclub.' Yet a certain ability to gossip might not have been enough if we had not lived so near. Until the Waughs moved to Combe Florey we never had to be asked to stay, a dangerous course if followed. And I think Jack had other qualities which Evelyn, far more perceptive than might be imagined, also valued. In a letter to Ann Fleming dated 13 March 1963, he wrote:

> Jack Donaldson is correct in saying that if you & any of your friends get to heaven you will rejoice individually in one another's company but he is pulling your leg if he suggests a continuation of common pleasures. Only the Mohammedans expect fucking in Heaven. ... What is certain is that we should be jolly different, beatified and perfect & united in the love of God and one another; each retaining individuality; not like Buddhists mingled into an eternal, undifferentiated unity. But no one knows or can imagine what our condition will be.

And to this Evelyn added: 'Jack will go to Heaven, I think.'

He believed in both Heaven and Hell. In Graham Greene's *The Heart of the Matter*, Scobie goes to mass with an unconfessed sin on his conscience in order that his wife should not learn something which would cause her much pain.

'What do you think happened to Scobie?' I asked Evelyn, and he replied with the utmost firmness: 'Scobie went to Hell.'

He could be extremely patient if he wished. When Ronnie Knox came to stay, he was thought to spend too much time and interest on crossword puzzles – he was so good at these that, instead of

---

* *The Diaries of Evelyn Waugh*, Weidenfeld & Nicolson (1976), p. 709.

doing them in the normal way, he had developed the habit of reading the solution of yesterday's puzzle and providing it with clues, discussing these as he went. All this bored Evelyn a great deal, but no one would have guessed it from his behaviour.*

Yet it has to be said that he was a bully and it was absolutely necessary never to show fear. When Cyril Connolly stayed with Evelyn or Robin Campbell with us, for reasons from the forgotten past fear invaded the normally pleasant room – in Robin's case I think because he had divorced his first wife and married Mary Dunn, who had also divorced Philip; a thing which, although no business of his, Evelyn chose to object to because Mary had been born a Catholic. An entry in his diary for 14 October 1956 reads 'Donaldsons to dinner bringing Robin Campbell who was surly, opinionated, and underdog', a combination of qualities which could coincide only in someone sensing a need to defend himself. This uncomfortable and detectable fear was not surprising or different from a necessary sensitivity, because no one wishes to call down unacceptable remarks upon his head, particularly from his host, since it is so difficult to leave. Nevertheless, it was fatal in dealings with Evelyn. We never showed fear – Jack because he did not feel it and I because I knew it would have exactly the effect one was anxious to avoid.

In fact, we never had any reason to fear. Evelyn came back with terrible tales of drunkenness and bad behaviour when he went to London, but at home he had to feel very ill to be rude or tiresome. In his diaries he says several times about the occasions when we dined there 'the Donaldsons got drunk' or 'the women got drunk', which serves to make one disbelieve a good many of the entries he made earlier in his life. We always had a good deal to drink since he mixed the drinks very strong, but I never get drunk because I feel ill first, and, although Jack, who drinks a lot when out, might have done, I do not remember that he did.

In 1947, when we first went to live in Gloucestershire, we did not know the Waughs, but we knew they lived there and I used to look wistfully at the signs to Dursley when we passed them, because it is frustrating not to know the most interesting people in the district where one lives. I have already recounted the circumstances in which we met but they were so typical of this unfriendly man's desire for friendship, it seems worth repeating them. Evelyn went to London to give lunch to Andrea Cowdin, an American who had

* Mgr Ronald Knox. Ronnie gave up crossword puzzles for Lent.

138

shown him much hospitality in Hollywood and who was a great friend of my father. 'Do you know the Donaldsons?' she had asked him, and when he said not, she explained that I was Freddy's daughter and said something about Jack. He returned to Dursley that night and Laura came to call the next day and asked us to dinner.

No biography of Evelyn will do justice to Laura. Christopher Sykes says that he knew her well and certainly she liked him and chose him for the authorized biography of Evelyn, but he exaggerates when he says he knew her well. He cannot bring her to life in the way he often does Evelyn, and in fact it would be difficult to do so. Later biographers get her ludicrously wrong. Humphrey Carpenter, referring to a remark Evelyn made when he first met her, says she was 'indeed a white mouse' compared with the 'strong self-assertive characters' of some of the heroines of Evelyn's books. It is true that Evelyn called her a white mouse but he also said: 'What is she like? Well fair, very pretty, plays peggoty beautifully. ... She has rather a long, thin nose and skin as thin as Bromo and she is very thin and might be dying of consumption to look at her ... she is only 18 years old, virgin, Catholic, quiet and astute.' And he also said that she was 'piercingly sweet'.*

It is difficult to set the record straight because Laura was an unusual person, as compulsively eccentric as Evelyn himself. She was the daughter of Aubrey Herbert, who was a younger son of the fourth Earl of Carnarvon, also an eccentric, and who became the subject of an excellent biography by Laura's daughter Margaret. A friend of Raymond Asquith, of the Grenfells and, incidentally, of Coney Jarvis's father, Charlie Meade, according to John Buchan Aubrey Herbert was 'the most delightful and brilliant survivor from the days of chivalry ... a sort of survivor from crusading times'. Laura's mother was born Mary Vesey, and through these two Laura was related to half the aristocracy, who are considerably inbred, since, apart from an occasional chorus girl, they seldom marry outside their own class. She never referred to this matter, but Evelyn often did, introducing someone into the conversation as 'your cousin So-and-so'.

Laura was, in an untranslatable phrase, *bien élevée*, and, aware of her privileges, she was also aware of her duties. I thought her a noble character. Considerate, kind and generous in all her under-

---

* *Mr Waugh and Mrs Stitch*, Letters of Evelyn Waugh and Diana Cooper, ed. Artemis Cooper, Hodder & Stoughton, (1991), p. 5.

takings, it is true that she was unusually shy, and although devoted to her two sisters, had few friends. Yet how could one have friends if one was married to Evelyn? She told me that on one occasion when they had asked people to tea, he got up at five o'clock, unable to stand it any more, and said that he had to take a bath. We had a special pull on her affections because we kept Ayrshire cows, but I think she would have made friends in the ordinary way in Gloucestershire if it had been possible. On the other hand, it is true that she found it difficult to become intimate with the people he liked, usually referring to them as 'Evelyn's friends'. All her interests lay in the country. I have said elsewhere that Evelyn lived in the country because if he had lived in London he would have spent too much time in White's, drunk too much and done no work at all. It is also true that he had to live in the country because Laura could have lived nowhere else.

In attempting to set this record straight, I must argue with their son Auberon, much as I dislike having to do so, for obvious reasons. In an article published in America he wrote:

> She, too, was always displeased by the Brideshead aspect, hating any form of ostentation or grandeur. 'Your dear mother', Evelyn would say to his children, 'is the kindest and most hospitable of women, but she has no sense of style.'
> 'And your dear mother', she would reply tartly, 'spoke with a Bristol accent.'

Bron goes on to say that this was as cruel as it was untrue. Mrs Arthur Waugh spoke with the gentlest and most ladylike voice, without any trace of regional or any other accent. To this one must add that it was not only cruel and untrue but also quite impossible. That is to say, not that Bron is reporting incorrectly, but that he must have missed some earlier exchange led by Evelyn and not by Laura, or some joke. There is no possibility that Laura could have said this simply as it stands. I think the fact that Mrs Waugh did not have a Bristol accent bears this out; as indeed does the fact that no one would have dared say it to Evelyn if there *had* been any truth in it.

It was fashionable among the friends Evelyn had made when young to believe that the break-up of his first marriage had a permanent effect on him. Christopher Sykes writes:

> Some of his friends saw, or believed they saw, a change in his character after August 1929 [the date of his divorce]; they saw a new hardness and bitterness and an utter disillusion which

showed itself in cruelty. This is a matter on which I cannot have a grounded opinion. I first met him with Cyril Connolly some months after the episode was over. I had no impression of an angry, broken man. If I do have an opinion it is expressed in a favourite expression of his own: 'He did not repine.' The evidence of his early life shows that he always had a tendency to cruelty; his every book, indeed almost every writing from his hand, shows a deep underlying bitterness; he had some illusions about the world, as appears much later, but they were fantastical; his serious thought was always free of illusion.*

I am even less entitled than Christopher to have a grounded opinion, but I have always thought the idea that his first marriage changed his character simply silly. Apart from the inherent improbability, no one who saw him with Laura would believe that theirs was other than a marriage made in heaven. Most important of all, she understood him. There are certain women who, without much education or exceptional intelligence, can nevertheless respond to genius. Servility was not in Laura's nature, but she tuned her mind so closely to Evelyn's that she could follow much of his thoughts.

I remember only one occasion when she refused to join him in some project he had in mind. Every Sunday Evelyn saw a girl in church who, with a veil tied round her head, had an appearance of Madonna-like purity and beauty. Evelyn wanted to ask this girl and her husband to dinner, but Laura, who had been too often made uncomfortable by his reception of his neighbours, refused to have anything to do with it. On the night this couple dined at Piers Court, Laura went to London and I took her place. She was of course right, and, without the veil and the pose of prayer, the girl both looked and was quite ordinary. Evelyn behaved impeccably, but the couple were never asked again.

At Piers Court Laura kept about five cows and had enough staff to look after forty; they also (although still at considerable cost) did the garden. When a change in the tax laws made it impossible to set their wages against Evelyn's earnings, Laura had to give up the cows and at Combe Florey she took to growing chrysanthemums, which she sold in Taunton. In this enterprise she had an assistant, not a full-time man but a pensioner who came when she wanted him. This man was called Coggins by Laura; Bron says he was really called Coggan. Because of his extensive knowledge of chrys-

* Christopher Sykes, *Evelyn Waugh: A Biography*, Collins (1975), p. 96.

anthemums, Laura thought of him as an oracle and quoted him on all sorts of subjects, particularly on the occult. She showed me once a brown mark on the doorstep outside the kitchen which she said was blood from a man who was murdered there which had risen through the step. She got this information from Coggins.

'Not to put too fine a point upon it,' Evelyn said when Coggins first appeared, 'Laura has a lover.'

When I read Auberon Waugh's autobiography, *Will This Do?*, I learned that he regarded Laura as almost as indifferent to her children as Evelyn was. Certainly Laura was not maternal – by which I mean she had no great feeling for very young children – while her whole upbringing inclined her to the employment of nannies. Yet I had thought that as her children grew up she protected them from Evelyn and became – as unmaternal women often do – someone whom they loved and felt close to, partly because she was not dependent on them. Bron gives the impression that she preferred her cows to her children and alludes twice to this in his description of her stay in Cyprus when he wounded himself so drastically.* When he says she went home 'to her cows' as soon as his recovery became certain, he forgets that she also had a husband at home; just as when he quotes a description of life at Government House from her first letter to Evelyn, he overlooks the fact that there must have been communication about the state of his health, if not by telephone because Evelyn hated it, at least by cable. I am astonished that Bron felt so deprived, and I wonder if this was also true of his brothers and sisters.

At Combe Florey Evelyn became more and more miserable and finally drove himself to death. He suffered from a boredom so overwhelming that for many years he had seemed to wish only to die. He drank too much and took hefty doses of some drug given him to make him sleep. The last time we stayed at Combe Florey, his mind was clear but his speech was slurred.

In a letter we had from Laura after he died, she said:

Thank you so much for your letter. It makes such a difference hearing from people who knew, loved & did understand him.

He died exactly the way he would have wanted to after Easter Mass & communion with Father Caraman in the house & with most of his children here & without any physical suffering. He had been most unhappy the last two years and I can only thank God that he is happy now.

---

* Auberon Waugh, *Will This Do?*, Century (1991).

Laura believed that she had no money after Evelyn died. Auberon says that this was the work of an over-cautious lawyer, and that in fact she was 'very rich'. I was surprised to read this, although I knew that certain adjustments to back income tax as well as the continuing sale of Evelyn's books soon relieved her of any actual poverty. In any case, during the period in which she believed she had not even the money to pay her son Septimus's school fees, she sold Evelyn's library to the University of Texas and, according to Bron, also much of the family furniture, which he has been told 'is still to be found in packing cases, or distributed through the offices of the English faculty'. What was certainly sent, unknown to Laura, who made an inventory of his books, manuscripts and lithographs aided only by one of her nieces, were Evelyn's diaries. These were found in Texas and edited by Michael Davie, appearing first in the *Observer*.

In order to understand the following excerpt from the last letter we received from Laura, it is necessary to know that A.D. Peters, Evelyn's literary agent, had died after the diaries had been sold to the *Observer* but before they were published.

> The *Observer* affair is beastly. I had no idea that the diaries – except the school ones – were like diaries. I thought they were only notes for Evelyn's travel books. I have not seen the last two and leave [for Greece] tomorrow. *Not nice.*

That was the last letter we received from Laura, who died suddenly of pneumonia when she was fifty-seven.

I think Christopher Sykes's biography of Evelyn is much underrated. It is not well structured and Christopher gives us too much information about himself, while he is confident but a shade naive as literary critic; but he knew Evelyn and I think no one writing without personal knowledge could ever understand him as Christopher did. Almost everything he says is perceptive and I find fault only with his description of Evelyn as a soldier. As I have said earlier, I met Evelyn only at home, where, contrary to general opinion, he was always at his best, but I cannot believe he was quite so uncouth when dealing with soldiers as he appears in this book.

Christopher was a long-time friend of Evelyn and used to travel with him. However, towards the end of Evelyn's life, something went wrong between them. In *The Ordeal of Gilbert Pinfold*, Evelyn wrote of Pinfold:

Sometimes he thought he detected a slight coldness among his old cronies. It was always he, it seemed to him, who proposed a meeting. It was always they who first rose to leave. In particular there was one, Roger Stillingfleet, who had once been an intimate but now seemed to avoid him. Roger Stillingfleet was a writer, one of the few Mr Pinfold really liked. He knew of no reason for their estrangement and, enquiring, was told that Roger had grown very odd lately.*

Roger Stillingfleet is based on Christopher, who, Evelyn often said at this time, avoided him and was no longer friendly to him. This is not surprising. Christopher was exceedingly proud in a good old-fashioned aristocratic way; he did not have Laura's personal modesty, and was the last man to take easily some chance barbed remark. I think – and this is the only real fault I have to find with his book – that he shows no mercy in his accounts of Evelyn behaving badly.

However, Evelyn did behave badly during the war and, because he made trouble everywhere else, Bob Laycock, commander of No. 8 Commando and later of Combined Operations, took him on his own staff. In Christopher's book there is no account of this, but both Evelyn and Bob confirmed it to me, as also the following story.

Evelyn was very cross because Bob would not take him when he went to high-powered conferences with the other commanders. One day Bob met the naval and air force commanders on board a ship. To his horror the conference had hardly begun when, with a certain amount of noise, Evelyn, his knees showing knobbly beneath his khaki shorts (Bob's account), scrambled over the side of the ship and took up a position behind his chair.

'Evelyn!' Bob said, horrified. 'What brings you here?'

'Loyalty, sir,' Evelyn said, saluting smartly and remaining at attention behind Bob's chair throughout the discussions which followed.

---

* Evelyn Waugh, *The Ordeal of Gilbert Pinfold*, Chapman & Hall (1947), p. 7.

15

···

Tony Crosland

The term 'the Hampstead set' came to be used about a group of people close to Hugh Gaitskell (who lived in Hampstead). I think no one who knew them would deny that Tony Crosland was the most valued by Hugh himself. We had not been long at Burden Court when Tony turned up there. Aidan and Virginia Crawley had told us that he would come as a candidate to the Labour selection meeting for South Gloucestershire, and they said that he was very bright and that we were lucky to get him. Jack went to the selection meeting, voted for Tony, and told him we would be glad if he stayed at our house when he visited the constituency. For several years he stayed with us whenever he was in Gloucestershire as our MP and afterwards he came four or five times a year both there and, when we moved, to Kingsbridge.

Although we had been members of the Labour Party since the thirties, we came, in different ways, from an almost entirely Tory society. Jack had known Denis Healey during the war when Denis was his staff captain, and the Healeys were and are great friends of ours. One of my earliest recollections of Denis is of travelling in a bus, Edna and I sitting on one side, Jack and Denis on the other, and hearing Denis say: 'But you're so happy, Jack, you've got no taste at all.' On another occasion, when Jack wished him to join something inappropriate, Denis said: 'It's all right for you, Jack, because you're expendable.' However, a considerable devotion has survived in spite of these remarks and, since they have a house near us in Sussex, we see them both often.

Apart from the Healeys, Tony was the first member of the higher ranks of the Labour Party we had ever met. When he first came to stay with us he was still a don at Trinity College, Oxford – lecturing in economics, I suppose. Before his death in 1977, at the age of fifty-eight, he had held six different ministerial posts in Labour governments, but, as Dick Leonard writes, 'it is almost certainly as a thinker and writer that Crosland will be most remembered. Already in his lifetime he had the rare satisfaction of reading the judgement of Professor Anthony King that he was the greatest socialist thinker of our time.'*

Tony had an unusually high moral sense and his philosophy, his politics and all his views were based on his feeling for man as an individual. He cared passionately not only about such issues as greater equality, but also about creating a society in which men could enjoy life. In a book called *The Conservative Enemy*, he wrote: 'Today we all accept some communal responsibility for overcoming poverty, distress and social squalor. The question is whether we do so gladly or grudgingly, and what priority we give it.' And he went on to quote from one of his earlier books: 'A socialist is identified as one who wishes to give this an exceptional priority over other claims on resources.'†

I do not intend to go deeply into Tony's political beliefs. I have not the understanding to do so. But since he was a close friend and a major influence in our lives for many years, it is necessary here to say three things.

First, he thought that equality could be obtained by steady economic growth and at the time he wrote the words I have quoted he believed this might be achieved, although he lived long enough to be aware of the difficulties. Yet it is a pity he died before Margaret Thatcher came to power, because it would have been so interesting to hear what he had to say about 'Thatcherism'. He was later to be accused of indecisiveness and unreliability, but I think he never lost his belief that a socialist was one who wished to give equality priority over everything else.

Secondly, he thought the control of industry through nationalization unimportant and disruptive, and he was with Hugh Gaitskell when he tried to fight Clause 4, the Labour Party's commitment to it in the party's constitution.

* David Lipsey and Dick Leonard, *The Socialist Agenda: Crosland's Legacy*, Jonathan Cape (1981), p. 9.
† Anthony Crosland, *The Future of Socialism*, Jonathan Cape (1956), p. 113.

Thirdly, for many years he spoke ardently in favour of entry into the Common Market, though he later denied its importance.

When Tony first came to stay at Burden Court, he arrived driving an open sports car and wearing a beret; that evening he made a speech to our local branch of the Labour Party. When he left the next morning he asked me to tell him truthfully what had gone wrong with it, since it had not, he thought, been well received. I explained that the audience had been unresponsive because they had not understood a word he said, but they had been flattered by being treated on such a high intellectual level. I added that he might learn to simplify the expression of his thoughts in future.

He was the second of the three people I have referred to (Evelyn Waugh being the first) who had such a command of the English language that they used an extensive vocabulary and so ordered their sentences that they spoke much as they wrote. (To avoid creating a mystery where none is necessary, Isaiah Berlin is the third.)

Tony was an immense pleasure to us at this time, and I think we were to him. He was in many ways very solitary and we were too busy to bother him or to wish to accompany him when he went for a walk. He was a curious mixture because while he had a genuine love of the country, he was entirely town-bred in many ways. He had to have it explained to him that we kept a bull because without calves the cows would give no milk and, for an ex-parachutist, he was unexpectedly nervous both of the bull and of the cows.

He made no concessions to our children Thomas and Rose, then in their teens, and did nothing to ingratiate himself with them. Yet he did ingratiate himself with them, and I think they were very proud of him, as we all were. Tony fancied himself very much driving a car and he once said that if he had not been a politician he would probably have been a racing driver. When he said this Rose got up and went out of the room. She returned with an album and showed us all a photograph of Tony's car, against the front tyre of which lay a white post, one of those meant to be holding up the chains which separated our house from the farmyard. Underneath she had written: 'Crosland comes to stay.'

Tony loved sightseeing and we sometimes went with him. The occasion I remember best was when we took a picnic and went to Dyrham Park which had just been taken over by the National Trust. It was some distance, and so when we got there and found that it was being repaired and not open to the public, we nevertheless decided to picnic on a bank facing the house. Presently a car drove by carrying two men, one of whom I had met somewhere and recognized as John Kenworthy Brown, the curator of Dyrham Park, although he did not recognize me. He got out of the car and came up to us.

'What brings you here?' he asked.

And, with no less formality, Tony replied: 'Your beautiful house.'

John Kenworthy Brown asked whether we had not seen all the notices denying us entrance and we agreed that we had. Then he asked us to pack up and leave as soon as we were ready.

I knew that Mr Kenworthy Brown was a friend of James Lees-Milne and next time I saw Jim I told him all this, and he repeated it to Kenworthy Brown. Jim later told me that the second man in the car had been the composer Aaron Copland and that when they drove off Copland had remarked: 'That conversation could not have taken place in America.'

Yet, if Tony was a constant pleasure, when I think of him I am often reminded of a splendid remark Isaiah Berlin once made. He had been describing the arrival of Diana Cooper on a yacht at Portofino, and of the disruption caused by her visit. When he had finished his story, I asked: 'But, Isaiah, didn't you find all that rather tiresome?'

'Oh, yes,' Isaiah said, 'but then I don't expect my friends not to be tiresome.'

Tony could be extraordinarily tiresome. He was always determined to put off meals until he felt sufficiently relaxed to enjoy them and he employed his considerable armoury in delaying tactics until the meals were often an hour or so late. He closed all conversations which did not interest him, and he never refrained from complaining about any lapse in the standards of comfort of the house.

Often he brought people who had spoken at his meetings to stay with us, and on one occasion he telephoned and said that he wanted to bring Tom Driberg. I do not know whether I learned from him or from Evelyn that the two of them proposed to go to Piers Court on the following morning. I was exceedingly annoyed about this because Evelyn had refused to meet Tony when we had asked to take him there, on the grounds that he could not meet socialists. (After his death Laura said this was all rot; the real reason was that he had met Tony before and did not like him.) In any case, I had believed Evelyn and I talked to him about the projected visit, pointing out that Driberg was also a socialist. Evelyn explained that Driberg had a particular interest for him because he believed him to be evil incarnate, and he had felt that seeing him involved allowing him to bring Tony. I forbade Tony to go and he obeyed me.

When he asked whether he could bring Driberg to stay, I knew that our friends David and Celia McKenna would be in the house and I told Tony that if they wanted food he must say so then, as I was not going to get it when they came. He had replied that they would be well fed at the meeting and would not need anything. However, when they arrived, Driberg, whom we did not know, came into the room with Tony following behind.

'Could we possibly have some food?' Driberg asked. 'We've had nothing to eat this evening.'

Driberg had written an article in the *New Statesman* the week before about Johnnie Ray, who was then singing in London. He had taken Ray to the House of Commons and he wrote: 'At Question Time in the House of Commons, he was much taken by one rather long-winded question: later, in his dressing-room, it amused him to read it out from the order paper in one breath – adding with a shout of laughter, "and some cat *answered* it".'*

I had thought this funny at the time and, after they had eaten the bacon and eggs I had cooked and come into the sitting room, I told him so.

'Ah!' he said. 'I think I may have that article with me.'

And, taking a copy of the *New Statesman* out of his brief case, he handed it in turn to everyone in the room until all had read it.

After this, he took the Whips' papers out of his case and explained that this one was a two-line whip, when one must go if possible, and this a three-line, when it was absolutely necessary to go. As the son of a well-known chancellor of the exchequer, David McKenna had probably spent his childhood making paper boats out of papers like these, but he too had to look at them.

The following morning Jack took Driberg to see Evelyn, and Tony mooned round me while I made the beds.

'What is the matter?' I asked.

'If I go directly after lunch, could you let Driberg stay the afternoon here and take him to a train later on?' (It was high summer.)

'Absolutely not,' I replied. 'We've got the McKennas here and we can't look after Driberg.'

Tony spoke in a voice of despair: 'But if I take him with me, he'll

---

* *New Statesman and Nation*, 11 April 1953, p. 422.

insist on stopping at all the pubs, which is simply unbearable and we won't get home for hours.'

When Jack came in, I warned him that Tony would ask him to keep Driberg, and, when he did so, Jack also refused. At lunch Tony leant over the table and said to Driberg: 'Tom, I have to go immediately after lunch. But I know Jack would take you to a train later on, if you would like to stay and spend the afternoon in the garden.'

Driberg accepted with pleasure.

Tony was jealous of John Kenneth Galbraith, or perhaps only disagreed with his theories on economics. Someone told him that Galbraith's famous phrase 'private affluence and public squalor' originated much earlier in classical literature. Tony's mother was a classical scholar and he put her to work to find the phrase. It took her more than a year, and then Tony used it only as a footnote as follows: 'To give credit where it is due, this phrase seems to have originated with Cato the Younger, who, when denouncing Cataline and the contemporary state of Rome, said, *"habemus publice egestatem, privatim opulentiam."* (Sallust, *Opera*, 1825 edition, p. 46.)'

Alan Watkins, whom I read every Sunday in the *Observer*, has a fondness for the story of Hippocleides, 'who behaved in a riotous manner on his wedding night, drinking too much and dancing on the tables. "O Hippocleides," someone said (for they used the vocative case a lot in those days), "you have danced your bride away." To which the young man replied: "Hippocleides doesn't care."'

Alan Watkins has usually applied this story to Nigel Lawson, to whom, he says, black spots are a matter of indifference, but on one occasion he said it also applied to Crosland.

Now this is an interesting point. Certainly Tony had Maureen Stanley's ability not to cry over spilt milk, but more than that he went out of his way to give an impression of not caring. Thus I think he is not merely the first but the only man in history to go to a side table and mix his own drink while being entertained by the Queen – I forget whether at Buckingham Palace or Windsor. Then, when he refused to wear a dinner jacket for some event at Covent Garden, he gave his refusal so much publicity that Roy Jenkins said to me: 'I don't think it matters much what Tony wears at Covent Garden, but I wish he wouldn't turn it into a *cause célèbre*.'

Yet my impression is that he took a good deal of trouble with, for instance, Mr Watkins, and I believe he minded very much on any occasion when, having worked hard to prepare a speech to the

House of Commons (or, as happened once, not worked enough), it had gone wrong in the delivery.

However, when he was young and visited us, I think he really did not care. He was still a don and soon afterwards he began writing *The Future of Socialism*. He worked incredibly hard and it was difficult to persuade him even out to lunch; and it was to writing rather than to practical politics that his magnificent gifts were most suited. In *Our Age* Noel Annan says that as a cabinet minister he was indecisive, putting strong arguments forward but capsizing when it came to a decision. This is a criticism I have often heard and which is illustrated in Roy Jenkins's book *A Life at the Centre*. Roy also says that he and his wife Jennifer decided that it was better to see Tony on his own as 'Famous for his flounces, and his unconcealed disapproval of those he might be asked to meet, he was too hazardous a guest for dinner parties.'*

I am not sure about the word 'flounces', but certainly Tony did not recognize merits that were different from his own or which he had not met before. He was also curiously emotional in his judgements. Thus when I asked him before the election of 1959, which Labour expected to win, whether Hugh would really have to make Harold Wilson chancellor, Tony replied: 'Yes. But he won't last three weeks.'†

Most people would agree that he had extraordinary intellectual ability (although Roy Jenkins had a far greater command of the House of Commons), yet other qualities determine success as a politician. In 1976 Tony led a motley group of lesser ministers, including Roy Hattersley, Shirley Williams and Harold Lever, in opposition to the Treasury line over the terms of a loan from the IMF, but when Callaghan made it plain he intended to back the Treasury, Tony's resistance crumbled. David Marquand tells this story, then goes on:

> Croslandism had been sacrificed on the altar of Labourism. Six weeks later, Crosland was dead.
>
> Even now, more than a decade later, the story seems to me unbearably painful. Even at the best of times, secretaries of state are two-a-penny. In the Labour government of the 1970s, they were a glut on the market. The labour movement – indeed, the whole progressive tradition in British politics – was collapsing from intellectual anaemia. It had no special need of competent

---

* Roy Jenkins, *A Life at the Centre*, Macmillan (1991).
† Wilson was well to the left at that time and regarded as a Bevanite.

apparatchiki; Callaghan's Cabinet was stuffed with them, and even Wilson's had a fair number. What it needed was a blood transfusion of ideas. Crosland was the author of one of the half-dozen greatest works of socialist theory written in this country in this century. For him to narrow his horizons to the Department of the Environment or even to the Foreign Office was, in a way, a betrayal – not of others, but of himself.

Why did he do it? This is the question that future biographers will wrestle with.*

If one were to hazard a guess as to why he did it, one would have to apportion the blame between Hugh Gaitskell and Tony's second wife, Susan. When Tony left the Gloucestershire seat because a redrawing of the boundaries made it unlikely that he could win it, it was at Hugh's instigation, and when he lost Southampton Test (by a margin far larger than that by which his successor in Gloucestershire was beaten) Hugh never rested until he had persuaded him to accept the safe seat of Grimsby. Susan was naturally ambitious and neither she nor Hugh could be expected to have seen what David Marquand can see so easily now. I have quoted Marquand at some length, partly because of his admirable attitude to cabinet ministers, but also for the more important reason that I believe that in his already published books Tony had reached the end of what there was then to be said about socialist theory. There were many notable left-wing theorists immediately before him – the Webbs, G.D.H. Cole, Harold Laski, Victor Gollancz, John Strachey – but who is there today?

Susan did not enter our lives until we moved to Kingsbridge, but she is so important to any account of Tony that having once mentioned her name I cannot leave it at that. Their marriage in 1964 was, like Evelyn and Laura's, made in heaven. Well-known to the public as a journalist writing under the name of Susan Barnes (only later as Susan Crosland), she was quite extraordinarily attractive both physically and mentally and a great addition to our circle. She had two children, both girls, by Patrick Skene Catling, from whom I think she was already divorced by the time we knew her. Tony had been notorious for his promiscuity before he met her and I believe they married on the understanding that he would continue to do as he liked as long as this was unimportant. He became almost immediately an entirely faithful and loving husband and his natural desire to have made only arrangements which

* David Marquand, *The Progressive Dilemma*, Heinemann (1991), p. 176.

suited himself served him well as a stepfather, since he treated Susan's children, Sheila and Ellen-Craig, without fear or favour and exactly as he would have if they had been his own.

He had an unfailing sense of humour. We went to see him in 1970 after the fall of the Labour government, and I asked him whether he would be in difficulties for money.

'Well, yes,' he replied. 'I have just been making a list of things that will have to be done.'

He showed us the list which had only one item on it: 'Susan must earn £3,000 a year more.'

16

....

The Power of Chance

We lived at Burden Court Farm for thirteen years, and during that time I wrote four books. The first was a technical book about milk production, of little importance at the time and of absolutely none now. The second was a biography of my father, Frederick Lonsdale.

Freddy had left America after the war but he never lived in England or even stayed there long. He lived almost entirely in France, always in the best hotels, sometimes visiting New York. He was bored and restless when he was old and he developed the recurring belief that life would be jollier somewhere else. In the winter he motored ceaselessly between Paris and Cannes, staying at the Lotti Hotel in Paris and the Carlton in Cannes. His attitude to money was extraordinary. He kept a large sum in the safe at the Lotti and he was always willing to lend money to people who were short because of the restrictions on taking money out of Britain immediately after the war. We used to stay with him every winter at Cannes, where he could only eat in the Carlton because of an advanced contamination complex. In hotels, too, he was never alone, a thing he could not endure. He knew so many people that almost always when he went into a hotel dining room someone would call out 'Freddy!' At night, rather than going to bed, he would sit up talking to the waiters.

He died suddenly in 1954 of an aneurism, as, accompanied by Sir John Marriott, he walked from Claridge's hotel home to his bed. He left no debts except current ones, almost no possessions except his clothes, and only the letters he had received in the last two weeks. Strangest of all he left only £7,000, enough for about eighteen months on my reckoning at the rate at which he lived. He had a trust in America which brought in about £1,000 a year and he still received some income from his plays – acted sometimes on tour or by amateurs, and occasionally in London – but this source of money was uncertain. At best he would have been reduced to about £1,400 a year and a way of living which would have driven him insane.

He always spoke of the play he was writing, and Rex Harrison questioned me closely in the hope that something viable had been left. Yet there were only a few opening lines on paper and I think he had known for some years that his gift had gone.

Walking in the gardens of the Tuileries one morning, when we were staying with Freddy in Paris, I had said to Jack : 'What is going to *happen* when his money has gone ?'

'That is a thing', he replied, 'that one cannot even contemplate until it happens.'

He was seventy-three when he died and one could only be glad for him he lived no longer. At least two of his plays have survived for more than sixty years.

My mother died of cancer a year later in Brighton, where she had lived for some years. Towards the end of her life she and Freddy quarrelled the moment they were in a room together, but they still retained a sense of belonging. Their reckless and improvident youth had bound them irrevocably.

Before Freddy died he told me to write his biography.

'But you must tell the truth,' he said. 'None of that business of daughters praising their fathers.'

I enjoyed writing *Freddy Lonsdale* very much ; I am sometimes told it is the best book I have ever written and I think this is probably true. In addition to being an eccentric, witty and charming character, my father had that exceptional blessing for a biographer, a talent for memorable speech. The book I wrote was much admired before publication and A.S. Frere, the chairman of Heinemann and husband of my friend Pat Wallace (daughter of Edgar), was so confident of its success that he printed 15,000 copies. (No one would do that now, but I suppose it was the equivalent of something like 5,000 today.) I was used to success through my farming books and I looked forward to publication, although I should have been warned by the fact that no newspaper wished to serialize the book. The truth was that the public had lost interest in Freddy Lonsdale, who had not had a new play produced for some years, and the book was a flop – not what Ian Fleming called a succès-flop-d'estime, but a complete flop.

The critics of all the main papers reviewed the book and they were not particularly nasty, but, with the one exception of Arthur Marshall, they wrote it off. The first review to appear was in the *Sunday Times* and was written, if memory serves, by a man called Kenneth Pearson. He referred to the twenties and thirties with light-hearted contempt as 'this ivy-clad age', and I knew from this one sentence that my hopes were forlorn. I walked down the valley to look at the cattle after I had finished reading, and nothing since has equalled the depth of disappointment I suffered then.

A.S. Frere was more than disappointed, he was angry. His flair and judgement were admired by other publishers and agents, and he had personally stood behind this book. For three months he used almost the whole of the Heinemann advertising budget to push it, using words of praise which Evelyn Waugh had written in a letter to me and kindly allowed to be published. This advertising made people believe the book was a bestseller, but there was no evidence that it sold a single extra copy.

I learned many lessons then, the first and most important being that, while the public may buy novels on the name of the author, they buy biographies and histories only if they are interested in the subject. I learned, too, not to bother whether or not my book was advertised by the publisher, and, more important still, not to expect any great return for truth, objectivity or research, only for lighting on a subject popular with the reading public. Over the years I have received many letters of praise for *Freddy Lonsdale*, some from people I knew, often from critics I did not know. The most amusing and also, I think, the most important was as follows:

Dearest Mrs Donaldson,
I wish I could call you Frankie as your father did. That biography you wrote of him is really ONE OF THE BEST I HAVE EVER READ. You are a natural and what a nice man he was. ... I don't think you need bother at all about the manner of his death. Jack Donaldson will tell you that people, whether they think Christ was God made man, or not, are given by the Management (a better word for God today) the sort of death suited to them. As you say, imagine him besieged by fear dying in a foreign hotel. Oh no! far better between Claridge's and Hill Street. No anxiety. No time to think. He lived fully and well. He used all his talents. Your book makes

me love him, though I would have hated the Garrick side of his life. I think as he did that 'Aren't We All' is his best play. Of course all the time he seemed idle he was thinking out scenes. ... You probably don't realize what a fearfully good book that biography is. Well here's an old hardened literary man who tells you it is & thanks you warmly for sending it.

The letter was signed John Betjeman. I had sat next to him at luncheon with Ann Fleming and, because he told me he had seen and enjoyed most of Freddy's plays, I sent him the book.

Yet *Freddy Lonsdale* remains a flop. Nowadays I receive some money every year for public lending right and in the column showing the number of times the book was taken out, *Freddy Lonsdale* is one of three books recording '0'.

Looking back on my life, I think it was the last book I wrote which was not suggested to me by someone else. This is not entirely through lack of education – sufficient intellectual curiosity might have made up for that – nor entirely through diffidence. I have few ideas, and lack confidence in those I do have unless they are endorsed by a professional. It was lucky therefore that I ran into Rupert Hart-Davis on Shaftesbury Avenue one night when we were both coming out of a theatre, a chance meeting which altered my life. Rupert had written to me praising *Freddy Lonsdale* and on this occasion he stopped and asked me what I was writing and, when I said that I was not writing at the moment, asked me to go and see him.

Solly Zuckerman used to wonder about the odds against a chance event of this sort. Certainly the odds against my running into Rupert at that particular moment were high. If I had not, I think I would sooner or later have written another book, because although I fear and to some extent dislike writing, there is also an urge which eventually makes itself felt, and I suppose someone would have picked me up. But I should, nevertheless, have depended on some outside encouragement of the kind I got from him.*

Rupert had been at Eton with Jack and I had met him once or twice. His firm had been taken over by Heinemann, although it still bore his name, so there was no difficulty in passing from Heinemann to him. (There is no difficulty in any case, since the clause in an author's contract giving the publisher the right to his next book is not easily enforced and is more often than not struck out.) As a result of the meeting outside the theatre, he published two books of

---

* It is curious that one volume of Rupert's autobiography is called *The Power of Chance*.

mine – *Child of the Twenties* and *The Marconi Scandal*. I might have stayed with him forever if he had not been sold by Heinemann and then retired. I say 'might' because he was not, I think – unlike some publishers, most notably George Weidenfeld – full of ideas for his authors. Rupert's great merits lay in other directions – he was an excellent judge and a marvellous editor. Any knowledge I have of the technicalities of a prose style I learned from him. He always covered my manuscripts with what he chose to call the 'blue pencil', but which in practice was red.

(Evelyn Waugh attempted to teach me the difference between 'shall' and 'will' with the following: 'No one will save me; I shall drown. No one shall save me, I will drown.' But, although I understand the differences here, I have never been sure of the application. Jack McDougall, the chairman of Chapman & Hall, tried to teach me the intricacies of 'who' and 'whom', which he said were far more complex than I realized. But I was unable to understand him and he finally told me to give it up and alter the form of the sentences.)

When I told Rupert that I would like to write another book but could think of nothing to write, he suggested an autobiography (the last resort of publishers and authors). I said that I had already thought of this but discarded the idea as impossible. Because he suggested it, I nevertheless went home and started immediately to write one. This was published in 1959 as *Child of the Twenties*, and recently reprinted as a paperback.

The second book, *The Marconi Scandal*, resulted from an argument between Jack and Evelyn Waugh, in which Evelyn said that Herbert Samuel was a politician 'who lost his honour in the Marconi case'. Jack denied this slur absolutely and spent time in the London Library trying to find out something about the case (which was a political scandal in 1911, involving not Marconi himself but a government contract with his company). It transpired that, although the Marconi scandal was given a few lines in every political biography of the period, no one seemed to know much about it.

There were two strands to the scandal, which occurred primarily because the managing director of the Marconi Company, Godfrey Isaacs, was the brother of Rufus Isaacs, the Attorney General, while Herbert Samuel, as Postmaster General, had awarded a contract to Marconi; and because all three were Jews an extraordinary weight was put on this. Indeed anyone who does not believe there was gross anti-Semitism in England in the early years of the century should read *The Marconi Scandal*. The first suggestion was that, because of these relationships, there was corruption in the placing of the contract; the second, that Rufus Isaacs, Herbert Samuel and the Chancellor of the Exchequer, Lloyd George, had used inside information and bought shares in the Marconi Company which, after the contract was awarded, had risen steeply.

Jack's researches produced the fact that two journalists, Wilfred Lawson, in a paper called the *Outlook* and later in the *National Review*, and Cecil Chesterton (brother of G.K.), in the *Eye-Witness* – a paper, founded, contributed to and for some time edited by Hilaire Belloc, although at this time by Cecil Chesterton – were publishing without restraint libels of the grossest kind against Rufus Isaacs and Herbert Samuel, and later against Lloyd George and the Master of Elibank, the Government Chief Whip. These libels were polished as well as extreme, and it was impossible to believe that their authors would have been allowed to continue unless there was something behind all this. In fact, a study of the Marconi case yielded interesting material sufficient for a book. Moreover, the research was so amusing that, although I would not have written the book without pressure from Jack, I much enjoyed doing it.

Both *Child of the Twenties* and *The Marconi Scandal* were flops, with the difference from *Freddy Lonsdale* that they were succès-flops-d'estimes. (I should perhaps say here that all three books sold about 2,000 copies, which paid for their publication but was not in the least what, from the reception of my books on farming, I had come to expect. Nor was the figure comparable with the same sale today, because at that time books sold much better.)

Child of the Twenties was well reviewed and was chosen and praised by Alan Pryce-Jones on the very popular radio programme, *The Critics*. It was on this programme, however, that I was first accused of an air of superiority and this has been said, not often but on occasion, about my other books. It must be the tone some people find superior, because they have difficulty in giving an example of what they mean. Thus on *The Critics* a man called Basil Taylor, having made this criticism, illustrated it by saying that in discussing a book by Pat Smythe I wrote that I had found it 'unexpectedly charming'. Yet Pat Smythe was our leading show-jumper and spent her whole day schooling horses or competing. I still think it unexpected that she should have had the time and talent to write a very amusing book. Similarly a critic reviewing *The Royal Opera House in the Twentieth Century* accused me of snobbery, giving as an example that I had supplied an appendix about members of the board but not about members of the management.

The truth was that I dealt with the board in this way in order to avoid the necessity of bringing them into the text; whereas members of the management appear on almost every page. On the radio Alan Pryce-Jones defended me strongly against the charge of snobbery and others agreed with him. So I repeat, it is the tone some people find superior. Yet I cannot alter it for them.

The Marconi Scandal never attracted the public. The title was against it, giving the impression the scandal had to do with Marconi himself, but at the time it seemed the only one possible. However, it was well reviewed and read by politicians. I have a copy of Hansard with 'Fame indeed' written on it in Tony Crosland's hand-writing because it had been quoted in the House of Commons by the Prime Minister; and it was much admired by Dick Crossman, leading later to an element in our friendship. It was an enormous disappointment to me, however, and I apparently told Penelope Dudley Ward (then married to the film director Carol Reed) that I would never write another book, since I could not work for two years on a project knowing that it led only to hope destroyed.

17

···

Covent Garden

W e were still living at Burden Court when in 1957, after some preliminaries, Jack received a letter from Lord Drogheda saying that at a meeting of the board at the Royal Opera House it had been 'unanimously agreed to invite you to become a director of the Company', and adding that he very much hoped Jack would feel able to accept the invitation. Before going into the effect this had on our own lives, I think it necessary to explain that the circumstances were not exactly the same as if one were asked to go on the board of the Royal Opera House today.

Until after the Second World War there was no permanent company at Covent Garden. In spite of being called the Royal Opera House, it was used for much of the winter as a dance hall; seasons of opera, for which singers and orchestra had to be specially engaged, were given mainly in the summer and through the backing of one group of enthusiasts after another. Between the wars the theatre was taken by other companies, such as the Carl Rosa, for spring or autumn seasons. Harry Higgins, the chairman of the Grand Opera Syndicate which kept Covent Garden open as an international opera house for twenty-five years from 1887, said that autumn seasons were always a loss; and summer seasons would have been a loss too but for foreign visitors and the private subscriptions for boxes and stalls, which depended to a great extent on fashion. Sir Thomas Beecham and his father Joseph Beecham had tried spring and autumn seasons in 1910 and lost a great deal of money; yet after the First World War Beecham, who also made great efforts to give opera in English, continued to lose money at the Royal Opera House until it was closed in 1939. After a few months it reopened as a dance hall for the duration of the war.

The Council for Encouragement of Music and the Arts (CEMA) was founded during the war to carry music, drama and pictures to places cut off by the circumstances of the time. Even before the end of the war its name was changed to the Arts Council of Great Britain and the responsibility for a public grant transferred to the Treasury. After the war the music publishers Boosey and Hawkes took a lease of the theatre and spent generously in returning it to its pre-war purposes. They were strongly assisted by the Arts Council, who at this period might almost be said to have been looking for clients. Lord Keynes, who was chairman of the Arts Council, also became chairman of the trust formed to run the theatre. This trust, over-looking the claims of all those who had been professionally con-cerned with presenting opera in England, appointed as general administrator David Webster, who had been chairman of the Liv-erpool Philharmonic Orchestra, had great experience as an organ-izer, but was without any professional experience in the opera world. At the same time the success of the undertaking was made even more doubtful by deciding to stage opera in English, in the belief that singing in translation and encouraging English poets to write libretti to the music of English composers would over the years result in a national opera and an English 'style'. To understand the almost inevitable failure of this intention, it is necessary to realise that until then British singers had been given so little encour-agement to appear in opera that, unlike today, there were very few to choose from; and secondly, to understand that from the begin-ning Webster was determined to keep all authority in his own hands and consistently blocked the appointment of a musical director. In 1946 Lord Keynes died and Lord Waverley was appointed as his successor, an appointment which I have remarked elsewhere was probably 'the strangest of all'. As Sir John Anderson, Waverley had had a notable political career. As Home Secretary and Minister of Home Security in 1939 he was responsible for the 'Anderson Shel-ters', so well-known in the war, and he was Chancellor of the Exchequer from 1943–5. Yet his biographer writes that the associ-ation of John Anderson with the world of arts 'is not one which springs immediately and spontaneously to mind', and adds that his wife Ava was immensely anxious that he should accept the invitation, 'while he realized what a fortunate medium of expression

Covent Garden would afford her social talents and aesthetic sensibilities'.

Probably nothing but the fact that the board at Covent Garden had succeeded in taking over the Sadler's Wells Theatre Ballet, a company under the general direction of Ninette de Valois which included Frederick Ashton, Margot Fonteyn and Robert Helpmann, could have kept the theatre open during the years before Garrett Drogheda became chairman. The critic Ernest Newman spoke for a great many people when in 1949 he asked the following questions:

> We ask ourselves once more how some of these people who are running opera ... ever came to occupy the positions they now do. Who appointed them, who gave us and opera into their keeping, and in virtue of what supposed qualifications? What were *their* qualifications for the shaping of the destinies of opera in this country?*

Although some improvement had been achieved through the appointment of Lord Harewood to the staff of Covent Garden, very little had changed when Garrett Drogheda was elected chairman in January 1958 and soon afterwards invited Jack on to the board. When Sir Georg Solti was asked some years later what was his first impression of Covent Garden, he replied: 'I thought there was no one there who knew anything at all about how to run an opera house.'

Garrett was determined to change all this. His success in doing so has been recognized in his obituaries, but even here I think his originality and achievements have been underrated. He was a very unusual character. Born at a time when an aristocratic upbringing was likely to promote certain recognizable characteristics, he had acquired both the good and the bad. The difference between him and anyone else I have ever met is that he managed to make as much use of the bad as of the good to further good purposes. He was absolutely confident and he was determined that Covent Garden should achieve excellence as an international opera house. He had given evidence of his personal attitude in a letter to the previous chairman, Lord Waverley, in which he announced his intention to resign from the opera subcommittee on the grounds that Webster had appointed a designer for *The Trojans* without reference to it:

In my view, if the Opera Sub-Committee is to fulfil its duties

* *Sunday Times*, 27 November 1949.

satisfactorily, all major decisions relating to the employment of conductors, producers, designers, etc. should not be taken by the Executive without reference to the appropriate Sub-Committee. ... The minutes of the Opera Sub-Committee ... are always circulated each month in time for the Board's monthly meeting, so that any proposal can be questioned if any member of the Board so wishes. This cannot be so if decisions are taken by the Executive without reference to the Sub-Committee.

Quoting this memorandum, Lord Harewood wrote : 'I could never have subscribed to such a view which seems to me to a great extent to beg an important question. Is an Intendant fully executive, or is he mainly the mouthpiece of a board or committee, to which he must refer decisions ?'

He goes on to say that he had never been put in the latter position, nor could he ever have accepted it, and he added : 'The chief executive of such organizations is to my mind appointed to carry out the Board's *policy*, and he in his turn accepts it as an implied condition of the job that major failure will lose him that job, and failure on a lesser scale will endanger it.'

Lord Harewood was undoubtedly right in principle, but people have to be in a much stronger position than Webster was to work entirely on principle. The 'trust me or sack me' attitude, carried out successfully by such talents as Sir Peter Hall, was not really available to him. No one, at this time or any other, really wished to sack him because he was a major personality, much liked by the musicians and executives in the theatre and a good organizer, who, in words often used at the time, 'always got the curtain up'. On the other hand, he had no intention of being sacked from a position he could never have reached in the conditions of today, and in which he had as yet failed to achieve much success.

In these circumstances Garrett had a good hand which he proceeded to strengthen. He appointed to the board only people with a central passion for music, but only those who could be trusted to get on with him. And it was here that he showed his originality, his belief in his own judgement and above all his willingness to take all responsibility in doing as he pleased. Sir Isaiah Berlin, Burnet Pavitt (chairman of the London branch of Roche, extremely musical and a good pianist) and the Hon. James (Jimmy) Smith (at that time chairman of the opera company at Sadler's Wells and later of the liaison committee between the two Houses) were already on the board and shared Garrett's views on the necessity for change.

164

Garrett now appointed Sir Thomas Armstrong to represent the world of academic music. His second appointment was Mark Bonham-Carter, an enthusiast for ballet, but of whom Garrett wrote: 'There were plenty of others who might with justice claim that their knowledge of the ballet greatly exceeded Mark's. I wanted him more particularly because of his very acute mind, his astringent wit and because he was a fighter for what he believed in and a splendid debunker of nonsense.'* Then with even greater insouciance, he appointed Jack, of whom he said that 'he was a tried and trusted friend of almost thirty years standing, with complementary tastes and reactions to mine, with whom in 1932 I had started the Quartet Society in London.'

Garrett explained that the Blech string quartet were living at that time in the house Jack had recently inherited from his mother and then said:

> Jack also conceived the idea of a small music society which would give both employment and pleasure. He spoke to me and we jointly launched the Quartet Society ... the members of which were drawn from among our friends and the friends of our friends. For a modest sum the members enjoyed about half a dozen chamber music concerts every year, given at first in different large private houses, but soon regularly at Wimborne House.†

All this was true, but Jack, having fought in the war and then lived and farmed first in Warwickshire and then in Gloucestershire, was known at that time neither to the other members of the board nor to anyone else in the musical world. In my view no one but Garrett would have had the nerve to appoint to the board of this splendid, if temporarily mismanaged, opera house, an unknown stranger on the strength of personal friendship and the Quartet Society.

However, I think he had one other reason for this appointment, because the first thing he asked Jack to do was to go and see Walter Legge, who was at that time in charge of the classical section of the Columbia Gramophone Company and consequently of great influence with singers. Walter had been assistant artistic director to Beecham at Covent Garden before the war and had been 'fondly confident' that he and Beecham would be in charge once more in 1946. Both Beecham and Legge (with some justice, it has always seemed to me) had been extremely angry when the newly formed

---

* Lord Drogheda, *Double Harness*, Weidenfeld & Nicolson (1978), p. 108.
† *Ibid.*, p. 36.

board failed to approach either of them, and Garrett believed, probably correctly, that Legge 'discouraged artists whom we wanted to
appear' from singing at Covent Garden.

Jack had known Walter since 1931 when he had been responsible
for a scheme by which subscriptions were received in advance to
cover the cost of issuing collections of recordings of great musical
works. Jack had subscribed to the Beethoven Sonata Society, which,
in fifteen volumes, included all the piano sonatas in recordings by
Artur Schnabel. He had met Walter again in Brussels towards the
end of the war, when Jack was once more running a quartet, this
time for the benefit of soldiers stationed there.

Walter, by now married to the soprano Elizabeth Schwarzkopf,
was a consummate musician, witty and charming, with great power
in the musical world, and generally regarded as a monster. Jack,
who likes everybody, saw only his attractive qualities and consequently was on good terms with him. I also met only his good
qualities, since I did not cross his ambitions, and I found him an
amusing companion. I remember running into him in the foyer at
Covent Garden after a world-famous mezzo had cracked on a very
difficult top note.

'What will she do?' I asked him in horror.

'Well, the first thing she'll do', he replied, 'is go home and kick
her husband.'

Jack returned from his first luncheon with Walter to report that
he had said his one ambition in life was to run an opera house. No
one seriously considered him in this capacity, but as a result of
Jack's meeting he was appointed to the board – much against the
wishes of David Webster and others. He was never a good member
in the conventional sense : his attendances were bad and he resigned
after five years, chiefly, I think, because he never gained the full trust
of the other members, particularly of the chairman. Nevertheless, he
played a part in the battle against mediocrity at Covent Garden,
since the administration was anxious to give him no cause for
criticism. 'W.L.'s presence', one of the directors said, 'is the greatest
single factor which at present keeps the administration up to the
mark and his resignation would genuinely lower the quality of opera
produced.' And in a letter which was in general congratulatory to
Garrett on his resignation in 1974, Isaiah Berlin said : 'I think the
brio has slightly gone out of our general condition, partly I think
because of our success ... a strongly critical voice or two – Walter
Legge did us no end of good – helps.'

Returning to 1958, I think no one but Garrett could have both kept Webster in his position and also achieved his own aims. Kenneth Clark, who had been on the board earlier, had said of Webster that he did not really know the field but would not turn to anyone who could advise him in case he should be over-shadowed; and his biographer tells us that dilatoriness was an essential part of his nature. For twelve years Webster had used dilatoriness to avert the appointment of anyone who might 'over-shadow' him.

Now he met a natural goad, and one who combined perseverance with an inability to prevent himself saying what he thought on every occasion. Garrett was described by Isaiah Berlin as 'a curious mixture of painstaking conscientiousness and aristocratic self-indul-gence and impatience; but one who does an excellent job and that is that'. Isaiah later wrote to Jack: 'All the same, I am glad that Garrett stuck one of his pins, which your flesh and mine have received so often, into the doubtless astonished and indignant Solti.' And on another occasion: 'The Headmaster has instructed us to re-draft the opera section of the Annual Report. I said that in spite of the hideous snub administered to us on the last occasion of our doing that, we had no vanity, no thought of self, and would once again bend our shoulders to the wheel.'

Garrett carried a notepad and pen with him at all times, on which he jotted down any matter he wished to take up the next day; the memorandums these notes inspired became known as Drogheda-grams. In six months from 1959 Webster received Droghedagrams on the following points: the exact arrangements for the Bedford box (next to the stage and reserved for Covent Garden Properties Ltd); the loan of Marie Collier to Sadler's Wells; designs for *Fidelio*; designs for the ballet *Two Pigeons*; a plea that he, Webster, would go backstage after performances; the question of presenting first nights at weekends; the suitability of Claire Watson for Sieglinde; a draught which caused movement in the cyclorama; questions affecting the British Council; his desire to dissociate Covent Garden from a protest being made by the West End Managers; appointments made to the press office.* This picture must be completed by saying that many of the notes were to remind himself to do something about a job for the son of a friend; or the situation of a retired dan-cer; or about the whole question of pensions in the opera house. And I think it is appropriate to say here that, when he was old and in

---

* Frances Donaldson, *The Royal Opera House in the Twentieth Century*, Weidenfeld & Nicolson (1988), p. 112.

need of money as well as work, he twice resigned from the board of a company he thought was not treating its employees well enough.

In 1958, there were two major issues at stake. The first was the policy of singing in English which had proved a failure because of the unwillingness of foreign artists to learn the traditional roles in translation, an unwillingness shared by our own best singers, who had to learn to sing in the original languages if they were to advance on the international stage. Here I must say that I think the importance of singing in the vernacular is much exaggerated. Once when I was being interviewed by Ken Davison (who ran the Friends of Covent Garden and edited the magazine *About the House*) in one of the lunchtime meetings in the crush bar at Covent Garden, he asked me some question about singing in English and I replied that I did not think it mattered very much because I could seldom hear a word in any language. I was surprised to find that this went down very well with the audience, who all seemed to agree with me. And in fact I have often sat through operas at the Coliseum – notably Britten's *The Rape of Lucretia*, in which the words are important because they were written by a poet – without hearing more than a word here and there. In any case, whenever more than one person is singing there is no question of hearing the words.

One of Jack's first actions as a board member was to ask for a comparison showing the difference in loss (there is some loss at every performance, thus the necessity for the Arts Council grant) on what were known as 'special' performances – those given with foreign singers at higher prices but with higher costs – and the ordinary performances sung by members of the resident company. This was apparently the first time this request had been made and everyone was surprised when the figures showed that, with very few exceptions, the loss on 'special' performances was considerably less than on the ordinary ones; and that the same thing applied to higher-priced performances of ballet – when, for instance, Margot Fonteyn (who was paid a special fee) was dancing.

However, singing in English was part of Arts Council policy and any change had to be cleared with Kenneth Clark, then chairman. He agreed, with the proviso that, if Covent Garden did not wish the Arts Council to interfere with its policy, it must not expect the Council to take sides in any controversy which that policy produced.

Far more difficult was the question of appointing a major figure as music director, a matter which Webster had fought off for four-teen years. Garrett dealt with this by meeting Georg Solti in a private house and presenting Webster with a virtual *fait accompli*. (Solti was to say many years after that he thought the reason Webster and Garrett were able to work together in spite of Garrett's often outrageous behaviour was because Webster could not resist his looks, which indeed were very fair.)

There now followed what in hindsight is seen as the golden age of Covent Garden in the twentieth century. At the end of his first year Solti said in *About the House*: 'There is an enormous amount of brilliant talent, both in this country and in the Commonwealth, and I feel that it must be given a chance to develop. However, we must bring internationally famous singers to this House, since the public has a right to hear them, and from them our singers can learn much.' What this policy has done both for the Royal Opera House and in the long run for the singers and opera companies of Great Britain is a matter of history. Even companies such as the English National Opera, which have made a success of singing in English, rely on an international outlet for their great singers. Covent Garden provided a doorway to the world stage. Solti may be quoted again at the end of his term at Covent Garden:

I had the fantastic luck to meet a very talented generation of English singers – fantastic luck, but with that luck I think I used my luck, giving them the chance. So here we are today with a very strange thing. Wherever you go in America or on the Continent the first choice is an English singer, even at Bayreuth; and that of course is a marvellous thing, but it is entirely new. I don't say it is entirely due to me, I just had wonderful luck and used my luck to give them the chance.

At Covent Garden in those years we had a superb *Don Carlos* under Giulini, with Christoff and Gobbi, Vickers and Brouwenstijn; Thebom and Vickers in *The Trojans*; Callas in *Traviata* and later as a memorable Tosca; and, among other outstanding performances, an unforgettable *Lucia di Lammermoor*.

When the management first suggested to the board that Joan Sutherland should be allowed to sing Lucia, they resisted it to a man. She had a remarkable voice but at this time in her career not much stage personality, and, although the management was anxious not to lose her through giving her too little opportunity, the board thought this would be too much for her. The only excuse that can be made for their judgement is that they insisted that she should be sent for six weeks to study the role under Serafin, who would conduct it. Jack and I went to one of the rehearsals and when

169

Sutherland came on in a coat and skirt in the second scene, and sang the aria '*Regnava nel silenzio*', we were both reduced to tears. We also had the privilege of telling the rest of the board that something very unusual was about to happen. It may be remembered that she inspired a standing ovation on the first night and soon was known worldwide as La Stupenda.

Another absolutely marvellous singer was Leontyne Price, whose Aida was beyond compare. Price was the first, or one of the first, black singers to appear at the Metropolitan Opera House and the story is told that, as she waited in the wings to make her first appearance, she was heard to say: 'God, you got me into this. Now get me out of it.'

Since this period coincided with the years when Ninette de Valois, Frederick Ashton, Margot Seymour and later Rudolf Nureyev were at Covent Garden, to say nothing of such dancers as Anthony Dowell, Merle Park, Lynne Fonteyn and Antoinette Sibley, we look back at a golden age comparable to that of Italian opera in the early nineteenth century, the French impressionists and post-impressionists, or the Victorian novelists. Such moments in art are unpredictable and inexplicable, but the circumstances must be right if they are to occur.

Jack's appointment to the board of the Royal Opera House was one of the most important single events in our lives. One of Garrett's first acts on becoming chairman was to change the arrangements for what is known as the royal box (second from the stage on the right of the auditorium). This box is always available for members of the Royal Family and for government entertaining, but otherwise it had been the exclusive right of the chairman and was often empty. Garrett immediately made it available to all the board members on a first-come-first-served basis, with the proviso that the chairman should have priority on first nights. In 1958, when many performances were of the routine repertory kind, this privilege was not much taken up and Jack and I were able to have the box at least once a week, sometimes even being asked to go by Webster's secretary so that it should not remain empty. As the performances gradually improved the box could only be got by immediate application on the day the season was announced, but even at the beginning it was one of the best 'perks' in London, exactly the same as being very rich. One could not only go to the opera whenever one chose, but everyone invited to the box was pleased to accept and to invite one to something in return.

Through the box we recovered Peter Cazalet. Some years after

Leonora died he married again, and Zara, a woman of strong emotions, was not in a hurry to know his first wife's friends. She could not resist invitations to the ballet, however, and we soon made a close and lifelong friendship. We were asked immediately to Fairlawne (in the days when Albert Roux of La Gavroche fame was chef there) and, until Peter died in May 1973 and the house was sold, went often. I still see a great deal of Zara, and also of Peter and Leonora's son, Edward, and his wife, born Camilla Gage, who are almost like our own children to us.

We also made new friends at Covent Garden. When one is near the end of middle age, one feels the time for making close friends has passed. This is quite untrue, and at this time we met Isaiah and Aline Berlin, to whom we have remained devoted. During the next twenty years we stayed with them every summer in their house at Paraggi (in the hills above Portofino) and often at Oxford. Aline is, unexpectedly, a first-class golfer, and in her youth won the women's championship of France. By the time we knew her she no longer played seriously and, until we grew out of the game through sheer old age, we used to play regularly with her at Oxford – once in the spring at Rapallo.

In 1963 Jack replaced Jimmy Smith on the board of the Sadler's Wells Opera Company, in order that he might act as chairman of the liaison committee between the two houses. After that we went to opera at one or the other theatre two or three times every week, staying at first at the Farmers' Club in Whitehall. We began now to say that, although Jack had always refused to spend his life in making money, he was adept in getting the things which money buys.

I first met Freddy Ashton in the Sadler's Wells bar.

'I hear', I said to him, 'that you are going to do a ballet on *Traviata*.'

'Yes,' he replied, 'but I'm not going to do all that father and daughter stuff.'

And he then proceeded to act both what he was not going to do and what he was.

The second time I met him was at a luncheon party. Freddy sat on my right and, for reasons I have forgotten, we were both annoyed by the people on our other sides. When Freddy turned to me, with anger in common, we discovered a love for each other which lasted, I am proud to say, until he died. Looking through his letters to me the other day I found the following, the first written when he received the Companion of Honour in 1970, the second when he received the Order of Merit in 1977. Freddy did not date his letters and he also had the strange habit of signing himself sometimes Freddie, sometimes Freddy.

8 Marlborough St Chelsea

Darling Frankie & Jack
I think Countess Carabosse in my own right would be more apt in this 'Travestie' world. Who are my other companions, do we have an annual dinner? at Browns? I worry about the people who say 'Why he and not me' but I really am delighted you are pleased and love the things you say.

> All love
> Freddy

8 Marlborough St Chelsea

Darling Frankie
I have my own list of oms and you are certainly one of them – I am sure there are many going round and wondering why me and not they – but I can honestly say I have never scrabbled for orders. My list of oms certainly does not extend to 24. Queen Elizabeth high on my list. She wrote me an enchanting letter with a funny drawing of a dancer on a pinnacle. She is a joyous person. I loved your letter as I love you.

> Freddie

I repaid his love by turning down one of the most interesting offers of a book to write that I have ever received. George Weidenfeld used regularly to try and persuade Freddy to write his memoirs and on one occasion he told him he would give him someone to help him. To this Freddy replied: 'Well, I think the only person I could work with is Frankie.'

George was immensely excited and so was I. Yet I immediately recognized this as the most certain way of ending a treasured friendship. I know very little about ballet and would have been full of unexpectedly ignorant questions, but even if that had not been so, I knew Freddy well enough to know that our friendship could not have survived the constant visits which would have been necessary. I discussed this matter with Camilla Cazalet, who at this time was closer to Freddy than anyone else I knew, and she agreed the danger. I did not refuse to write the book, but I did not take the matter up. George took a bit of pacifying, but Freddy never mentioned it.

18

....

Golden Eye

In 1960 we sold Burden Court Farm and bought Kingsbridge Farm in Buckinghamshire from Aidan Crawley. We had often been to Kingsbridge, most notably on the occasion when in 1950 we were asked to lunch to meet Clement Attlee. We arrived first and were there when Aidan said to Virginia (his wife, an American writer and war correspondent in the Second World War): 'Now Virginia, you are not to mention the Schumann Plan.'

The Schumann Plan was a proposal for the pooling of French, German and other European coal and steel production and was the first step towards the EEC. Attlee was prime minister at the time and had to defend in the House of Commons his reluctance to join without a more explicit understanding of the principles involved. This he did in June and November 1950, using arguments with which in the last years we have again become acquainted.

When we sat down to lunch, just the six of us, Virginia turned immediately to Attlee and said: 'Now Mr Attlee, what about the Schumann Plan?'

The Prime Minister waved the question off. 'Oh,' he replied, 'that is nothing but a blueprint.'

The other thing I remember about this visit is that after lunch Attlee was introduced to the Crawleys' bailiff and his wife, who did the cooking; and while he was quite unable to summon up either graciousness or conversation, the bailiff's wife made good all his remissions, speaking in the most charming way and keeping the

173

conversation going by explaining to him their loyalty to the Labour Party.

We moved to a smaller farm for various reasons, but most importantly because Jack was no longer content with being a farmer, at which I was always better than him, and wanted to return to the kind of unpaid but important work he had always seen as his function in life. The opportunity came as a request from Frank Longford that he should become secretary of a committee formed to look into the problems of discharged prisoners. This involved visiting one hundred prisoners at ten different prisons, and meant that Jack was away a great deal and, in consequence, that I spent too much time on such matters as a single-handed attempt to get the cows out of the corn. The report finally issued by Jack's committee was critical of the Discharged Prisoners' Aid Society, formed at the end of the nineteenth century and entirely financed by local voluntary contributions, and the secretary of this society, named if memory serves Haig, suggested that Jack should join the committee and see if he could do better himself. The upshot of this was that the Discharged Prisoners' Aid Society was disbanded and reformed with substantial government aid as the National Association for the Care and Resettlement of Offenders (NACRO). Jack became its chairman.

NACRO and the Royal Opera House meant that we needed a room in London and we were lucky to acquire the servant's bedroom on the top floor of K3 Albany, which belonged to Harry and Catherine Walston, together with the use of their bathroom. We had not known the Walstons for long but we had quickly made friends with this rather odd couple. We originally met them when they asked us to a Labour Party weekend, to meet George Brown in order to discuss a policy for agriculture. On the day we arrived at their house, then the farmhouse described by Evelyn Waugh in a letter to Nancy Mitford,* Harry greeted us by saying they had spent the day trying to telephone us to put us off as in the end George Brown had been unable to come. This was typical of Harry and one got used to being greeted with a remark such as: 'We didn't expect you until tomorrow.' He had a natural friendliness which persuaded one that these remarks were revealing only of the truth and might not have been said if he had not been well pleased to see us.

Catherine was another matter. She was at this time at the height of her love affair with Graham Greene, which since the death of both Graham and Harry has been well publicized. An article in the

---

* *The Letters of Evelyn Waugh*, Weidenfeld & Nicolson (1980), pp. 283–4.

Sunday Times of 9 June 1991 insists that she was the great love of Graham's life. I know nothing of his life after he parted from Catherine, but I find no difficulty in believing this to be true. Certainly he was completely attached to her at that time and when she used the word 'we' – as in 'when we were in Paris' – there was no way of knowing whether she had been accompanied by Graham or Harry. The writer in the *Sunday Times* says Harry turned a 'blind eye' to the whole affair. This may be true, but none of their friends had any idea what Harry thought or felt. When, in the words of the writer in the *Sunday Times*, Catherine's affair 'spluttered to an end', Harry told me that they had at last forbidden Graham the house because he would criticize the food.

Catherine was exceptionally beautiful, slightly dotty and even more adept at discouraging her guests than Harry, and I always thought less kind. When they moved to the big house that Harry had inherited from his father, they entertained many Labour politicians and their wives. The wives had naturally taken trouble over their clothes and went down to dinner the first night in their best dresses. Catherine would appear in jeans. Accordingly the guests would go down the next night in day clothes to find Catherine in a long evening dress. Probably she had done this to keep them company, but it was very disconcerting.

The Walstons had very good modern pictures and some small statues by Henry Moore which they had bought together when young. I never found out which of them was responsible for these purchases but they bought ahead of general recognition, certainly in the case of Henry Moore.

They had a farm on the West Indian island of St Lucia, and they used to go there each year, staying on Rat Island, formerly the quarantine island, just off the mainland. After we left Burden Court and before we could get into Kingsbridge they asked us to stay there and we went, stopping off on the way to stay with Ann and Ian Fleming in Jamaica.

The invitation to stay at Golden Eye came from Ann, not Ian. We had not known her for long, but when she chose to make friends she did so very quickly by the method of asking intimate questions about oneself and one's life. Since her interest was genuine and everyone likes to talk about themselves, she skipped whole stages in the normal growth of friendship and in addition knew more about people she chose to make her friends than anyone else did – discussing freely with homosexuals their love affairs and with heterosexuals their troubles with their wives.

I speak of those she 'chose' to make her friends, because she was extremely difficult to please. Her function in life was that of a hostess and she shared with Pam Berry the reputation (earned in both cases) of being the last of the notable practitioners of this historic role. Those whom she chose to like adored her, everyone else disliked her very much because she made no attempt to disguise not wanting to know them. Everyone she did not wish to know was designated 'a bore'. She was really fond of gardening and gardens but once when I told her there was an exceptionally beautiful one near her at Sevenhampton which we should go and see, she replied: 'Oh! I've spent years avoiding that woman. I cannot go and see her now.'

In a marvellous address at her memorial service, Noel Annan said:

> Ann thought that life would be a very tame affair if everyone made conventional responses and had a conventional regard for rules and regulations. This belief is not pagan. Gerald Manley Hopkins in one of his great poems 'That Nature is a Heraclitean Fire and of the Comfort of the Resurrection' pictures the world as a huge, self-fuelling bonfire which creation perpetually replenishes: where life is endurable only if we recognize that everyone and everything in it is produced by discord and strife. Annie lived by this principle. She herself was not above rolling an apple of discord in among the goddesses. She loved turmoil, she provoked, she led her friends on, she wanted movement and hated the pale and the placid.

So it is no wonder that those who did not love Annie were inclined to hate her. Personally I loved her as much as anyone outside my immediate family I have ever known. She had a warmth of affection and of hospitality which made it an exceptional pleasure to enter her house, and if she had an easy, unconsidered willingness to offend those she described as 'bores', she was entirely loyal, absolutely loving to those she made her friends. Sir Nicholas Henderson wrote of her that 'as if by the light of nature, she sought to give pleasure ... giving pleasure to others was part of her being, part maybe of her way of enjoying herself.' This was true, and it was very noticeable when she entertained that she was concerned with the amusement of others, rather than seizing attention for herself.

She was a tremendous gossip, which accounts for her status as correspondent-in-chief to Evelyn Waugh after Nancy Mitford left England. At the beginning of the war Oliver Stanley said that the telephone was out of order but luckily the tel-annie still worked.

Ian Fleming had built Golden Eye before he married Annie: it is a long, low bungalow with wide apertures along the whole of the garden side which faces the sea. Noël Coward, who also had a house in Jamaica, called it Golden Eye, Ear, Nose and Throat.

Ian had a Jamaican servant called Violet, who had been with him before he married and who loved only him. The day we arrived both Flemings took us into our bedroom and Annie said to Ian: 'Ian, those flowers are really awful. Please have them taken away.'

Ian sent for Violet.

'Violet,' he said, when she came in, 'those flowers are too beastly for words. Take them away at once.'

'Yes, Commander,' Violet replied and took them away.

'That is the sjambok method of making love,' Jack said after everyone had gone.

In an appendix of names at the end of his collection of Ann's letters, Mark Amory writes of me:* 'A closer friend than might be imagined from these letters, she preferred Ann in quieter mood, finding her social manner and sometimes her writing style, particularly to Evelyn Waugh, a little forced.'

I think it is true that I was closer to Annie than the book of letters suggests, because, although I have kept a great many of her letters, I thought many of them too intimate for publication; and I can easily believe I made these remarks to Mark because they are true to what I felt. On the first morning we were at Golden Eye, looking out of my bedroom window, I saw Ann dressed in a cotton blouse and short cotton skirt, feeding some animal, I think a bird, and I thought at once: 'How nice.' It was on this visit that we really made friends not only with Ann, but with Ian, too.

This couple, who had been passionately in love and to the end of his life remained devoted to each other, were completely unsuited. Ian liked golf and solitude and undemanding people. He told me once he liked men who talked about silage. Ann liked entertaining Evelyn Waugh, Cyril Connolly, Lucien Freud, Kenneth Clark, Francis Bacon. Chosen for their talents and intellectual achievements, none of her friends could pretend even to have read Ian's books. So if he went into Victoria Square when Ann was giving a dinner party, he would go by the dining-room door and up to his rooms. At Golden Eye he could stand Jack and me precisely because we were not smart and had no pretensions to great intellectual

* *The Letters of Ann Fleming*, ed. Mark Amory, Collins Harvill (1985), p. 432.

achievements. Yet both he and Annie, apart from being irresistibly charming, were what nowadays is described as 'one-offs' and, in spite of all, were worthy of each other.

Ian used to work in the mornings and again in the evenings. I asked him once whether in the evenings he revised what he had done in the morning. He shivered.

'Good God, no. I couldn't possibly go on if I read what I had written.'

I did not believe this to be true and I do not think he meant me to, but it expressed a certain attitude of mind.

On Jamaica there lived someone whom Ann always referred to as 'Ian's Jamaican wife'. Once when we were motoring she said: 'On the left is the house that belongs to Ian's Jamaican wife. You may look, but I cannot.' Because she spoke so flippantly I did not think she was serious, or, if so, I thought this was something she did not mind. Later in that year she wrote to thank me for something and added: 'Curiously the most helpful thing you did was to boost my morale by coming to Jamaica.'

I did not understand this at the time, but I think she had to go to Jamaica although she hated it because of the 'Jamaican wife', so the fact that we got on with Ian made it easier for her. When we left she wrote: 'PS. We *loved* having you both here, and you were sadly missed. PPS. Ian sends love.'

At Golden Eye we learned for the first time the pleasures of snorkeling, floating about on the top of the sea, looking at the fish that swam beneath us. The beach was below the end of their garden and we used to go down before breakfast and again later in the day. Ian was unexpectedly nervous and always in a state because Jack would swim out too near the reef.

Once we went to dine with Noël Coward. I had known him when I was seventeen and he a famous playwright not in the least interested in me; now I felt for the first time his prodigious charm. Ann says somewhere in her letters that Noël was always slightly attracted to Ian and certainly Ian bitched him quite a lot. The only conversation I can remember was when Ian explained to Noël that he did not understand the difference in the French pronunciation of 'an' and 'on'. Noël was not best pleased but Ian was undoubtedly right and I feel sure Noël's pronunciation was correct in the future.

When we left to go on to St Lucia, Ian came with Annie to take us to the airport. I am not sure that I ever saw him again.

19

....

Kingsbridge

I have lived in many different houses in my time, since my parents were great movers, and, although without a war Jack and I might have stayed forever at the Wood House, the move to Kingsbridge was our third since leaving there. Of all the houses I have lived in, Kingsbridge was the one I loved best. It was too big and grand for us and, when Hugh Gaitskell said that allowing for inflation we had lost much money since the beginning of the war, he was speaking at Kingsbridge, on which too much of it had gone.

The main part of the building was the usual 1880s farmhouse, but someone had added on a really lavish room, measuring 30 by 20 feet, and above that two bedrooms and a bathroom. It had eight bedrooms in all and three bathrooms. The Crawleys had left us a good tennis court and a large but basic swimming pool without heating apparatus, which we loved.

At this time I met Paul Anstee, the only interior decorator I have ever known who had the knack of following the style of a house without leaving his mark on it. He nevertheless suggested some irresistible but extremely extravagant improvements and, by the time the builders were in and we on our way to Jamaica, I was already in despair about the cost.

We had intended to have a dairy herd but Jack turned a large enclosed Dutch barn into a hen battery and installed in it 6,000 hens. By the time we had paid for these we had no money left for a dairy herd and we therefore grew wheat, which, since the land was very fertile, yielded well. We also reared beef calves.

In a letter to Evelyn Waugh, Ann Fleming expressed the views of many of our guests about the hen battery. She wrote: 'Jack is uneasy about his chicken battery, and so he should be. Three in a cage, they are mad and miserable, it is a horrible sight. It is an occupation unbecoming to the high-minded Jack. He does not openly admit it but it is quite clear.'

Now, although this expressed a widely held view, it was not one which either Jack or I agreed with, and as a description of hens in a battery it is absolute rot. The hens had rather more room and freedom of movement than Ann said, and they were always warm and always well fed, while they were preserved from the two things from which hens suffer most: the pecking order, and the wet and mud of much so-called free range, often consisting then of small wire enclosures. People find the sight of hens in batteries unattractive, but they do not listen to them. Ours clucked cheerfully away all day. No one knows whether hens, showing every sign of being comfortable and happy, nevertheless feel seriously deprived of something. We took the view that there was no evidence that this was so, and we neither of us felt unhappy about the battery.

Yet there is so much prejudice on this score that many people believed, as Ann did, that the hens were 'mad and miserable'. Someone who read this account soon after I wrote it told me she thought hens in batteries had their beaks cut off and also their wings. I think the former may happen in what is called 'deep litter', where the birds, usually raised for killing and eating, are together in one large shed, but after doing it once Jack thought it unnecessary and never did it again.* One thing we proved to several of our guests is that a fresh egg is one under twenty-four hours old, after which, however it is produced, it loses taste.

At Kingsbridge we began immediately to play tennis which we had not done since before the war. We were surprised how many of our guests wanted to play too, in particular Tony Crosland, who, having played as a child, was very much better than one might have expected. I gave him a white cotton milker's cap to keep his hair out of his eyes while playing, and he proceeded to wear this all over the world and at the most unsuitable occasions until, as foreign secretary, he lost it in the China Sea. Susan's biography contains a photograph of him wearing it.

---

* These words were written some time in 1991. On 16 October of that year Germaine Greer described in the *Independent* the horrendous deaths of the young hens Peaseblossom, Cobweb and Mustardseed, by pecking from older hens, and being told of the necessity to debeak these. This is on free range. She should also have been told not to put young birds with old.

Tony never introduced us to any of his friends in the Labour Party, but I think it was when we were first at Kingsbridge that, staying with Solly and Joan Zuckerman, we met Hugh and Dora Gaitskell. All too old to waste time, we immediately became great friends; and we met Roy and Jennifer Jenkins through the Gaitskells. Denis Healey we already knew. We never learned why Tony was reluctant to have us meet his friends, whether he thought we were too pink or just that we would bore them. In any case all these people stayed with us at Kingsbridge.

Hugh Gaitskell was such a nice man. I had known a good many ministers or Cabinet ministers before I met him, and it was noticeable with all of them that every car and driver, Private Secretary, Permanent Civil Servant added weight to their personality. They dominated any room they were in and, even when someone one had known and previously disregarded, was made an under secretary, the force feeding by the Civil Service added immensely to the importance of his personality. Hugh had been Chancellor of the Exchequer and yet he was not in the least like this. He had absolutely no side on him at all.

Until we met him in Solly Zuckerman's house I had seen him only on television – ours was black and white in those days – and had thought him slightly portentous and grey in personality. My first reaction was surprise at how much nicer he looked in the flesh – brown of face and blue-eyed. My second was of his entire lack of self-importance. And this was a correct impression. I often saw him at his own table listening with kindness and courtesy to someone telling him something he knew more about himself.

He was extraordinarily obstinate in small ways, and had a penchant for rewriting which annoyed his colleagues. We experienced this when he asked Jack to help him run a concert given at the Festival Hall to mark Labour's anniversary. Jack wrote an introduction to the programme and Hugh told me he did not think it right and explained why. I told him I would rewrite it myself, making the points he wanted made. I was surprised when I saw the programme to find it rewritten once more.

He gave the impression of a man who had been too serious in youth and was making up for lost time. But I am not sure that was true; he may merely have loved dancing and not cared that other people thought him funny. He liked gossip and I remember that once when he was preparing some irises to give me, I did the digging, because he had a bad back, and he cut the leaves, while gossiping in a not particularly malicious way the whole time.

'You should not trust George Brown,' I said to him.

'I should not trust anyone,' he replied.

Once when Tony was beefing about Hugh, which he quite often did, I said to him: 'Well, if you think Hugh so often wrong, why do you continue to back him?'

And he replied: 'Because he is head and shoulders above the rest of us.'

I think all the 'Hampstead set' thought this, but it was not apparent in ordinary life. An unsurpassable description of him is to be found in Roy Jenkins's *A Life at the Centre*, and I cannot resist quoting much of it here:

> He would not have been a perfect prime minister. He was stubborn, rash, and could in a paradoxical way become too emotionally committed to an over-rational position which, once he had thought it rigorously through, he believed must be the final answer. He was only a moderately good judge of people. Yet when these faults are put in the scales and weighed against his qualities, they shrivel away. He had purpose and direction, courage and humanity. He was a man for raising the sights of politics. He clashed on great issues. He avoided the petty bitterness of personal jealousy. He could raise a banner which men were proud to follow, but he never perverted his leadership ability; it was infused by sense and humour, and by a desire to change the world, not for his own satisfaction, but so that people might more enjoy living in it.*

Denis and Edna Healey came to Kingsbridge with their daughter Cressida; the photograph of the Healeys was taken by Denis with an auto-timer. Roy and Jennifer Jenkins came, and Roy sometimes came alone on his way to London from his constituency. While he was Home Secretary he brought a detective with him who was an extremely musical man. Roy likes to work to music and he occupied the big sitting-room which we called the long room all morning, while the detective chose the records and put them on the gramophone.

The first letter we had from Evelyn Waugh when we went to Kingsbridge was addressed 'Steeple Claydon, Near Pambury, Bucks'. This was a reference to the fact that the Berrys – Michael and Pam – had a house a few miles away at Oving to which they came at weekends, Pam on Friday nights and Michael only late Saturday

* Jenkins: *Life at the Centre* p. 148.

182

after the *Sunday Telegraph* had been put to bed. Pam was alone on Fridays and often asked us to dinner.

She had more intellect than Ann Fleming, whose name was so often bracketed with hers as the last of the great hostesses, and more wit; but she had less affection and less desire to please. She was seriously interested in politics and from the choice of guests at her luncheon parties one could have successfully guessed which political party was in power. She herself was a hardened Tory, but, when the Labour Party formed the government, her curiosity and her love of power were too strong for her to be able to resist them. One or two remained a permanent part of her life, Dick Crossman telling me once that he really loved her, while I think she returned his feeling. Certainly they were in many ways well suited.

Pam entertained to please herself, unlike Ann who wished to please her guests, and one could tell the order of importance of those present by observing who sat next to her. However, on Friday nights at Oving there were only small parties. On the night I first met Dick Crossman, I sat on his right with Pam on his left, and soon became conscious that she was having difficulty in holding him because he wanted to talk to me. When he finally broke away and turned to me, I found that my attraction for him arose from his desire to abuse Hugh Gaitskell to someone he knew to be a friend of Hugh. When I got a chance to speak, I said that I thought anyone who believed that people whose opinions differed from his own must be either a fool or a knave was likely to be one or the other himself. This was an instantaneous success and Dick remained a friend until he died in 1974. David Marquand, having said of him that he had the reputation of an intellectual bully, goes on to say: 'Unlike the true bully, however, he wanted to get as good as he gave; the purpose of the exercise was not to trample on others, but to provoke them into standing up for themselves.'*

I think there was even more to it than that. Several years later Jack and I were visiting a National Trust house and, walking round the garden, we ran into Dick and his wife, Anne. That week Dick, then a minister, had taken a terrible drubbing in the House of Commons, yet I overheard him say to Jack: 'As a matter of fact I rather enjoyed it.'

I do not think either Marquand or Anthony Howard, Crossman's biographer, conveys how purely mischievous Dick was. Someone who had known him most of his adult life once said of him: 'He

---

* Marquand, *The Progressive Dilemma*, p. 139.

bites the hand that feeds him even before it has had time to feed him.' We never suffered from this. On the contrary, when, some years later, after we had left Kingsbridge, we spent a winter in Warwickshire near the farmhouse (belonging to Anne) where he spent his weekends, we went there often and received much kindness.

Marquand remarks that for all his bump of irreverence, there was a curious strain of diffidence in Dick, a fact I can confirm in a most curious way. Towards the end of his life he was writing a life of Chaim Weizmann and apparently in difficulty. He was an admirer of the book I wrote on the Marconi scandal, and he asked me to dinner in order to discuss his biography with me.

'But what is the difficulty?' I asked. 'You've got all those letters.'

And then this double first, this fellow and tutor of New College, this noted journalist and essayist, replied: 'It's the bits in between I find difficult.'

So strange is this remark that I would not repeat the story, in case I had made some mistake, but for the fact that, when I told it to Elizabeth Longford, she replied that he had asked for her advice in the same way.

Pam Berry also introduced me to George Weidenfeld. (Rupert Hart-Davis had by now retired.) At that time Weidenfeld had some agreement with Michael Berry and the *Sunday Telegraph*, by which George published books and the *Sunday Telegraph* serialized them. Pam now persuaded George that he ought to find a subject for me.

George was always a comfort to me, not only because he considered it his duty to find ideas for his authors, nor because he was a gifted and successful publisher, but also because he gave such a spirited performance in the role, asking authors to luncheon in expensive restaurants, and bustling between Frankfurt and New York and back again to London, leaving a barrage of telephones unanswered because he had gone somewhere else. I have already said that for many years I could not visualize myself in the role of writer, and was inclined to feel that to pretend to it is an affectation better kept from one's friends, an attitude of mind inhibiting in the extreme. I found George's unaffected posturing a comfort because it added a theatrical touch to my own position.

He asked me immediately to luncheon at the Ritz, and, of more real importance, suggested that I should write a book on actor-managers, as part of a series to be edited by John Gross. This seemed to be something I could do. No one told me exactly what was wanted so I wrote of the great Victorian actor-managers, purely as a potboiler – that is to say, reading everything already published (much of which is very interesting, in particular the dramatic criticism of Leigh Hunt, Hazlitt, Bernard Shaw, Max Beerbohm and Henry James) but not attempting to find new information. Later, when George asked me whether, if he increased my advance to £1,000, I would write the book at greater length and allow him to take it out of the series, it added even more to my self-esteem. Rupert had given me an advance of £250 for each of the two books I wrote for him.

Evelyn Waugh died in 1966, and both Pam and George put pressure on me to leave *Actor Managers* for the moment and write a book about him. I did not immediately jump at this, partly through diffidence, but also because I did not know how Laura would take the idea. Eventually, I complied and wrote the book which was published as *Evelyn Waugh: Portrait of a Country Gentleman*, one of the two most successful books I have ever had published.

In 1967 Jack was made a life peer. Roy Jenkins was Home Secretary at the time and had suggested to Harold Wilson that Jack might be useful in the Lords because of his work with NACRO and also as chairman of the board of visitors at Grendon Prison, which was near us in Buckinghamshire. Wilson had once been our guest in the royal box at Covent Garden and we had asked Freddy Ashton to meet him. I think this visit probably had some influence on his immediate decision to agree to Roy's suggestion. Since an account of it is interesting in itself, although slightly irrelevant to the present theme, I give it here.

Wilson talked fluently and knowledgeably about the ballets he had seen in Russia, mentioning dancers whose names Freddy knew but whom he had never seen. He also recognized that there was music not usually used in the ballet we were watching – which I think was *Swan Lake*. He might have been briefed, and he might have read about the extra music in newspaper reviews of the ballet, but we did not think so. In any case, it was a masterly performance and Freddy wrote to me afterwards as follows:

Royal Opera House

Dear Frankie

Thank you very much for last night. I liked the leader very much, in reality he presents a more pliable personality than the image put over by the press & she is a Doll. I am glad Sibley was in good form as the poor girl was up against the top rankers which Mr Wilson had seen in Russia. He is the first politician who has seen a ballet & remembered anything about it after. I hope Jack becomes Minister of Fine Arts. I want to be Minister of Works & stop London being turned into Tokyo & get my garden done for nothing. Love & thanks.

Freddie

When Roy Jenkins proposed Jack for a peerage, Wilson asked only one question: 'Will he work?'

When Jack replied in the affirmative, it was more than ever necessary for us to have a bedroom in London. The Walstons had changed their flat in Albany and there was no room in the new one for Jack and me. Ian Fleming had died in 1964, and Ann asked us to stay with her at her house in Victoria Square. We had the two rooms and a bathroom on the top floor which had belonged to Ian. Ann said to me that she hoped Jack would bring people back to Victoria Square at any time.

'Oh, no,' I said, shocked. 'He wouldn't do that.'

And she replied: 'But I would like him to. I like to have people in the house.'

She entertained a great deal in the evenings. We seldom went to these parties because we were either at the opera (Covent Garden or Sadler's Wells) or at home at Kingsbridge. I now remember only two things about the entertaining at Victoria Square. One was that Jack met a member of the House of Lords who had been there the night before at a party for Princess Margaret.

'I felt so sorry for her,' he said, and when Jack asked why replied: 'She hasn't the faintest idea of what anyone is like. When she came into the room we all changed.'

I know exactly what he meant. Some years after this I had to destroy a photograph of myself talking to Her Royal Highness at some function and grimacing horribly in an over-extended effort to please.

The other thing I remember is sitting next to Hugh Gaitskell at luncheon in Victoria Square in 1962. This was immediately after his Labour Party conference speech against entry into the Common Market in which he had evoked 'a thousand years of British history', which had greatly surprised his closest friends and allies and so pleased the Left.

'I'm fed up with you,' I said to him – the splendid thing about Hugh being that you could make that sort of remark to him.

When he asked me why, I explained that it was on account of his speech about the Common Market.

'Oh! You needn't mind,' he said hastily. 'When I was in Paris I saw de Gaulle and he told me he would prevent our entry.'*

This was the last time I saw Hugh, although he rang up to wish us a happy Christmas from the Manor House Hospital in Hampstead. He was thought to have some kind of influenza but said that he was better and going home for Christmas. Three weeks later he was dead.

When Hugh died the most brilliant of his front bench were too young for the immediate succession, but Jack and I have always thought that if any one of three – Tony Crosland, Roy Jenkins and Denis Healey – had been backed by the other two for future leadership, the history of Britain might have been different. But this is a constantly recurring situation in British politics, where selflessness has never been in great supply. Tony and Roy had been close friends since they were together at Oxford, but politics put a strain on their relationship. Although both were intellectually brilliant, Roy was more naturally successful as a politician; while in office he and Tony had leapfrogged each other into departments of ascending importance. It was impossible for Tony to welcome Roy's appointment as Chancellor in Wilson's government in July 1967 after Callaghan resigned the office, partly because he was himself the most obvious choice, but more especially because for a week after Callaghan's resignation, at which time he was thought to be going to the back benches, Tony had reason to believe he had been chosen to succeed him. I was much in touch with Susan at this time because one of her children was ill, for which reason she feared having to move into No. 11. When it was decided that Callaghan should not go to the back benches, the only department which could be offered him was the Home Office, then occupied by Roy. Wilson later told Roy that Tony had never been considered for Chancellor and had certainly not been offered the job. All I can say is that for a week he thought he had been; and I think this episode spoilt his relationship not so much with Wilson, as logically it might have done, but with Roy.

---

* Philip Williams says that 'close advisers like Denis Healey predicted the French veto'; and in retrospect Gaitskell's widow thought that his decision had been crucially influenced by the expectation that there was no chance of Britain entering – though that outcome was still speculative when he made his speech at Conference. Philip M. Williams, *Hugh Gaitskell: A Political Biography*, Jonathan Cape (1979), p. 728.

PART IV

....

London

20

....

The Duke of Windsor

In the end, Jack and I were more or less forced out of farming by the technical advances in egg production. It was soon clear that very little stockmanship was necessary on the battery system and that, with a small amount of supervision, girls from the village could do the work. It then became merely a matter of having sufficient capital to do the thing in a really big way, and, whereas when we first went to Kingsbridge the 6,000 hens we kept seemed a perfectly reasonable unit, we realized in time that we should not be able to compete with units five, six or even ten times as large. In 1968 we had virtually completed the education of our children and we decided to retire.

We went to London with a total capital of £40,000 which, as Hugh Gaitskell had remarked, taking inflation into account should have been a great deal more, and an income of about £2,000 from the third part of a trust Freddy had left, which I shared with my two sisters. We had lived well and educated our children and we had no fears, largely because the Stock Exchange had shown a sustained rise for a number of years and we expected to do as many of our friends had done, and live on the appreciation of capital.

We bought a very pretty house in Chalcot Crescent, from where you could see Primrose Hill. We paid £14,000 for it, but it had been converted very cheaply into flats and we had to spend a further £7,000 before we could move in. We took out a mortgage for this last sum, not because we needed it but because it saved tax.

During the time this house was being got ready for us, Peggy

Willis (earlier Peggy Dunne) lent us a cottage at Radway in War-wickshire. It was at this time that we often visited the Crossmans. We spent Christmas of 1968 in Jerusalem in company with Isaiah and Aline Berlin, and we began soon after to visit the Berlins every summer at their house in the hills above Paraggi, where is the beach for Portofino. Sometimes we went by air to Genoa, but more often we motored down, spending two nights on the way there and two on the way back, and usually going on, sometimes to stay with the Blakenhams at Cannes, sometimes with Michael and Pam Berry at St Tropez.

This was all very jolly, except that we had now entered the slump of the seventies, and money invested on the Stock Exchange no longer appreciated in the way we had expected and which had been a basic essential of our financial calculations. Since we were both over sixty, it needed something of a miracle to get us out of trouble. We were lucky in experiencing not one miracle but several.

Soon after I finished *Actor Managers*, I got a letter from Robin Denniston, then working for Hodder & Stoughton, saying that he had an idea for a book which might suit me and would I go and see him. I had not been long in his room before I realized he had not really got an idea and was merely fishing. I was not surprised at this, since all publishers do it, seeming to take more trouble with authors not on their lists than with those who are. However, after Robin had suggested various silly ideas, he suddenly said: 'How about a life of the Duke of Windsor?'

I laughed at the suggestion as I had at several others, but, in some sphere which is a mixture of intellect and emotion, I recognized the subject instantly. This recognition, which I cannot define more closely, is absolutely essential to me if I am to write with any pleasure or originality. I had not the slightest idea where I would get any information about the Duke, although I was quite certain it would not be from the archivist at Windsor; but I thought that I knew more about him already than might have been learned from the pictures of the smiling Prince. At this time he was still alive, but he was old and ill, and it was clever of Robin to think of getting a book written which would be ready when he died.

When I left Hodder & Stoughton I had not agreed to do this book or even to think about it, but Robin must have been aware of my inward response, because soon after this he asked me to go and meet Ed Burlingame, the managing director of the American publishers Lippincott. They offered me an advance of £5,000, a figure which in 1970 terms seemed enormous and probably was about five or six times as much as it is today. I agreed to do the book if I could get help either from Martin Charteris, who was married to Jack's cousin and was Secretary to the Queen, or from Freda Dudley Ward – not otherwise. I knew that Martin would be a fairly hopeless bet, although, being more enterprising than most of the Queen's servants, I think he would have helped if he had been able to, on the grounds of better me than some unknown. Nor had I much real hope of Freda, who had a reputation for secrecy on the subject.

I got nothing, or very little, from Martin, but Freda, after a lifetime's discretion, decided to tell me at least as much as she wanted known – enough to persuade me to agree to the book. When people asked her why she decided to talk to me, she replied, 'I've known her since she was a child'; an insufficient reason in my opinion since she had known me so little, although she knew Jack quite well because he was a friend of her elder daughter Pempie (Penelope). But I suppose she decided that at the end of her life she would like something of her own story told. This stayed well within limits set by her, and she was too formidable for me even to ask for the letters her daughter Angie (Angela) gave to Philip Ziegler twenty years later.

I felt that I ought to see the Windsors if possible, and I asked Biddie Monckton, widow of Walter Monckton, who acted for the King at the time of the Abdication, to persuade them. This she did when, as quite often happened, she stayed the weekend with them in Paris, and she always reported good progress. I suppose it must have been also through Biddie that I was able to see the Monckton papers. These were at that time in the offices of a firm of solicitors called Allen & Overy, and I was too ignorant even to know that this was the firm which had acted for the King at the time of his abdication. I was surprised to be told that, although I could see the papers, this had to be arranged on a day when Sir Godfrey Morley, then head of the firm, was available to see me; and even more surprised when, as I began to look at the papers put out for me, Sir Godfrey came into the room and sat down to talk. He questioned me in some detail about what I was doing, and, although I did not understand his interest, I saw no reason not to answer him. At the end of about twenty minutes he said:

'You see, I am interested because I also act for the Duke of Windsor.'

To which I replied, 'Well, you might have said so about twenty minutes ago.' And we both laughed.

However, although I had by now collected a certain amount of information, all was not plain sailing because I soon heard that James Pope-Hennessy, not merely well-known for his excellent biography of Queen Mary but a friend of the Windsors, intended to write a biography of the Duke which would be authorized by them. It is an indication of my interest in the subject that, although I refused to sign a contract and said that if James was doing it I would not, I continued to study the available material.

Then one day, when I went into our house in Chalcot Crescent, Jack told me that Sir Godfrey Morley had telephoned and said that the Duke of Windsor wanted to see me and, if I would say when it would be convenient for me to go to Paris, he would make the necessary arrangements.

'There's something wrong about that,' I said to Jack. 'It's me who wants to see the Duke of Windsor, not him me. I shall go and see Sir Godfrey Morley to find out what it's all about.'

I was given an appointment almost immediately and when I got there Sir Godfrey explained to me that the Windsors had called off the biography with James Pope-Hennessy – I never knew quite why. One version was that they had decided he would be too much of a nuisance in the house, since he drank a lot and had odd friends; another that, when it came to the question of the carve-up between the writer and the sources of his information, his agent, had been to see the Windsors and had opened her mouth too wide for this exceptionally mean couple.

Sir Godfrey Morley gave me the first of these two versions and then he said: 'So I suggested to the Windsors that, as you were writing a biography in any case, you might as well take James's place with them.'

'I don't think you understand what I am doing,' I replied. 'The Windsors have had their say in two books and I am trying to write an objective account.'

'What is the difference?' he asked.

And I replied: 'Well, I wouldn't give them a veto.'

I needed to say no more and I went away a little crestfallen, not merely because of the opportunity for an exciting life I had just turned down, but also because, having refused to work with the Windsors, I could hardly ask to see them. But I told Isaiah Berlin what had happened and he said: 'Quite right. You don't want to see the Windsors. Write it as history.'

I think this was very good advice and afterwards I was glad I did not see them. If I have even a cup of tea with people, I find myself faced with a breach of trust, either to them or to readers.

With James Pope-Hennessy out of the way I went to see Tony Godwin, who was then editorial director of Weidenfeld, and told him I wanted to do a book with Hodder & Stoughton. He replied that this was quite all right, they never minded an author leaving for one book, and he did not ask me what the book was. Pam Berry did, however, and when she told George Weidenfeld, in the words of Ann Fleming, 'he got it in one'. He was almost alone in this, however. The Windsors had been forgotten in England except by a few old women to whom the Prince had been polite as a young man. The only people who knew anything about them were those who actually met them in Paris, and they regarded them as a sad and shoddy little couple. Tortor Gilmour begged me not to do the book on the grounds there was nothing worth saying, and Noel Blakiston, at that time running the Public Record Office, made no attempt to hide his contempt for the idea. And in case this is taken for a minority upper-class view, I must add that we were staying with Frank and Kitty Giles the weekend the Duke of Windsor died, and I told Frank I had written the first half of the book, reaching the point where the Prince became King but not dealing with the Abdication. He said at once that he would show it to the people who chose the books for serialization at the *Sunday Times*. They refused even to read it on the grounds that 'the Windsors are really not our style'. The *Sunday Telegraph* bought it and sold every copy, not merely all over England but in most of the cities of western Europe. The enormous public feeling for royalty of any kind was not completely appreciated then as it is today, and there began an interest in the affairs of this couple which has scarcely been satiated by about a dozen books.

I was immediately lucky in my sources, some of whom I still cannot reveal. The only failure I had was one I expected. We had met Tommy (Sir Alan) Lascelles often in Gloucestershire when we dined with Eny Strutt. I knew that he had been Private Secretary to the Prince of Wales but had left his service after a number of years, on the grounds that he could stand no more ; also that having been appointed Assistant Private Secretary to George V, he had rather surprisingly – in view of his earlier resignation – remained in this capacity when Edward VIII succeeded.

Although all these sad things were long past, I did not want to try to see him when I started to write *Edward VIII* because I was sure he would refuse me. However, people kept on asking 'Have you seen Tommy ?' and finally I thought I had better get it over. I wrote telling him what I was doing and asking in very modest terms whether he 'would at least put me right on points where my views were wrong or where my opinions might be regarded as biased'. Here is his reply:

Dear Frankie,

I pay you the compliment of sending a non-circumlocutory answer to yr letter. It is No.

Throughout the past half century, I've wasted so much time, energy and ink on the subject under review that I cannot, in my few remaining years, waste more. Let me say, as an ex-Archivist, that those who succeeded me are entirely right in refusing access to the papers in question. If they did not do so, they would be guilty of a gross breach of trust to me and to others, living and dead.

Since you've asked my view of yr project, here are two points which I make in all sincerity: (i) if you have not known this particular subject *personally* and at least 80 per cent well, you will never paint a worth-while portrait. (ii) when you speak of a 'fantastically contradictory character' you are starting from the fundamentally false premise from which have started so many would-be biographers. The character in question is neither fantastic nor contradictory; it is essentially simple and wholly consistent.

> Yours ever,
> Tommy

I took mild offence at this: not because Tommy refused help – this had been predictable – but because of the remarks concerning the archivists, about whom I had said only that I could not expect their help. I therefore wrote as follows:

17.4.71

Dear Tommy

Thank you so much for your letter, which was not unexpected. I have never questioned the correctness of the actions of the Royal Archivists, and I meant only to refer to them as one of the factors in the case.

> Yours,
> Frankie

However, I did not forget, and when I came to write the book I took a good deal of trouble to annoy. In a chapter called 'No Doubt of the Young Man's Capacity For Goodness', I quoted from Keith Middlemas and John Barnes's *Baldwin* a letter from one of the Prince of Wales's Household which contained that phrase. To this I added the footnote: 'This writer remains anonymous but the magisterial tone suggests Captain Lascelles.' In fact, I had been told that in the library at Cambridge there was a letter addressed to Baldwin which contained these words and which was signed Lascelles. But I had been refused permission to see Baldwin's abdication papers without permission from the Royal Archivists, and this was not obtainable.

After my book appeared, Tommy made handsome amends, as follows:

Dear Frankie

On 16/4/71, I wrote to tell you that I couldn't fall in with yr kind suggestion that I might give you some help with yr projected life of Edward VIII.

My letter was, I think, quite civil, & wholly sincere. If I had to write it again, I wouldn't alter a word of it.

But what I must do now is tell you how very glad I am that the book has had such a triumphant success. I see few people nowadays, but, of those I bump into, one and all have said what a good, fair book it is, and what a valuable contribution it is going to be to the future history of our troubled age. It is a model for all biographers.

I quarrel with none of it, save the note at the foot on p. 134. I don't think I've ever earned the adjective 'magisterial'. Rather the contrary. Ld Stamfordham [illegible] once told me that K.G.V. had said to him: 'That man Lascelles puts jokes into my son's speeches. Nobody ever put jokes in my speeches.' And, incidentally, I shd. never have used the words quoted about the Prince – never, though I may often have felt their less pompous equivalents. I certainly never wrote in that sense to S.B., though I did once extract from him a *verbal* promise to try & make HRH act more rationally.

    Yrs ever,
      A. Lascelles

The only other person I can remember refusing to give me any information was Colin Buist, a friend of the Duke of Windsor since his early days. Georgia Sitwell took me to lunch with him and was more embarrassed than I was by his rather surly attitude.

Mrs Humphrey Butler was a relic of the 1920s, born into an aristocratic family and married to an equerry of Prince George, the Duke of Kent. I had been told by a friend of hers that she would see me. However, she telephoned and in a very crisp 1920s voice asked:

'Lady Donaldson, what is the purpose of this book?'

Without thought, I replied: 'Oh! I don't know, to make some money, I suppose.'

She melted immediately. 'Ah!' she said. 'Of course you have to have some money.'

And I sealed an already budding friendship when, in answer to some clipped comments, I said: 'Well, if you are simply going to lecture me, there is no point in my coming to see you.'

She repeated this remark immediately on the telephone to Freda Dudley Ward and several times to me.

Mrs Butler, known to her friends as 'Poots', had been on the famous cruise on the *Nahlin* and it was she who gave me the information that after some time the King's mood spoiled the tour: 'No lip-service to courtesy disturbed his melancholy, no concern for his guests diminished an unremitting fit of the sulks. . . .'

After she had told me this, Mrs Butler spoke of the occasion when the conversation turned to the relationship of King George of Greece and the woman who was his mistress.

'Why doesn't he marry her?' Mrs Simpson asked.

It was Mrs Butler herself who replied in tones of astonishment that it was impossible for the King to marry a woman who was a commoner and already married.

'I don't think that it could have been that which upset the King,' she said. But it was clear to me that she did think so and also that nearly forty years later this thought still disturbed her. She said that the difficulty had been that Wallis was unable to understand that a divorced woman could not be Queen.

'It's a fairly simple proposition,' I said, but she insisted. She also said that Mrs Simpson had no idea of the limits of the King's power, and to illustrate this she told me that one day Wallis had been reading a comment in a British newspaper which was critical of the King.

'The fools,' she said as she threw it down. 'They'll lose him if they go on like that.'

Best of all the unexpected sources was Baba (Lady Alexandra) Metcalfe. When she came to lunch with me in answer to my request for help, she brought with her a briefcase.

'These are Fruity's letters to me written from Paris during the war,' she said.

Fruity Metcalfe had been hand-picked by the Prince of Wales when he met him in India, and was taken home on his staff. He was thought unsuitable by George V but he joined the Duke of Windsor when he went to Paris to join the British Military Mission at the beginning of the war, and the letters were written at that time. Most people liked Fruity, but no one would have expected him to be adept with the pen. Yet, reading his letters that night on the sofa in the sitting room in Chalcot Crescent was one of the most exciting moments of my writing career. I had never had the slightest idea how I was going to deal with the period after the Abdication, when, presumably, sources would be less plentiful, but here was the answer to a large part of it, not merely cut and dried, but written by a man with an unexpected talent for lively description.

Lord Mountbatten told me directly everything in my book which appears to come from him, and he also gave me Sir Etienne Dupuch. Dupuch, a native of the Bahamas then staying at the Savoy Hotel, consented to see me at Mountbatten's request if I came armed with a list of questions written down. He had been knighted in recognition of his services to the Bahama Islands and to the War Materials Committee during the Second World War. The proprietor and editor of the Bahama *Tribune*, he was half-French, half-black. When I saw him he told me that before he answered any questions I should understand that he did not like the Duke. This was only partly due to the Abdication ; he had first taken against him years before when, as Prince of Wales, he had made some remarks which had offended Dupuch and which would today earn the term 'racist'. He could not forgive him because, as Governor of an island in which so large a part of the population was of mixed race, he 'invariably and openly assumed the natural superiority of the whites'. And Dupuch accused him of being largely responsible for the riots which took place during the Duke's period in the Bahamas, because, in the building of airfields for the Americans, he refused to appoint as liaison officer a man not only competent to do the job but known to the workers, on the grounds that he was black. After I met Sir Etienne Dupuch, in an attempt to supplement what he had told me, I read a history of the Bahamas. However, it soon became apparent that the authority for the account of the Duke of Windsor's governorship in this book was the same as my own – Dupuch.

He was at that time the chief witness to the Duke's views on colour, but Lord Mountbatten told me that, after visiting the Bahamas, he had asked the Duke whether it was true that as Governor he would not permit black or coloured men to enter through his front door. To this Windsor had replied that he had regarded it as important to successful administration that coloured people should be kept in their right place when visiting Government House.

The statements of both men have recently been entirely cor-
roborated by the release of papers under the Thirty Years Rule,
which show that in 1941 the Secretary of State, Lord Moyne,
circularized colonial governors urging them to broaden the nature
of executive councils and in future to select for appointments to the
Executive Council from various sections of the community and said:
'I trust that no one, otherwise reasonably suitable, will be excluded
from consideration because of social or racial reasons.'

To this the Duke replied that any suggestion of the sort would be
most unwelcome in Nassau and went on to say:

> Were the coloured element to be introduced, the social colour
> bar would automatically be lifted. The coloured member of the
> Executive and his wife would have to be invited to Government
> House on official occasions and it would undoubtedly follow that
> the coloured members of the Legislative Council and the House
> of Assembly would eventually expect to be invited with their
> wives to Government House as well.

Even so, I feel my account of the Windsors was unduly harsh in
the chapter devoted to their period in the Bahamas. It can be relied
upon for the facts given, but, having read both Michael Bloch and
Ziegler, I think that, if not one-sided, it is at the least unsympathetic.
Philip Ziegler, who visited the islands recently, says there are still
those who remember both the Duke and Duchess with affection
and speak of them as having worked hard, the Duchess in the local
Red Cross and war charities. I wrote that travelling Englishmen
brought home reports that they were doing well; in particular that
Sir John Balfour had told me that Brigadier Daly, who visited Nassau
as Inspector for the War Office, said that he found the Duke of
Windsor to be the most capable of the various colonial governors
he visited. But I was perhaps too much affected by the fact that the
Windsors were known to have hated the Bahamas and also by their
immediate and extravagant expenditure on Government House. It
is Michael Bloch's account of the conditions and climate in the
Bahamas and also of the state of Government House when the
Windsors arrived there which, provoking my sympathy, has
inspired this attempt at partially correcting, not the facts, but the
impact of my own account.

However, they made mistakes and, with their peculiar mixture
of vanity and bad judgement, some important ones. Thus when Sir
Harry Oakes, a Canadian millionaire, friend of the Windsors and
the Bahamas' richest resident, was murdered, instead of leaving the

matter to the local police or calling in Scotland Yard, the Duke engaged an American private detective because he knew him personally, who, on cross-examination by the defence lawyer, proved to have faked the evidence which had put Oakes's son-in-law on trial for his life. As a result, the real murderer has never been found.

Some time during the period when I was writing this book, Robin Denniston left Hodder & Stoughton and went to Weidenfeld. As I knew no one else at Hodder and Weidenfeld had published my last two books, I asked and received permission to follow him there. This was agreed and so Weidenfeld published the book after all.

Lippincott published *Edward VIII* in America and Ed Burlingame, then managing director, lured me into a publicity trip of about ten days through many of the towns in America. During this time I was interviewed on the wireless or television several times every day. I remember clearly only two things. The first was landing at New York, and, on reaching the last of the compartments where various matters concerning arriving travellers were dealt with, I noticed people standing outside clearly awaiting someone. Among these was a girl whose face I unusually and immediately took a liking to, and I wished that she was there to meet me. This in fact was Dianitia Hutchison, who accompanied me throughout my trip and with whom I fell immediately into terms of considerable intimacy. The other was being interviewed at 6 a.m. one morning by Barbara Walters, famous throughout America and usually rather tough. I was inclined to ascribe the fact that she let me down very lightly to my answering 'Yes' to the question whether I knew Antonia Fraser. On the train to Philadelphia that morning I was recognized instantly as having been on the Walters' programme.

21

....

The Duchess of Windsor

My book on the Duke of Windsor was written twenty years ago but the interest in the Windsors has produced a great many others, the last of which, Philip Ziegler's excellent official history, sanctioned by the Queen, must take precedence over all others. In his introduction Ziegler says: 'Before I embarked on this book it was my conviction that every biographer must owe *something* to those who had worked in the field before him. My study of certain recent books dealing with the Duke and Duchess has disabused me of this.'* And it is true that most of the books about this couple have been romantic or scurrilous, quite untrustworthy and largely invented. Ziegler goes on to say that his source notes will reveal how much he owes to other writers, but two must be specially mentioned – myself and Michael Bloch.†

No one writing about the Duke and Duchess of Windsor can ignore Michael Bloch's five books, published between 1982 and 1990, since he has been given freedom of the Windsors' papers by their French lawyer, Maître Blum. However, Michael Bloch has accused me in print not merely of having 'a down' on the Duke of Windsor, but of being 'determined to award him low marks'. This is offensive and presumably meant to be, while it directly impugns my integrity as a biographer. My book was reviewed extensively here and in America and no one else has ever made this accusation.

* Philip Ziegler, *King Edward VIII*, Collins (1990).
† Michael Bloch, *The Reign & Abdication of Edward VIII*, Bantam Press (1990).

The Duchess of Windsor

Mr Bloch has never attempted to disguise the fact that his own books are devoted to special pleading on behalf of the Duke of Windsor, or disputed the idea that it was for this purpose he was given the Windsor papers. In fact we owe him a debt for presenting their side of the case so that one can understand the unhappiness and bitterness which inspired their actions, but he writes as an advocate and has never pretended to the objectivity of the uncommitted observer. Nevertheless, if he can persuade the reading public that the only book beside his own which Philip Ziegler thought worth mentioning was written by someone with 'a down' on the Duke of Windsor, he obviously adds plausibility to his own account.

In fact I have disagreed with him on many points, but only one need be brought up here. It is important because my book contains a very serious charge against the Duke, one which has caused many people to tell me that it was the thing which finally turned them against him. This was his treatment of Fruity Metcalfe when, in May 1940, the Duke left Paris to join his wife in Biarritz. It is necessary therefore that I should restate it to be true or that I should withdraw it.

Metcalfe had accompanied the Duke to Paris expecting to be formally accepted as his equerry. Only on arrival had he discovered that this was not so – that he was to be neither attached to the British Mission nor paid by the Duke of Windsor. He nevertheless remained with him until the end. I describe how every evening after the real war had begun and the Duchess gone to Biarritz, the Duke and Metcalfe, still in Paris, would make plans for the next day:

> One evening towards the end of May the two parted in the evening without any precise plan. 'Goodnight, Sir,' Metcalfe said, 'see you tomorrow.' The following morning at 8.30 he telephoned to the Boulevard Suchet and was answered by a servant. He asked to be put through to His Royal Highness and he received the reply 'His Royal Highness left for Biarritz at 6.30 this morning.' Metcalfe, who was on nobody's pay roll, attached to no military mission, who had served the Duke all these months as an unpaid and unacknowledged aide, slowly took in the news that he had been left without a word to find his way back to England as best he could.*

Bloch does not refer to this account in any way, but he throws doubt on it with the publication of a letter written by the Duke of

---

* Donaldson, *Edward VIII*, Weidenfeld & Nicolson (1974), p. 357.

Windsor on 4 June 1940 to Major Gray Phillips which caused Philip Ziegler to think that there had been 'a total breakdown of communication between the two men', for which all the blame was not necessarily on one side. In this letter the Duke says: 'I have heard from Fruity that he is returning to England which is by far the best thing he could do, only I do think that he should first of all have submitted his intention for my approval and not left without my permission. However, it is a typical Fruity gesture and one would not expect him to behave otherwise.' Michael Bloch has added a footnote to this letter as follows: 'Metcalfe appears to have quarrelled with the Duke in Paris and parted from him there. Afterwards, each of them seems to have regarded himself as abandoned by the other.'

Yet both Michael Bloch and Philip Ziegler overlook the fact that the Duke's letter to Major Phillips was written from Biarritz, making it certain that Fruity left Paris only after the Duke had gone. Moreover the sentences quoted by Bloch occur in a letter in which the Duke has previously written:

> Those days of inactivity in Paris were intolerable, and exposed more definitely than ever the fact that the futile role I played at the Mission died a natural death with the German offensive. It is not in my make-up to sit in Paris without a job when I should be with the Duchess who, in view of the uncertainty of Italy's attitude towards the war, I cannot and will not leave here quite alone.*

These remarks do not make the whole of Fruity's version true, but they do make it difficult to believe that it was Fruity who abandoned the Duke or that he had no reason to feel abandoned himself. Indeed, it seems to me certain that he was left 'on nobody's pay roll, attached to no military mission' to look after himself as best he could.

However, if, as I have said, I did not have 'a down' on the Duke of Windsor, I soon acquired one on the Duchess. Since Michael Bloch may one day come across these words, I must add that for that very reason, as far as possible, I wrote of the Duchess only in her relationship to the Duke, and in as much as she affected his public life. Thus it was assumed by some reviewers that I did not know of her sensational friendship with the Woolworth heir. On the contrary, since this occured after Windsor had retired from

---

* Michael Bloch, *The Secret File of the Duke of Windsor*, Bantam Press (1988), p. 155.

public life, I had thought it of purely personal rather than historical importance.

In an effort to explain an event so unlikely as to be unknown in previous history, it was much put about after the Abdication that the hold of the Duchess of Windsor upon the Duke was a purely sexual one – that he was previously incompetent and that Wallis was the first woman to overcome his difficulties. Several writers have gone further and suggested that she was able to do this because of sexual tricks she learned in a Chinese brothel. As far as I know no one has been able to produce any evidence for this, although recently several writers have referred to a document they call the Chinese Report, allegedly produced by the security services on the orders of Stanley Baldwin on behalf of King George V. It is difficult to take this report very seriously, since none of the authorities who might be expected to have asked for it or received it has left any record of it.* I must also make the point here that if the Duchess had with her husband visited a brothel in China as a *voyeur* (which is what is alleged) it would not have been so very much out of the way, since at that date this was a fashionable exploit for English-women in Paris.

While I was writing my book I asked the late Peter Scott (the psychologist known to the public as the adviser to the police on psychological warfare against men holding hostages) whether it was plausible to believe that the clue to the Duke's actions was that, having as a child been to all intents and purposes rejected by Queen Mary, he had spent the rest of his life in search of a mother figure. This theory to explain the Duke's character and the Windsor marriage has since been put forward by other writers, including Michael Bloch, who has had access to so many papers and who writes: 'Throughout his first forty years he sought in a succession of amours with older married women an ideal mother figure; and this he found in Wallis.'†

In fact for sixteen years he had relied on Freda Dudley Ward to fulfil this role, and she might have held him forever if her desire to dominate had been as strong as her successor's. The question I asked Peter Scott arose in my mind because when I asked Freda whether she had at any time been in love with the Prince of Wales, she replied: 'Oh! no. You couldn't be. He was too slavish.'

---

* Since these words were written Philip Ziegler has denied the existence of this report.
† Michael Bloch, *Wallis and Edward, Letters 1931–1937: The Intimate Correspondence of the Duke and Duchess of Windsor*, Weidenfeld & Nicolson (1986), p. 110.

Peter Scott replied that the suggestion was perfectly plausible, but for the Prince to achieve satisfaction, he would have to find a woman with a complementary experience in childhood: domination, perhaps, by an unpredictable and bullying father. The Duchess of Windsor's father had died when she was young, but her Uncle Sol, who held the purse strings and doled out money irregularly – placing different sums to her mother's account every month – substituted admirably in this role.

> For a long and impressionable period, he was the nearest thing to a father in my uncertain world, but an odd kind of father – reserved, unbending, silent. Uncle Sol was destined to return again and again to my life – or more accurately it was my fate to be obliged to turn again and again to him, usually at some point of new crisis for me and one seldom to his liking. I was always a little afraid of Uncle Sol.*

There were reasons other than Uncle Sol and the general poverty of her childhood which might have made Wallis Warfield assertive. When I was writing *Edward VIII*, it was arranged for me to go to Baltimore to meet some ladies who had been at school with her. They were all in their seventies, and we met for luncheon in their club. It was an unusual occasion because Jack, who was travelling with me, insisted on coming to the luncheon. There were six or seven of our hostesses (I have forgotten the exact number) and earlier we had met another of Wallis's contemporaries in New Jersey. None of them would admit to having liked her, although they had kept on terms with her because she was a magnetic attraction to the boys. Wallis was described by these Baltimore ladies as rather fast; and she was isolated in her youth by the circumstances of her mother's second marriage to a Mr Raisin. This took place not quite in time, since he had been known to be her lover for some while before the marriage; worse still, he drank.

In any case, for whatever reason, Wallis grew up with a strong desire to dominate, while the evidence of the Duke's willing subjection to her is extremely convincing and spoken of in all the books of those who knew them personally. One is bound therefore to question her disclaimers of influence on the King at the time of the Abdication, as in all other important matters.

I first acquired a dislike and mistrust of the Duchess through reading her book *The Heart has its Reasons*, and this was not only

---

* Duchess of Windsor, *The Heart has its Reasons*, Michael Joseph (1956), p. 21.

for her style and her jokes, although both are unfortunate, but for her pretentiousness over class. There is no doubt at all that the families of her father and mother – the Warfields and the Montagues – were two of the leading families of Baltimore. Alistair Forbes has said that she came from a far higher stratum in society than 'say, Princess Grace of Monaco, Jacqueline Bouvier or the Jerome or Vanderbilt ladies of the nineteenth century. By present English standards she might rank rather below two recent royal duchesses and rather above two others.' (These words were written in 1972, before the advent of the most recent royal duchesses.) I cannot quarrel with what Ali says because he knows much more than I do about this kind of thing, but I should have thought the Warfields and the Montagues could better be compared to those English country squires and younger sons who, although not the peerage, are the next in rank – the gentry.

Yet the Duchess writes of them in the kind of pretentious terms usually employed only by the insecure. Here, for instance, are some passages – which have received less attention than they deserve – about her family's reception of the news that she proposed to divorce her first husband. Her Aunt Bessie, a stalwart character who has passed into history, is said to have greeted it with the exclamation 'It's unthinkable', and the Duchess writes as follows:

> Aunt Bessie said much more. I had been too young to know what I was doing when I got married, and I was still too young to appreciate what a divorce meant. ... As a divorced woman I would be entering a wilderness – the shelter, support and companionship of marriage would all be behind me; and as a woman who had already failed as a wife, I could hardly hope to achieve these things again. ... Suddenly Aunt Bessie stopped. At last she said, in a tone of absolute finality, 'The Montague women do not get divorced.'

Aunt Bessie then sent her niece to see her Uncle Sol. In a long conversation he 'reserved his emotion for the disclosure of my intention to profane the family traditions'.

'I won't let you bring this disgrace upon us!' he announced. 'The Warfields ... in all their known connections since 1662, have never had a divorce. What will the people of Baltimore think?'*

From a woman who, two divorces later, believed she could marry the King of England; who believed, if only for a short time, that she

---

* Duchess of Windsor, *The Heart has its Reasons*, pp. 89–91.

might be Queen and certainly that she could become the King's morganatic wife with appropriate titles and position ; this is surely a bit rich.

Yet in spite of all this claptrap, when I was writing *Edward VIII* I believed that the Duchess of Windsor was at her best and most attractive during the early years of her marriage to Ernest Simpson. He was kind and well-off, had an interest in architecture which took them at weekends to country hotels and the cathedrals and castles of England, and had a knowledge of antique furniture which gave them a shared happiness in furnishing a flat. The Duchess seemed to me in those years to be glad to have at last reached harbour, to have no startling ambitions, and to find sufficient exercise for an inborn perfectionism in shopping for food and some quite unadventurous entertaining. I thought her sights were not set inordinately high, and that, but for the accident of meeting Lady Furness and through her the Prince of Wales, she might have been content with her second husband for the rest of her life.

'The Duchess of Windsor', I once wrote, 'may be said to have had greatness thrust upon her.'

Yet recently her letters to her Aunt Bessie have rather surprisingly been made available to us in two books edited by Michael Bloch. Reading them, I realize that I believed exactly what she intended me to believe. After her mother died Mrs Simpson wrote regularly to her aunt, and, except on rare occasions, quite openly. What strikes one immediately is how different her life was when she arrived in London from the account she gives in *The Heart has its Reasons*.

First, and most important, the Simpsons were not only not well-off, they were at times frighteningly insecure, and soon after their marriage unable to sustain the level of new clothes, servants and entertaining which were so important in Wallis's life. Then Ernest Simpson's father, who in the Duchess's memoirs is shown as both rich and generous, in the letters is shown to be uninterruptedly mean.

In 1931 Wallis wrote to Aunt Bessie as follows :

Everything everywhere seems to get worse and worse and you can't help but be depressed by it all. We have nothing but a series of unpleasant business or family news – and much cutting down in office staff and closing of branch offices. Mr Simpson is in a panic and so disagreeable. He would not give a penny as I wrote you. He chopped £3,000 off the loan he agreed to make to E and as you remember last year he didn't give us an Xmas cheque so you can see he would let us rot here before helping us home. We appreciate all your generosity but really can't move away from all our debts – they need nursing! I got the food bills down £15 last month – but of course we hardly ever entertain which I miss as I think it's so true that people forget you or don't ask you as much if they don't think you can return the cutlet.*

This theme is repeated again and again. The picture of an unambitious but satisfactory life from which Wallis was persuaded only through exceptional chance, although carefully cultivated in her book, is absolutely untrue. There are sixty or seventy pages of letters to Aunt Bessie between 1931 and 1937, and in all these thousands of words it would be difficult to find one reference to the great events of the day, to politics, to any book, music or play (beyond the bare statement 'went to the theatre'), or, until she meets the Prince, to anything except the lists of those she has entertained or been entertained by, requests for clothes to be bought by Aunt Bessie and sent to England, servant troubles, complaints about her father-in-law and so on.

Almost all writers on the Windsors have attempted to give an explanation of why the Royal Family, in particular the Duchess of York (now the Queen Mother), disliked Mrs Simpson. There is a theory that she in some way annoyed or insulted the Duchess when she stayed at Balmoral in 1936. This may or may not be true, yet the point surely is that no explanation is necessary for the fact that the royal family, with their enormous sense of dedication, their almost religious belief in the consecration of the crowning ceremony, and their upper-class attitude to life, could possibly have liked this wisecracking, purely pleasure-loving, twice-divorced woman.

However, the Duchess of Windsor cannot be entirely blamed for her part in the Abdication, because she was so tremendously misled first of all by the King himself, but also by Lord Beaverbrook and Duff Cooper. Lord Beaverbrook probably merely enjoyed a little mischief-making, but Duff Cooper urged delay. He said afterwards that he had thought that, if the whole thing could be shelved until after the Coronation, the King might well have grown out of his obsession. At the same time Winston Churchill urged the King to fight for the morganatic marriage proposal, by which Wallis could

* Michael Bloch, *Wallis & Edward, Letters 1931–1937*, p. 45.

marry the King without becoming Queen, but with appropriate
titles and status. In spite of what Poots Butler thought, it seems
probable that Mrs Simpson did not for long entertain any idea
that she might be Queen, but she was very much taken with the
possibility of a morganatic marriage, as well she might have been
on the combination of advice given by Duff Cooper and Winston
Churchill. The publication of the letters between her future husband
and herself makes it fairly clear that what they argued about so
painfully after their marriage (see *The Heart has its Reasons*, pp.
229–30) was her belief that if the King had gone through with the
Coronation and after several months shown himself determined to
marry her, his position would have been so strong that he would
not have been forced to abdicate. On Sunday, 6 December 1936,
she wrote to him from the Herman Rogers villa, Lou Viei, in Cannes,
where she had gone on leaving England, a letter which Michael
Bloch says is barely coherent and evidence of the exhaustion and
despair in which it was composed. The letter is incoherent, but I do
not find it either obscure or highly creditable. In it she asks the King
to stay until the autumn (that is, until after the Coronation) and
then (apparently) reopen the question of marriage :

> My idea [presumably the morganatic marriage] might go in Oct
> so it would appeal to the world. We would have made a gesture
> which is sporting fair. If B[aldwin] turns it down in Oct – there
> would be an uproar. No one but Baldwin and the dominions
> want you to go and as the Aga Khan telephoned they haven't
> given you a fighting. The people in the press are clamoring for a
> word from you. You owe it to them to tell them something and
> if you made that gesture by radio – by October Mr B couldn't
> afford to say no and I think the Dominions could be won over.*

Michael Bloch accompanies this letter with one to Lady Colefax
in which Mrs Simpson writes : 'If only they had said, let's drop the
idea now and in the autumn we'll discuss it again. And Sybil darling
in the autumn I would have been so very far away.'†

In deciding whether Mrs Simpson was lying to the King or to
Lady Colefax, one has to take into account that she had previously
lied to Lady Colefax about the King's intention to marry her, as she
had to her friends the Hunters. In the light of her predicament,
these lies were probably necessary, but I think it extremely naive
that we should be expected to believe them now. No one who was

---

* Bloch, *Wallis & Edward, Letters 1931–1937*, p. 220.
† *Ibid*, p. 223.

involved with the King at the time believed that any of Mrs Simpson's publicly proclaimed intentions could be taken seriously, except when at the very end her lawyer, Theodore Goddard, issued a statement saying she was willing to instruct him to withdraw her divorce petition, by which time it was clearly too late.*

However, what I think so unattractive about Mrs Simpson's letters in the series published by Michael Bloch is not the twisting and turning, which is at least understandable, but the fact that in the whole correspondence there is hardly to be found one word of regret for the dereliction of duty, or sorrow for all those who loved and trusted the King, or even any appreciation or sympathy for the sacrifices which he made for her. In the letter of 6 December in which she outlines her plan for delay she begins by saying: 'I am so anxious for you not to *abdicate* and I think the fact that you do is going to put me in the wrong light to the entire world because they will say that I could have prevented it.'†

Letter after letter concentrates on this theme and on her belief that Baldwin was an enemy who had quite unnecessarily created bad will both in the country and with the new King. At times one cannot help feeling sorry for her, since her expectations are so great and her understanding so small. Thus the following excerpts from her letters.

Late December 1936:

I am getting rather worked up about what support we are going to get from your family for our wedding. It is so important – everyone around me realizes the importance of it re announcement etc. After all we have done nothing wrong so why be treated that way.‡

And in an undated letter early in 1937:

What have I done to deserve this treatment? I have never had a word said in my defence or a kind word in the press. Surely your brother can protect me a bit – not to be the butt of musical

---

* According to both Walter Monckton and Sir Edward Peacock, who were at Fort Belvedere at the time, the King was actually a party to the statement she made under Lord Brownlow's influence when she first arrived in Cannes. 'He was most anxious', Monckton wrote, 'that Mrs Simpson's position should be improved in the eyes of the public, and it was with his full approval that she made her statement on Tuesday, 8 December, from Cannes that she was willing to give up a position that was both unhappy and untenable. This was published, was looked upon as being perhaps the end of the crisis, but we at the Fort knew of the statement before its publication, and that his intention was quite unchanged.' (Monckton Papers.)
† Bloch, *Wallis & Edward, Letters 1931–1937*, p. 219.
‡ *Ibid.*, p. 238.

comedy jokes on the radio etc. If they knew your family approved
our wedding when free, things would be so different for me. . . .
It has been such a lone game against the world for me and a
woman always pays the most.

And then to the poor wretch who had given up so much for her:
'And you my sweet haven't been able to protect me.'*

* Bloch, *Wallis & Edward, Letters 1931–1937*, p. 263.

22

....

Royal Highness

Probably all biographers and historians distort history at times but, with some exceptions, the writers least to be relied upon are the diarists. To record the events of the day in a manner casual enough to suggest a private record but easy and attractive to read is a separate gift, and one not necessarily given to even the most talented writers of prose. Yet it does not guarantee truth, objectivity or even opportunity. The two writers most quoted on the Abdication are Chips Channon and Harold Nicolson – both diarists. Yet no one who knew Channon during his lifetime would have paid much attention to anything he had to say on public matters. Indeed, the only person I know who belonged to the social and political world of his day told me that if I believed the opposite of everything he wrote I would get nearer the truth than if I believed him. He was a diarist of talent, yet lightweight and rather malicious and he thought, as Mrs Simpson did, that anyone with a mind more serious than his own was a bore. (He speaks, for instance, of 'that gloomy Oliver Stanley – "Snow White" as we all call him'. As I have shown earlier, Oliver was admired not only for his exceptional gifts and character, but also for his wit.)

Harold Nicolson was rather a different matter. He was not spiteful and he had both greater intellectual understanding and a more sensitive taste. Above all, he was a close friend of Sir Alan Lascelles, Assistant Secretary to George V.

A second difficulty for writers of the present day is that all biographers have a natural tendency to exaggerate the importance of their subject, and in the case of the Abdication they are writing about people – Baldwin and the Royal Family themselves – who were directly concerned with it and who did take it extremely seriously. As someone who lived through it, I am not sure that anyone else did. Yet Michael Bloch writes:

> The Abdication aroused passionately strong feelings among the ex-King's subjects. It is not unfair to say that *nothing in the last hundred or more years has caused so much controversy among British people – and the controversy rages to this day* [my italics]. At the time, reactions differed sharply. On the whole, the working classes and thinking people of liberal views sympathized with the former sovereign and found it tragic that he should have had to leave under such circumstances, while the conservative middle classes tended to regard his decision as a dereliction of duty. *There was a widespread sense of dismay that so apparently gifted a ruler, trained so well and so long for his task, should be handing over his crown to an untrained, reluctant and embarrassed successor of far less obvious gifts* [again, my italics].*

Speaking as someone who lived through the Abdication, I can only say that I think both the italicized passages rubbish. I cannot of course speak for the working classes, although like everyone else I came in contact with a number of them. Yet if I come from what is here described as 'the thinking people of liberal views', at that time almost all my friends were Conservatives. I am sure that, whereas some of the working class sympathized with the King, particularly some of the women, and others disapproved, to many of them the Abdication was a matter of no importance at all. To myself and to most of the people I knew, it was a particularly enjoyable nine days' wonder. Jack and I were actually pleased because, thinking it absurd when the Stock Exchange fell, we bought shares and almost immediately made £100 (equivalent to about twenty times as much today). For some time at dinner parties Jack used to drink to 'the King across the water' and I remember no occasion on which anyone took exception either to the sentiment or to the obvious irreverence with which it was expressed.

Even more important, I believe it is quite untrue that there was widespread dismay that the crown should be handed over to 'an untrained, reluctant and embarrassed successor of far less obvious gifts'. As far as I can remember, we knew nothing about all this at

* Bloch, *The Secret File of the Duke of Windsor*, p. 4.

the time, and I believe it is the stuff of biographies which have been written since. The Duchess of York was extremely popular and had already exhibited a natural talent for royal jobs (it was said that she planted a tree as though she had discovered a new and delightful occupation), while the King, although handicapped by a stammer, immediately showed a good deal of authority. There is a widespread (not merely British) desire for royalty, which has not received the analysis it may deserve, but which ensures a devotion not dependent on great gifts. Also, it must be remembered that Edward VIII had even as Prince of Wales begun to show in public his boredom with the job. I myself saw him driven round the ring at an agricultural show without once looking out of the car or waving to the public.

Michael Bloch quotes both Nicolson and Channon in support of a statement that Hardinge, the King's Private Secretary, and Lascelles, Assistant Private Secretary, 'regarded the Duke of Windsor with an intense and irrational personal loathing'. And he writes: 'With the accession of the conservative George VI, who was happy to leave things as they were, the Court breathed a sigh of relief and closed ranks, determined to exclude the man who had tried to interfere with their settled ways.'* The word 'conservative' is here used in a pejorative sense, and Michael Bloch is making the suggestion, so dear to the Windsors themselves, that the courtiers disliked Edward VIII because he tried to bring the practices of the Court into the twentieth century.

If the King had wished to bring innovations into the royal role, such as our present Queen has done, the courtiers may well have resented it – who knows? The facts are that they were glad to get rid of him because he was opinionated and conceited and not up to the job. Once when I attended a luncheon given in my honour after signing copies of *Edward VIII* in a bookshop, I sat next to a man who had for many years been one of the Prince's equerries. I felt a little nervous as I asked him what he thought of my book, and I was taken by surprise when he replied: 'Well, I don't think you quite got across how awfully tiresome he was.' He then told me the following story. The Prince had to visit two regiments in one day and after the first visit it was necessary for him to change his coat and spurs before going to the second. This he for some time refused to do, finally succumbing only after much persuasion. Years later my neighbour met the Duke of Windsor, who in conversation said to him: 'Do you remember the day when I nearly sacked you after

---

* Bloch, *The Secret File of the Duke of Windsor*, p. 32.

an argument about my changing my coat?' The incident was not very serious by itself, but if, as I think, it was given as an illustration, one can understand the feeling that looking after a spoiled boy is not a job for a grown man.

The King's staff complained of his unpunctuality, inconsequence and conceit, of his lack of consideration. Most unexpected, since he had been generous in his youth, was his stingy preoccupation with money. An extraordinary example of his almost pathological concern with small sums is given by Michael Bloch himself, quoting Philip Guedalla:

> He [the King] said that he never took lunch, and used to have a good look round when they [presumably the Royal Household] were at theirs. He described finding in the bowels of the earth an enormous room packed with candles, also a troglodytish individual who seemed to sleep there. When he asked about this he was told he was a pensioner: and when he asked why he was there he was told that 'he helps with the candles'.*

This is a story of two men in the bowels of the earth concerned with candles – one the King of England.

Still, in books written recently about the Windsors a good many *canards* are spread simply for the joy (and benefit to sales) of spreading them. Among the most important is the suggestion that Mrs Simpson may have been in direct touch with the Germans both before and during the war. Charles Higham seldom asserts anything definitely himself, but he tells us that the most improbable things were 'widely believed': for example, that while she was in China between her first two marriages, Mrs Simpson became pregnant by Count Ciano and had an abortion which 'destroyed her chances of ever having a child'; and, more important, that in 1936 she was 'having an affair with Ribbentrop and that he was paying her directly from German funds in Berlin to influence – as if that were necessary – the King'.†

Mrs Simpson denied absolutely that she had met Ribbentrop more than once or twice, both times in public, and there is every reason to believe her. In the first place, because of worry on the German score, both the King and Mrs Simpson spent his reign under the surveillance of security officers. At Fort Belvedere the windows of the drawing room are well above the ground, supported by a high

---

* Michael Bloch, *The Reign and Abdication of Edward VIII*, p. 19.
† Charles Higham, *Wallis: Secret Lives of the Duchess of Windsor*, Sidgwick & Jackson (1988), pp. 45 and 121.

wall. Lady Hardinge (wife of the King's Private Secretary) told me that during the King's reign security officers were stationed beneath the windows and against the wall every evening after dusk, where at least in summer they could hear much that was said inside. When I asked Tommy Dugdale – Parliamentary Private Secretary to Stanley Baldwin – whether any of this was true, he replied: 'Oh, yes. But they gave us the slip at the end, because the car that took her away to France went down the back drive and was not noticed.'

A consequence of this surveillance, it seems to me, is that it provides one of two incontrovertible reasons for discarding the suggestion that Mrs Simpson was a German contact. If, during the course of their duties, these security officers had come across any evidence to support it, in the ordinary course of leakages we should by now have heard what this was.

Far more important, when the Windsors passed through Spain and Portugal during the war, the Germans plotted to induce them to stay in Spain pending the successful invasion of England. Yet in the many captured papers giving instructions about the Windsors to the German agents in Spain and Portugal – some direct from Ribbentrop – there is no mention of any previous contact with the Duchess or any suggestion that she was a tool who might be useful in this case. Surely it is inconceivable that, if she had had previous contact with Ribbentrop or any other German, this fact would not have been used.

Although, as I have made clear, I think Michael Bloch's books should be taken in evidence only in company with my own or Philip Ziegler's, he has told us much to make us more understanding of the Windsors' lifelong anger about the way they were treated. This is so even when one's sympathies are with the King and Queen and their Court. He has also made it necessary for me to correct my account in several places.

From his last two books, *Wallis & Edward, Letters 1931–1937: The Intimate Correspondence of the Duke and Duchess of Windsor* and *The Secret File of the Duke of Windsor*, we learn the extent of the Duchess of Windsor's early expectations and the consequent size and bitterness of her disappointments. The ex-King and his wife were at all times unable to understand the sense of the enormity of his behaviour felt by his family. The fact that the rebuffs he received were so unexpected and so deeply distressing was a result of his belief that he could, without consultation or any regard for his family's feelings, abdicate and then in effect change places with his brother – after a short time returning to Britain to do the kind

217

of work for which his previous life and training had fitted him.

However, as in all family rows, he had some reason to believe himself badly treated. Michael Bloch explains the causes of the Windsors' grievances under four headings: their relationship with the Royal Family; the denial to the Duchess of the title Royal Highness; the breach of an agreement made by George VI about the financial arrangements for the Duke's future; the question of the Windsors' return to Britain.

The first of these is not a matter for discussion. However, there seems to be general agreement today that George VI had no power to deny the title HRH to the Duchess or to make terms for the Windsors' return to Britain. His actions were based on the advice that the Duke in abdicating had ceased to be a Royal Highness, since this attribute was due by right only to persons who were in line of succession to the throne. It was argued that, since the Duke was no longer in the line of succession, he had ceased to hold royal rank. Following this advice, George VI issued the Letters Patent of 1937 restoring the Duke's rank of HRH but not conferring it on the Duchess. The reason given for this inflammatory action was that the Prime Ministers of Great Britain and four of the Dominions had advised against conferring royal rank on the Duchess and it would therefore have been unconstitutional to do so.

The legal precedents cited in support of this view were the Letters Patent issued by Queen Victoria in 1864 and those issued by King George V in 1917. So far, my own account accords with the facts, and I give some space to the views of those who said at the time that there was nothing to support the view that the title HRH is due only to those in line of succession to the throne.

However, today this view is generally accepted because there is nothing in the Letters Patent of 1864 and 1917 to uphold the 'lineal' argument. The advice given by Sir William Jowitt that no Letters Patent were necessary to create the Duke of Windsor Royal Highness, because 'he was at birth and had always been entitled to that style', is generally accepted. From this it follows that the Duchess was also automatically entitled to the title. Michael Bloch quotes the editor of *Debrett's Peerage* as follows:

As was made perfectly clear by Mr Baldwin to the former King during his reign, we have no system of morganatic marriages in Britain. A wife, whether the illegitimate daughter of a milliner, as was the Duchess of Gloucester, sister-in-law of George III, or an Emperor's daughter, as was the Duchess of Edinburgh, daughter-in-law of Queen Victoria, takes her style from her husband.*

Mr Bloch also quotes Lord Devlin, in 1937 a junior to Jowitt, as follows:

Legally the only way of depriving the Duchess of royal status was to deprive the Duke first. If that had been done, a large body of opinion in Great Britain would have resented it. On the other hand there would also have been some resentment at having to treat the former Mrs Simpson as royalty. The clever solution to appease both sides was to 'restore' royalty to the Duke without 'conferring' it on the Duchess. It was in its way a good political solution; but it banked on the willingness of the public to overlook a technical illegality, and it was mean and ungenerous and absurd. It was mean in that it was a poor return for Edward VIII's decision not to fight for his crown in 1936. It was absurd in that a government which had advised the King that he could not make a morganatic marriage was now legislating to make morganatic the marriage which he did make. This was my view and I am sure Jowitt would not have disagreed with it. ....†

It is impossible to understand the events of 1937 if one believes the title was withheld from the Duchess as a good political solution to appease both those who would have resented the Duke being deprived of his title and those who would have resented the Duchess bearing it. The best evidence suggests that the reason for withholding the title was because it was believed the Windsor marriage would not last.

The ex-King had been entirely under the domination of Freda Dudley Ward for sixteen years, until he met Mrs Simpson. Freda, however, was never in love with him. Probably for this reason, although he visited her almost every day and treated her, as he would his future wife, as a kind of mother figure, contrary to what was put about after the Abdication he also indulged in a great many light sexual affairs, not only with well-known members of English society and the well-publicized Lady Furness, but according to rumour with women who took his fancy all over the world. The Royal Family knew more of his promiscuity than of his unswerving attachment to Freda Dudley Ward. They believed that he abdicated while suffering an obsession of an almost pathological kind – but

* Bloch, *The Secret File of the Duke of Windsor*, p. 76.
† *Ibid.*, p. 76.

one that could not last. In addition, it has to be said, with how much truth I have never bothered to find out, that Mrs Simpson was reputed to have a crowded sexual past.

What an appalling vista therefore opens to the imagination. The King had reminded the Prime Minister that once a person has become Royal Highness there is no means of depriving him or her of the title; and Baldwin wrote to his niece that 'his family [the Duke's] are all wondering what will become of him when at last he opens his eyes and sees the sort she really is.' I quote what I wrote before on the subject:

> And what would become of her? Where would Her Royal Highness go? What do? Once the idea enters one's head the possibilities are limitless. Would there be marriage and remarriage? More than one Royal Highness? The King and those nearest him were still under shock from the Abdication. Was there no limit to the possible damage to the throne?*

This passage shows quite clearly where my sympathies lay and I must admit still do. Yet, if the depriving act was actually illegal, one must also sympathize with the Duke and Duchess of Windsor – particularly as, when Jowitt became Lord Chancellor, he ignored the Duke's request that he should now take some action.

After reading what he has to say on the question of the financial arrangements, one suspects that Michael Bloch has what he calls 'a down' on me, since he misquotes me in a manner which suggests this. He opens his chapter on the subject of the financial agreement by saying that it has often been alleged that the King was paid an enormous sum to abdicate, 'that he had to be bribed, as it were, into agreeing to renounce the throne'. I am not nowadays a great student of these affairs, and I may have missed something in the many books that have been written on this subject, but this is the first time I have ever heard this suggestion. I have always thought it was generally accepted (except by the Duchess of Windsor, who believed in plots) that the King abdicated because he wanted to marry Mrs Simpson.

Nevertheless, Bloch follows the remark that it was 'alleged the King had been bribed' by quoting me as saying that according to 'informed sources' he *exacted* (my italics) a cash settlement from his successor of £2 million in addition to a pension of £60,000 a year.†
What I actually said (having explained that, under the wills of

* Donaldson, *Edward VIII*.
† Bloch, *The Secret File of the Duke of Windsor*, p. 43.

Queen Victoria and King George V, Edward VIII had a life tenancy of Sandringham and Balmoral) is as follows:

> Any satisfactory settlement had to be based on the transfer of those to his brother. Naturally no one but their financial and legal advisers was a party to the settlement, but informed guesses put the figure for Sandringham and Balmoral at one million pounds and the yearly income at £60,000. Over and beyond this the Duke of Windsor is believed to have taken substantial sums out of the country from other sources.*

The 'informed guesses' were wrong on both counts, but Bloch has exactly doubled the figure I gave for the two estates; more important, by the use of the word 'exacted' he entirely changes the meaning of what I wrote.

The disagreement over money arose because, at a meeting to arrive at some financial arrangement for his future, held before the Duke left England, he had failed to disclose the extent of his private fortune, and in consequence of this George VI felt entitled to repudiate what he had signed. There is evidence it would be difficult to discount that in the summer of 1936, before the death of George V, the then Prince of Wales took one million pounds out of the country, investing it originally in a trust for Mrs Simpson, although she returned it to him after their marriage. This is to some extent confirmed in the Duchess's published letters to her Aunt Bessie, which make it clear that there had been some substantial settlement upon her. However, the arguments about finance enraged the Duke and Duchess of Windsor, who saw George VI and his advisers as in breach of an agreed settlement.

It was during the arguments about his finances that it was first proposed that the Duke's return to England should depend on the King giving him permission to do so. Here for the second time George VI and his advisers were acting in breach of the laws of England. The Crown may under certain circumstances prevent its subjects from going abroad; only an Act of Parliament could rob a British subject of his right to return to England. Both the Duke and his advisers found the suggestion outrageous.

Yet once more it is impossible not to feel sympathy for the Court. No one has ever attempted to explain the hold of the myth and magic on the ordinary mind, but royalty is royalty no matter who wears the crown. If the Duke and Duchess of Windsor had lived in

---

* Donaldson, *Edward VIII*, p. 292. A rough guide to the value of all figures in today's currency is to multiply by thirty.

England – with their eighty-four pieces of luggage, their equerries, secretaries and servants in uniform, with their wilfulness and complete lack of understanding of how to behave – they would have become a centre of gravity for the press. I have no doubt that those who served George VI accepted without too much questioning any expedient which would preserve the monarchical principle from continuing, uncontrollable and humiliating publicity; and, although there is clearly room for difference on this point, I think they were right. One can nevertheless understand the Windsors' resentment, particularly as all those, even Monckton, who had been their friends and advisers seem imperceptibly to have changed sides.

Bryan and Murphy, who wrote from personal knowledge, say the question of the title for the Duchess rankled for the rest of the Windsors' lives. They quote the Duchess as saying that, since her husband had given up the most exalted of titles, it was hardly worth quibbling over a lesser one. Then they go on: 'But quibble she did, and not only quibble but rage within.'

There is much evidence to support this view; and speaking of the Duke, Bryan and Murphy say: 'What he could never bring himself to admit, but what she – especially when in a foul humour – never let him forget, was that he had failed again. . . . This was the source of the shame and sorrow that awaited the poor Duke: the dreadful realization of his ineffectuality.'*

* J. Bryan and Charles J. V. Murphy, *The Windsor Story*, Granada (1979).

23

···

Northern Ireland

Sometime soon after the election of 1973 I was sitting at my desk, ostensibly working, when the telephone rang. The voice at the other end asked for Jack and, when I said he was out, asked where he could be got.

'This minute', I replied, 'he is in Wormwood Scrubs.'

The voice then said he was Number 10 Downing Street speaking and would Jack telephone as soon as he emerged.

Harold Wilson wanted Jack to go to the Northern Ireland Office as Parliamentary Under-Secretary to Merlyn Rees. Jack asked for time to consider this and to consult with me, and Wilson gave him until the afternoon, not later. He also said that if he preferred it he could go under Shirley Williams, Secretary of State for Prices and Consumer Protection. There was never any doubt which Jack would choose, since the problems of Northern Ireland were actually of interest to him; and, although he had never stood for Parliament nor sought a political life, he went to the Northern Ireland Office with some enthusiasm. This involved speaking for Northern Ireland in the House of Lords, and, in his first speech in this capacity, he said that he believed he was the oldest Under-Secretary ever appointed (in his sixty-seventh year). This claim was disputed by Lord Mitchison, but was otherwise correct.*

* Lord Mitchison had been Under-Secretary for the Ministry of Land and Natural Resources from 1964 to 6, starting at the age of seventy-four. But he had been an MP, whereas Jack had had no previous political ambition.

I was surprised how easily and confidently Jack took it on, but
he is a very confident character, although not ambitious. This was
in the days just before Direct Rule. A house at Stormont, of which
Lutyens had been the architect, was still in process of being converted for the use of the ministers and civil servants, who in the
meantime lived at the Culloden Hotel, just outside Belfast. This
made it possible for me to go over at weekends, travelling in the
RAF plane from Northolt which took the ministers backwards and
forwards.

I was often alone in the hotel, and the first time this happened I
walked to the nearby golf course, which is situated near the beautiful
Belfast Loch, and immediately decided to take up golf again. Both
Jack and I had played when we were children, and until the war,
but not for more than thirty years.

I decided to have a few lessons as a start and as a result of this I
learned to live in Northern Ireland as most people had lived in
England during the war – that is to say, without thinking about
things until they happened. It was, I think I am right in saying, a
particularly bad period, the IRA threatening ordinary civilians with
kneecapping to force them to drive bomb-laden cars, and when
people in England heard we were going to Belfast they pulled long
faces. On the second day that I had booked a lesson with the pro,
a car stopped beside me as I was walking along the road to the golf
course, and the driver opened the far door for me to get in. I felt a
thrill of fear and I bent down to look in the car only because I could
think of nothing else to do – to see the face of the golf professional
who was offering me a lift. After that I never remember feeling
personal fear again.

The security arrangements always seemed to me a bit odd. The
moment Jack arrived in Northern Ireland he had two cars, an armed
man sitting beside the driver in the car in which he (and I with
him) rode, with two armed men in another car in front. Yet the
moment he returned to England he proceeded without a guard. In
Ireland the job of the security men was very closely defined. When
we walked together two of them followed us, but if Jack turned left
and I right both men followed him. In the same way, when we
played tennis on the hotel court a guard was stationed near us the
whole time; but when Jack, in a hurry, left me to pick up the balls,
although there was a shrubbery which might have made a splendid
hiding place immediately beside the court, the guard followed him
without ever looking back. Best of all were the golf games. Two of
the security guards were golfers and they used to play immediately

behind Jack and me. It amused us to turn and watch them putting, since their whole attention was always given to this difficult task.

They were very nice men. I think in Northern Ireland all men are country men because there are no big towns. In any case, one of the golfers was an authority on birds and Jack, who was President of the RSPB, used to go out birdwatching with him. At the weekends we went for picnics, sometimes on the hills, sometimes driving past Mount Stewart, where Freddy used to stay with the Londonderrys and where we dined once with Maureen Stanley's sister, Mary, and on to Castle Ward. Northern Ireland is as beautiful as anywhere in the world, only spoiled by the fact that the farmers cut all the trees, having I suppose so little land that they cannot afford to waste any of it.

When the conversion of the Lutyens house was finished, although everyone had been taught to look forward to the move, it turned out that the plans had been passed before the days of Direct Rule, and there were bedrooms for only two ministers. Now that there were three, Stan Orme being Minister of State, there was no room for Jack except on the top floor among the secretaries. He therefore moved himself to Hillsborough, where I think some of the ministers have lived ever since, but which in those days had the drawback that the married couple running it went home at the weekends. For this reason I more or less gave up going to Ireland because there was no point in going in the week.

As an under-secretary Jack was paid £5,500 a year – not a princely sum and much exceeded nowadays, but for us it amounted to the second miracle, as it allowed us to save the money I earned from *Edward VIII*. With some of that we built the house facing the downs in East Sussex which we still have. We had looked for a house we could buy (as a second house) for two or three years, but everything I saw was both too expensive and too beastly. A great many houses, both in the country and in London, have been ruined lately by people who, proceeding without the benefit of architect or interior designer, have distributed inglenook fireplaces and patterned tiles all over England. Then one day in 1974, when we were staying with Pat and Dione Gibson, Pat said: 'If you can't find a house, why don't you build one?' and then revealed that he owned a site at the corner of his farm in East Sussex which, because there had been a cottage on it before, had building permission. This site, which is about one acre, has one of the most beautiful views of the South Downs, and, although when we first went there it was a wood of sapling elms, it has a natural fall which makes the garden lovely without too much help from us.

Pat was very generous over terms, so, almost before we had time to think about it, in 1975 we were once more building a house – if you count the four cottages I built at Gipsy Hall, our sixth. Our first was the Wood House, one of only two houses Walter Gropius built in England and the only one in the countryside. This decided us to employ once more an architect who would design in the style called 'modern'.

We were very much restricted, not only for money but because the rule governing building permission in Sussex allows only the size of the house that was on the site before, plus 10 per cent. Our architect, John Winter, also threw in the space allowed for a garage, although he built a car port. He designed a bungalow because he said the permitted space could not be well used for a two-storey house. Inside he managed a large sitting room – approximately twenty feet by twenty feet – a dining room leading into a kitchen, three bedrooms, two bathrooms and a separate gents lavatory.

No one could deny the convenience of this house, but there is considerable disagreement about everything else. John made two terraces, one in front of the house, looking at the view, and one behind, and beside each he put high garden walls designed to grow climbers as well as to keep out the wind. At first the bare walls added to the general criticisms of the house, although now that they are well-covered by creepers we hear no more of this one. For the rest, it is a matter of taste, and I can only say that many people besides ourselves like the house. When Jim Lees-Milne came he described it as 'like a little orangery', while Diana Cooper said, 'I love your great blazing room.' Neither phrases could, I think, have been used in an effort to cover disapproval. Yet it might be difficult to sell to members of the general public or to the Prince of Wales. It has the enormous advantage that the large windows reach to the ground. This feature, beloved of modern architects (and of the Georgians) and so unsuitable in towns, where the windows have to be curtained to prevent the life inside being revealed to passers-by, works in the contrary sense in the country. Thus, as I sit at breakfast, I watch the birds in the garden going through their daily routine just as if I were not there. In addition to the small specimens, there is a very large cock pheasant and several wives who seem to have been living with us for years, and from time to time there are rabbits. The behaviour of these simple animals, as you watch them taking their breakfast while you take yours, becomes of absorbing interest.

One of the pleasant things about a weekend house is that, since the choice is relatively less in the country, one sees so much more of other people who come nearby for the weekend than one would in London. I had known Edward Cazalet all his life and Camilla since she married him, but we see them far more often in the country than we would in London. The same applies to June and Jeremy Hutchinson, who have a cottage near Alfriston and to whom we have become very close.

In 1976, the year we took possession of our country house, Harold Wilson resigned and Jim Callaghan, the new Prime Minister, made Jack Minister for the Arts, a position he held for three years until the election of 1979, which the Labour Party lost to the Conservatives.

As Minister for the Arts, Jack added visiting the National Theatre and all the museums and picture galleries of Britain to what could be described as his duties. He was quite a good minister and all the heads of museums would say so; but he was bad with the press, who consequently regarded him as a faceless man, which I fear will make his obituaries unworthy. One of the major changes when one's husband becomes a minister is the car and driver which take one out at night. When the Labour Party was defeated in 1970, I remember asking either Roy Jenkins or Tony Crosland – I forget which – whether he minded very much, to receive the reply that he was still trying to find out how to get about London.

When Jack was Minister for the Arts we began to travel. We do not belong to the generations who have learned to travel cheaply on tours, and we had never had the money to pay for ourselves. We had gone every winter after the war to Cannes to stay with Freddy, as long as he was alive, and later for many years to Portofino to stay with the Berlins. So we knew something of France and a little of Italy; Jack had walked in the Pyrenees in Spain before we met and we had spent one Christmas in Jerusalem with the Berlins. I had been several times to New York and once on a writer's tour through many other cities in the USA. While Jack was Minister for the Arts we went twice to Teheran, to Budapest, to Belgrade, to Kansas City and to the Festival of Music at Aix-en-Provence. Three years after this I wrote a history of the British Council, and in order to see its work we both went to Egypt, Kenya, India, China, Hong Kong, Nepal and Brazil, while I went alone to Poland; in addition we went to Spain, to Venice to see the Biennale, to Lisbon to see the great Henry Moore exhibition, and to Frankfurt to the book fair. We were well treated at weekends and trouble was taken so that we might see the neighbouring sights. But this is not a traveller's tale and out of all this wide experience I can find very little to say.

For this there are two reasons. The first is that we stayed at the best hotels, which differ very little all over the world, and were collected by a car and driver every morning, sometimes driving into the country to see, for instance, an agricultural college, but often going no further than the British Council offices in the town.

But the second and more important reason is that I am a dull traveller, having neither knowledge enough of history, of peoples or of architecture to have anything other than bromides to offer. I learned things which have been of value to me, but which, with more intellectual curiosity and a greater desire to see the world, I should not have needed to learn.

24

....

Four Books

In February 1979 I had an operation followed by pneumonia. It took me nearly six months to recover and during that period I read a very large part of the *oeuvre* of P.G. Wodehouse. I had a reason for doing this in relation to which the operation was a fortunate circumstance. Edward Cazalet, Wodehouse's step-grand-son, had asked me to write the official biography and offered me access to all the papers.

I was in many ways the most suitable choice as I had known Plummie, as we called him, as well as anyone outside his own immediate circle, and understood him more completely, through Snorky, his step-daughter and my friend. I could be relied on to cover accurately the period during the war when Plum, captive in Germany, had broadcast to America.

Edward wished the truth of this episode to be established and he thought me the best person to do it. In the introduction to the book, I quoted Wodehouse as saying in a radio interview which referred to the fact that it was at first believed he had broadcast propaganda for the Germans: 'I don't think you'd ever get rid of a thing like that. If people get an idea like that in their heads, I don't think they'd ever let go.' This has unfortunately proved to some extent true. Because his actions had been much misunderstood and most evilly presented at the time, there were still people in England who believed that he had broadcast propaganda for Germany or wittingly used their medium in return for special favours. There is no doubt that he committed a technical offence, but the Cussen Report published here in 1980 established that he was essentially an innocent man.

The truth is that, having been interned in a prison camp for a year, Wodehouse was suddenly let out and taken to the Adlon Hotel in Berlin, where, as if by accident, he was met by someone who had been a friend of his in Hollywood. Soon afterwards he was asked if he would like to broadcast to America and he agreed to this, using humorous talks about his experiences which he had already given in the camp and which contained no word of propaganda. He emphatically denied later that he had made any bargain with the Germans or that he realized he was doing them a service. Here is his own statement made to Major Cussen, who interviewed him on behalf of the British government in Paris, immediately after the French capital was liberated:

> I should like to deal with my motives. ... I was feeling intensely happy [on being released] and at the same time I was very grateful to all my American friends and very desirous of doing something to return their kindness in sending me letters and parcels.
>
> There was also, I am afraid, a less creditable motive. I thought that people, hearing the talks, would admire me for having kept cheerful under difficult conditions but I think I can say what chiefly led me to make the talks was gratitude.

In the Introduction to my biography of him I said:

> Wodehouse made a very stupid mistake but one that surprised no one who knew him well. He was not a very complex character but he was a very peculiar one, and only those who knew him well enough to recognize and respect his peculiarities can understand (if not entirely explain) the reasons for this mistake. Here, after all, I have a special qualification, and it is because of that Edward Cazalet has approved the suggestion that I should write a biography and has put so many previously unpublished letters at my disposal.*

The best description of Wodehouse's character was given, not by someone who knew him, but in a note by a civil servant on the Cussen Report. I quoted this in my biography but think it worth repeating here:

> The report, combined with Wodehouse's statement and his radio

---

* Frances Donaldson, *P.G. Wodehouse: The Authorized Biography*, Weidenfeld & Nicolson (1982).

script gives the impression that he lives in the same world as his characters, a cosmopolitan, a-political world, into which conceptions such as the state and the nation do not intrude. He seems to be keenly interested in individuals but to have little sense of collective entities (other than my American public), and while he probably would not help 'the enemy' he has no very clear idea of what the enemy is and has difficulty in recognizing as such the individual German with whom he finds it easy to get on. Even, therefore, if he was specifically invited to broadcast and not given the impression, as his statement suggests, that he was being allowed to do so as a favour, he would be much more likely to think of himself as doing a good turn to the friendly Plack [who invited Plum to broadcast] than as 'assisting the enemy'. Had he seriously wished to help the enemy he could have given them much more help than we have any indication of; and it is difficult to believe that he would have thought it worth making such a bargain with them in order to get out of internment, when he was reasonably content in camp (there could have been little hardship there during the summer) and believed that he would be automatically released in four months' time [on reaching the age of sixty].

No one can beat this as an analysis of Plum's character and, as far as such a thing is possible, I think it exact.

However, it was not for any reason connected with this episode that I spent two years reading Plum's books. I was not in my youth an aficionado and it had been an embarrassment then, since I saw him often, that I did not like his books. What I wrote about this is continually misquoted. Having said that the Wodehouse world was one of purely masculine fantasy, in which all his literary grace, his talent for dialogue and his inspired humour were put at the service of knockabout plots, I went on to say that, with many exceptions to the rule, this put him out of the reach of the female sex 'who, because of their greater imagination, do not care for music hall jokes, farcical comedy, or any humour which relies on total disregard for the sufferings of innocent characters; while, because of their need to involve themselves, situations of mistaken identity or serious misunderstanding merely arouse their anxiety'. Then, having said that in my youth it was a source of embarrassment to me that, like so many other women, I could not read his novels with any pleasure, I went on:

For fifty years or more I made no attempt to remedy this state of

affairs and it was only when ... I began to read him with a
professional interest that I understood what all the fuss was
about. 'What an enormous uncovenanted blessing', Evelyn
Waugh wrote, 'to have kept Henry James for middle age.' What
luck, then, to have found Wodehouse at the age of seventy. And,
in case there should be any doubt of my sincerity, I must say
that, the task made easier by three months' convalescence from
illness, I have during the last two years read almost every book
he ever wrote, many articles and lyrics, and much that has been
written about him. No one has the stamina to do that except for
pleasure.

The biography of Wodehouse was on the whole a *succès d'estime*
but not a great seller (in terms of today, its sales would be regarded
with considerable pleasure). I remember only one bad review (there
may have been others) and that was by Brigid Brophy, memorable
because she took the opportunity to be extremely rude about Jack
as Minister for the Arts. He had nothing to do with the case but
had apparently annoyed her in some undisclosed way over the
unconnected subject of public lending right for authors. He was
strongly in favour of PLR, and as Minister for the Arts did much to
bring it about.

In the course of writing the book I had made a study of the letters
Plum wrote to Denis Mackail, which are among the best he ever
wrote, and which had made me think there might be something to
go for in editing a book of letters. There were two difficulties: neither
Michael Sissons, my literary agent, nor George Weidenfeld, my
publisher, was very interested. Michael had seen the letters to
Wodehouse's friend and collaborator Guy Bolton (which Guy had
unavailingly tried to get published some years before) and knew
that, taken as a whole, they were extremely dull, being mainly
about long-departed musical comedies, while George offered only a
very small advance. Plum wrote hundreds of letters, but not with
an eye to publication, and he had nothing much to say except about
his dogs and his work – too often, on the second matter, saying
merely that he had come to the end of a novel and had for the
moment no ideas for a new one. The whole question of a book of
letters was therefore dropped.

Edward Cazalet, Wodehouse's step-grandson, has a room in his
house given over to Wodehouse papers, first editions and so on. In
1988 he bought from Denis Mackail's daughter and two grandsons
the whole of the Wodehouse letters to Mackail, and this naturally

brought up once more the question of publication.

It is previous to discuss here the book which was finally published, but it follows too naturally for it to be inappropriate to do so. At the time the idea of publication was once more dropped, but Edward asked me if I would make a selection of the best letters to be bound into a file for his archives. I read most of the letters again, and could not help noticing that, although there was much repetition and very few letters that were of interest as a whole, there were many good things in them. I suggested to Edward that, as the book was for his archives, I should take the best bits out of the letters and group them under headings, e.g. dogs, lyrics, war, and so on.

This was agreed and when Edward read the result he thought, as I already had, that this might be appropriate for publication. He showed it to Hilary Rubinstein, literary agent to the Wodehouse Estate, and I showed it to Michael Sissons. After that it went out of my hands. Hutchinson bid a large sum for the book and the *Sunday Times, Observer* and *Sunday Telegraph* all bid for the serial rights, the *Sunday Telegraph* outbidding the others. I was generously treated by the Wodehouse trustees and I made as much money from editing this book as if I had written one myself.

One or two of the critics, notably Anthony Powell, were doubtful about the method of grouping excerpts under headings (none of them had of course seen the original letters) but the book, published in 1990, was on the whole very well received.

In the spring of 1982 I was resting in bed after a late night when Graham C. Greene, then chairman of Jonathan Cape, rang me up and asked whether I would write a history of the British Council. By luck I had sat next to the Director General of the British Council at some luncheon, at which I was present only because Jack was Minister for the Arts, and therefore, unlike 99 per cent of my countrymen, I had a hazy idea of what it was. Left to myself, I am not sure how I would have answered Graham Greene, but Jack was very keen and Jeremy Hutchinson said one should always do anything one was asked to do for the arts. Curiously enough, in spite of its unrevealing name, the British Council is about the arts. Its function is to spread abroad knowledge of the English language and of British literature, art, science, parliamentary institutions and way of life, as a means of encouraging understanding and good will on the part of others. It was formed in 1934, long after France, Italy and Germany had realized the necessity for something of the sort. In 1933, before the British Council came to life, Sir Charles Mendl, Press Attaché at the British Embassy in Paris, reported that the Alliance Française (the nearest equivalent to what the British Council has become) was by far the largest, best organized and most powerful instrument of cultural propaganda which France possessed, subsidized by the ministries of Foreign Affairs, National Education, and of the Colonies, by the governments of various French colonies and protectorates, by the city of Paris and by a number of *conseils généraux* throughout France. And Russell Galt of the American University of Cairo concluded a pamphlet on the difference between French and British educational philosophies in Egypt by saying that the French pen had proved mightier than the British sword.

Against this formidable competition, as well as that of Germany and Italy, the small, unnoticed British Council was formed. Now it has offices in countries all over the world and in 1982 it had a budget of £123.2m.: £31.5m. contributed by the Foreign Office, £64.7m. by the Overseas Development Administration, £14.2m. from contracts with international governments and so on, and £12.8m. from direct earnings on educational programmes. It is responsible not merely for teaching the English language in most of the countries of the world, and for bringing foreign students to Britain, but for sending abroad drama and dance tours, ranging from the National Theatre and the Royal Opera to small theatre workshops, and exhibitions of the work of artists ranging from Henry Moore to students at the Royal College of Art. Like all other cultural organizations, it has suffered from the philistine lack of generosity towards the arts which characterizes our Treasury, but, in the fifty years which I was asked to cover, it had become one of the arms of our diplomacy, although in most countries it operated at different levels of society from those of the Diplomatic Service. Clearly the history of its first fifty years was an attractive project.

The research for the book was done by Dr Harriet Harvey Wood, who had served in the British Council all her working life, as had her father. She naturally had a great influence on me, although the enormous suitcases of papers I took away every weekend was proof that she did not consciously try to guide my views. Sir John Burgh was Director General at this time and he and his wife are now my friends. Sir Charles (Dick) Troughton, lately resigned from the chairmanship of W.H. Smith, was Chairman. Dick died the other day and I think I can best add my tribute to him by telling the following story.

The Foreign Office had given us access to their records, including those not yet in the public domain, but they naturally retained a veto over what we published, made more important to them and more difficult for us by the fact that the book was unusual in being brought right up to date. One of the factors in the case was that the staff of the British Council were never absolutely sure whether the Foreign Office were entirely on their side or not, particularly as part of their budget came from there. When I found a recent record of a senior civil servant, not merely speaking in sympathetic terms of the Council to the Foreign Secretary, Lord Carrington, but giving views which had the effect of influencing events in their favour, I quoted this directly. The Foreign Office asked for this to be cut, for no good reason that I could see except that it was up to date, and I wanted to retain it. I therefore went to see Dick Troughton to say that, with his permission, I proposed not to cut anything, but to put the civil servant's advice into the mouth of Peter Carrington, who I felt sure would not care, and who in fact signed the letter in which those words reached the British Council.

I had not got very far in my attempt to explain all this when Dick interrupted me to say : 'Look here, anything you do, I'll back.'

Even before I had finished the book on the British Council, Claus Moser commissioned me to write a history of the Royal Opera House in the twentieth century. This was a book Jack and I enjoyed. Jack did much of the research, going most mornings to the offices in Floral Street opposite the Opera House itself. I worked in the morning at home and then joined him for a sandwich lunch from Ponti's in the office which had been allotted to us, and an afternoon looking through the papers he had produced.

Until I wrote the British Council book and then the one about the Opera House, I had always had good-to-very good reviews. For both these books I had many good reviews, but for both I also received some so discreditably vicious in tone that to read them was like being hit in the face. (I am reminded of Evelyn Waugh who said he never read the critics because 'they cannot give me pleasure but they can give me pain'.) If all reviews were bad, however reluctantly one would have to accept that one had failed. When the book has been praised, directly to oneself but more importantly to other people, and also received some good reviews, it is impossible to know what to think. Nevertheless, cruel notices are damaging, as I suppose they are intended to be.

I believe it is dangerous to write of an institution, since some of the flak is really directed at that. In the case of the British Council, one writer of a particularly poisonous review actually used some of his space to complain that, when he visited one of the major cities of the world (unique ground for the sightseer if nothing else), the British Council representative had left him to look after himself during the weekend.

The venom of some reviews of the book about the Royal Opera House at least showed that those who dish it out cannot take it. The London music critics are generally regarded as among the most cruel and unpredictable in the world and I had said this, as also that many international artist will not sing in London for fear of them. I also made the fundamental mistake of singling out some critics for praise, not noticing, as no one else concerned did, that this was bound unnecessarily to annoy those not mentioned.

Before leaving this subject I must recount one story connected with it. Soon after these condemnations in the press had appeared, I met David Pryce-Jones in the foyer of the Royal Opera House.

'You had a splendid review in *The Times*,' he said.

'How can you say that?' I asked. 'It was one of the most terrible reviews I have ever seen.'

'Oh! I didn't *read* it,' he replied, confirming that, as publishers believe, what matters is not what the critics say but the space they use to say it in. This is not much help to an author, however, and I can truthfully say that, whereas I have never particularly looked forward to the publication of a book, now, if I were young enough, I should go to India until it was all over. The writer's life is a lonely one and writing a private occupation. Yet it is inevitably attended with more publicity than office workers get in a lifetime.

EPILOGUE

··

A nd so to the end. I think it was Roy Jenkins who said it was so difficult to end an autobiographical work since the line drawn by death is not yet there.

Having so improbably lived long enough to see the rise and fall of the USSR, the splitting of the atom leading to nuclear capacity, the changes in sexual behaviour and the arrival of Aids, I must record these changes because they have altered the complexion of life. Yet they are cataclysmic, not impinging directly on me and entirely outside my control, while this is merely a chronicle of the trivia of personal experience.

To return, therefore, I must record that Jack and I both became members of the SDP and Jack, who still had a public position, joined the alliance now called the Liberal Democrats. I had been an enthusiastic member of the SDP, thinking not merely that it embraced a political attitude reflecting what had been my own position all along, but that it had some real chance of 'breaking the mould'. When instead it broke up, the shattering negation of all it had stood for in my mind and that of so many others seemed to me then, and seems to me now, evidence that original sin is as strong in societies long civilized as in the rest of the world; the difference being that it is arranged that temptation is smaller. So I will confine myself to the changes in ordinary life, almost all of which are in the social or domestic sphere.

First, and as remarkable in its speed and thoroughness as that of the loss of influence of the aristocracy which I have referred to in the introduction to this book, is the fact that for the first time in history women are no longer dependent on marriage to rescue them, if not from poverty, at least from an unfulfilled and humiliating life. I have related that my own parents, having three daughters, more or less forced me into an entirely unsuitable first marriage which I was both too weak and too much under their influence to reject. The fact that I did as I was told is not understood today, since it was due to the enormous influence they both – in different ways – had upon me, something modern parents give away quite early. For years I believed that they behaved as they did in an attempt to avoid the shame of having three unmarried daughters; only lately, thinking about it, I have realized that, with Freddy's uncertain income, they must have viewed our financial future as too hazardous to be left to chance.

Because girls had to marry they also had to remain virgins and this produced a race called spinsters, those who had passed the marriageable age without sexual experience. There was also a male equivalent called bachelors, but, since these could have married if they chose, one is apt to wonder now whether they were all homosexually inclined. If so, very few were more than inclined. In a book published posthumously Rebecca West explains that, when her brother had to go abroad because he had gone unwittingly to a club for homosexuals and had been caught there in a police raid, it was impossible to explain to her mother why he left, since she knew nothing about such things.

The houses my parents lived in were thought quite small at the time, but one of them (admittedly with some additions) is now an hotel. They always had at least three servants living in the house, even when they were being kept by Mr Conran. So did Jack and I. Our house was kept beautifully clean – I remember being astonished when my sister-in-law, Molly, told me it was not really necessary to have the house cleaned every day – but the food we ate was very bad, as it was in most hotels, since no one knew how to cook, least of all, except in the houses of the very rich, those who were paid to do it. This was partly because they were paid so very little – as far as I can remember Jack and I paid the cook, housemaid and nanny about £27 a year each, although we kept them (except for their clothes) – but also because, as I have explained earlier, those who employed them were as uneducated in this as in other ways. The English learned to cook only when the middle classes had to do it themselves; then Elizabeth David came along and taught them how. Until we left Kingsbridge I had a morning and an afternoon daily who would come also at weekends if one needed them. Today, with luck, I have (in both our houses) someone who comes to clean for three hours a week.

London was so lovely when I was young and the water carts cleaned it at night. No high-rise flats, no modern and no post-modern buildings, no crowds on the pavements and no couples barring the way by holding hands as one tries to pass along the streets. The latter is one of the strangest features of modern life because it is not only the young who do it; is the need for reassurance so strong, or is it to show off a relationship?

In other ways the middle and working classes (what does one

238

call them now without offence ?) have freed us all from the bondage of aping the aristocracy and the rich. This is particularly true in the matter of clothes. Fashion throughout history has started above and percolated down, whereas now the opposite is more often true, and a good job they have made of it. When I was young, it was absolutely necessary to have at least two coats and skirts – tweed for the country and dark blue or black for London – and once when I stayed in a country house one of the other girls staying there told me that she had expected me to go earlier than I did because on the fourth night I wore the same dress as on the first. All this made public appearances a misery, since one was quite unable to afford all the necessary clothes.

Having written the above, I read in the *Independent* that a perfectly ridiculous dress, shown in a photograph and made in Paris, cost the owner £15,000. Not only that, but in a later paragraph the writer says that the Duchess of York and Princess Michael of Kent wear couture, but only 'thanks to the munificence of Yves Saint Laurent or Dior' – that is to say that, while no money is actually exchanged, they wear these clothes as an advertisement for the firms that made them. If that is true, what has happened now to the mystery and the magic ? Perhaps it is not true.

This has not been intended as an entirely personal memoir, but I cannot finish it without some mention of my family. My son Thomas may be remembered for refusing to help the war effort by picking peas, and Rose for her cold hands while doing so. Kate was born after the war. All three remain very devoted to Jack and me, and Rose and Kate, who live in London, come to see us every week. Between them the three have given me eleven grandchildren and a computer. Of the grandchildren, six are Thomas's, three belong to Rose and the other two, who are still at school, to Kate. They all seem eminently satisfactory and are a pleasure to me.

Rose and Kate are both professionals in the computer world and the computer was given me for my eightieth birthday. They boast that I learned to use it at that age, but the truth is I belong to the generation which cannot read an instruction book and I learned only by constant recourse to the telephone when in trouble. Counting the Wodehouse letters, which I selected and edited, I have used it for three books and it has been a great pleasure to me. My method is to write one morning and correct the next and this, which was very boring on a typewriter, is amusing on the computer.

Because of my advanced age, I am unable to find words to bring this chronicle to an end, and I have been forced to resort to using the words of other people. I have had a difficulty over this because, searching for an ending, I looked first at the books of the famous, who quite naturally assume more talent and more importance than I would care to do.

I cannot use the words of Diana Cooper who says, 'The long custom of living disinclines one to dying', because she adds, 'Besides before the end, what light may shine?' – Since I have insufficient faith. So instead, I end with the words of Professor C.D. Broad in a book of lectures on psychical research:

> In the known relevant *normal and abnormal* facts there is nothing to suggest, and much to counter-suggest, the possibility of persistence of the psychical aspect of a human being after the death of his body. On the other hand, there are many well-attested *paranormal* phenomena which strongly suggest such persistence. ... One can only wait and see, or alternately (which is no less likely) wait and not see.

INDEX

···

Index